F

Spring /
1

Completed in 1891, Wedekind's notorious play *Spring Awakening* had
to wait the greater part of a century before it received its first complete,
unadulterated performance in Britain in 1974. The production was
highly praised, much of its strength deriving from this translation by
Edward Bond and Elisabeth Bond-Pablé, 'scrupulously faithful both to
Wedekind's irony and his poetry'. Charles Lewsen, *The Times*

Lulu: A Monster Tragedy is based on Wedekind's first manuscript and
presents the original sexually voracious heroine to a British audience
for the first time. 'The Bonds' version is sharper and funnier than its
predecessors.' Michael Billington, *Guardian*

Also included in the volume are the translators' general introductions,
specific notes on each play and three *Lulu* poems by Edward Bond.

FRANK WEDEKIND (1864–1918) was a journalist, advertising
manager, secretary to a circus, cabaret artiste, satirist, convict and
actor as well as the author of twenty-one plays, many of which
reflect aspects of his extraordinary career. He himself paid for the
publication of *Spring Awakening* (1891), though it was not staged
till 1906. (In England it was banned from public performance until
1963). *Earth-Spirit* (1985), the first of his plays to be seen on stage
(1898), introduced Lulu, who also figured in *Pandora's Box* (1904)
and subsequently in Alban Berg's opera (*Lulu*, 1935) and in Peter
Barnes' conflation of the two plays seen in England in 1970. Other
notable plays include *The Marquis of Keith* (1900; British premiere,
1974), *King Nicolo* (1902), *Castle Wetterstein* (1910) and *Franziska*
(1912). Wedekind was greatly admired by Brecht, and his satiric
songs still have considerable bite.

Methuen World Classics

FRANK WEDEKIND

Plays: One

Spring Awakening: A Children's Tragedy
Lulu: A Monster Tragedy

translated and introduced by Edward Bond
and Elisabeth Bond-Pablé

Methuen Drama

METHUEN WORLD CLASSICS

This edition first published in Great Britain 1993
by Methuen Drama
an imprint of Reed Consumer Books Ltd
Michelin House, 81 Fulham Road, London SW3 6RB
and Auckland, Melbourne, Singapore and Toronto
and distributed in the United States of America by HEB Inc.,
361 Hanover Street, Portsmouth, New Hampshire NH 03801 3959

Reprinted 1993, 1994

Spring Awakening first published in 1980 by Eyre Methuen
and corrected for this edition. Copyright © 1980, 1993 in this translation by Edward
Bond and Elisabeth Bond-Pablé.
Lulu: A Monster Tragedy copyright in this translation © 1993
by Edward Bond and Elisabeth Bond-Pablé
Original German text entitled. Frank Wedekind: Die Büchse der Pandora. Eine
Monstretragödie. Historisch-kritische Ausgabe der Urfassung von 1894. Hrsg. v.
Hartmut Vinçon. Copyright © Verlag Jürgen Häusser.
General introduction first published in 1980 by Eyre Methuen
and substantially revised for this edition. Introduction
copyright © 1980, 1993 by Elisabeth Bond-Pablé.
A Note on *Spring Awakening* first published in 1980 by Eyre Methuen,
copyright © 1980 by Edward Bond
Using *Lulu* copyright © 1993 by Edward Bond
Lulu poems copyright © 1993 by Edward Bond

The translators have asserted their moral rights

ISBN 0-413-67540-8

A CIP catalogue record for this book
is available at the British Library

Typeset by Hewer Text Composition Services, Edinburgh
Printed and bound in Great Britain
by Cox & Wyman Ltd, Reading, Berkshire

Front cover: *Wally with Red Blouse* (1913) by Egon Schiele.
Gouache, watercolour and pencil 31.8 × 41 cm, signed and dated
lower centre: Egon/Schiele/1913. By kind permission of Collection Serge Sabarsky,
New York, USA.

Contents

Frank Wedekind:
A Chronology

1864 24 July: Emilie Wedekind, née Kammerer (1840–1915) gives
birth in Hanover, Germany, to the second of her six children:
Benjamin Franklin (Frank) Wedekind. Father: Friedrich
Wilhelm Wedekind (1816–1888), doctor of medicine. The
parents had just come back from America.

1872 Dr. Wedekind purchases Castle Lenzburg near Aargau in
Switzerland where the family settles. Frank attends the
'Gemeindeknabenschule', then the 'Bezirksschule' from 1875,
then from 1879 the 'Kantonsschule' in Aargau.

1879 He writes *Der Hänseken*, a children's epic for his youngest
sister; writes poems and scenes (mostly parodies), in which he
acts himself, for the school literary society.

1884 Matriculation. Enrols first at the University of Lausanne to
study German philology and French literature. In the autumn,
at his father's insistence, enrols at Munich to study law.
Theatres, concerts, the circus remain his principal interests.

1886 Starts his first play. Meets Michael Georg Conrad and becomes
a friend of Karl Henckell. Open quarrel with his father.
November 1886 to July 1887: advertising manager of the Maggi
soup firm near Zurich.

1887 Contact with the socialist group 'Young Germany' around
Gerhart and Carl Hauptmann and John Henry Mackay. Starts
to write several plays and novels. Contributes to the *Neue
Züricher Zeitung*. September: makes his peace with his father.

1888 11 October: sudden death of Dr. Wedekind.

1889 May–July: in Berlin. Then Munich. Contact with Otto Julius
Bierbaum, Oskar Panizza, Hans Freiherr von Gumppenberg.
Friendship with Willy Rudinoff and Richard Weinhöppel.

1890 To Easter 1891: writes *Spring Awakening*.

1891 December: to Paris, where he stays – with interruptions –
until 1895.

1892 Fascinated by the theatre, ballet, variétés and the circus, whose way of life will help him to shape his philosophy. Friendship with Emma Herwegh; probably first contact with Willy Grétor. Begins 'Lulu' plays.

1894 January–June: in London. Meets Max Dauthendey, Georg Brandes; back in Paris, meets Albert Langen, his future Munich publisher.

1895 Returns to Germany: February in Berlin; summer in Munich. Tries to get his plays performed, without success. Autumn: Lenzburg, then Zurich; gives public readings mainly from Ibsen's plays, using the pseudonym Cornelius Minehaha. Starts his best known novel *Mine-Haha*. Langen publishes *Earth-Spirit*, the first of the 'Lulu' plays.

1896 Summer in Munich. Has more contributions than any other author in Langen's successful new periodical *Simplicissimus*.

1897 Contact with Curt Martens of the Leipzig Literary Society. Readings.

1898 25 February: first performance in Leipzig of *Earth-Spirit (Erdgeist)*. Under the pseudonym 'Heinrich Kammerer', Wedekind plays the part of Dr. Schön. The director, Carl Heine, and his wife Beate along with Curt Martens become lifelong friends. Heine tours *Earth-Spirit* with his 'Ibsen Theater': Wedekind is actor and theatre-secretary. Back in Munich Georg Stollberg, director of the Schauspielhaus, employs him as a dramaturg, director and actor. On 29 October, after Munich premiere of *Earth-Spirit*, Wedekind is given a hint that he is going to be arrested because of some political poems published in *Simplicissimus* under the pseudonym 'Hieronymus Jobs'. Flees to Switzerland, then to Paris. Roughs out *The Marquis of Keith*.

1899 With *The Marquis of Keith* complete, he hands himself over to the German police in June. Accused of lèse-majesté and sentenced to seven months imprisonment, a sentence later commuted to confinement in a fortress ('Festungshaft'), in fact, Königstein near Leipzig. While Wedekind is still there, *The Singer*, also known as *The Tenor (Der Kammersänger)*, has its first night in Berlin (10 December).

1900 3 March: back to Munich. Contact with Max Halbe and his literary circle. 28 September: *The Love Potion* (*Der Liebestrank* or *Fritz Schwigerling*) premiered in Zurich.

1901 April: joins the new cabaret The Eleven Executioners ('Die Elf Scharfrichter') in Munich, and is the only member *not* using a pseudonym.

11 October: first night in Berlin of *The Marquis of Keith* (*Der Marquis von Keith*).

1902 22 February: first night in Munich of *King Nicolo* (*So ist das Leben* or *König Nicolo*).

1904 1 February: first night in Nuremberg of *Pandora's Box* (*Die Büchse der Pandora*) – the second, more hostilely received of the 'Lulu' plays. 23 March: confiscation of the first published edition.

1905 1 February: first night in Munich of *Hidalla* later entitled *Karl Hetman, the Dwarf-Giant* (*Karl Hetmann, der Zwergriese*).

29 May: single club-performance in Vienna of *Pandora's Box*, organised by Karl Kraus, who plays Kungu Poti; Lulu: Tilly Newes; Jack the Ripper: Wedekind.

1906 1 May: Wedekind marries Mathilde (Tilly) Newes (1887–1970). Until 1908: residence in Berlin.

2 May: first night in Nuremberg of *Dance of Death* (*Totentanz*), finally called *Death and Devil* (*Tod und Teufel*), with the Wedekinds in the main roles.

20 November: Max Reinhardt's production of *Spring Awakening* (*Frühlings Erwachen*) opens at the Kammerspiele in Berlin. Wedekind is the Masked Man. It is to stay in the repertoire for twenty years and make Wedekind's name.

12 December: birth of first daughter, Anna Pamela.

1908 11 January: first night in Nuremberg of *Music* (*Musik*).

2 April: first night in Munich of *The World of Youth* (*Die junge Welt*). September: the Wedekinds finally settle in Munich.

1909 27 July: first night in Munich of *Censorship* (*Die Zensur*) as part of a Wedekind-cycle. Battles all the time with real censorship, which will go on until long after Wedekind's death.

Begins *Castle Wetterstein*.

1911 6 August: birth of second daughter, Fanny Kadidja.

20 December: first night in Munich of *Oaha*.

1912 June: first Wedekind-cycle in Berlin.

      30 November: first night in Munich of *Franziska*.

1914 24 January: first night in Berlin (as it had been banned in Munich) of *Simson*. Many honours on Wedekind's fiftieth birthday. A Wedekind-cycle in Berlin, another in Munich.

      29 December: appendicitis; operation not successful; wound doesn't heal. Hernia. More operations over the next few years. Wedekind continues to act and to write plays which get more and more abstract and are no longer performed today.

1915 25 March: death of Wedekind's mother.

1917 May to October: last tour with his wife as his partner in Switzerland.

      17 November: first night of *Castle Wetterstein* (*Schloß Wetterstein*), with Wedekind and Elisabeth Bergner.

      30 November: back to Munich. Given the news that his wife has tried to kill herself.

1918 2 March: last hernia operation.

      9 March: Wedekind dies in Munich. Tilly Wedekind lives on until 20 April 1970.

Introduction

The flesh has its own spirit.

Art is knowing what to leave out.

Frank Wedekind

A hundred years ago Frank Wedekind paid to have his 'Children's Tragedy', *Spring Awakening*, printed. In the same year he began to write the 'Monster Tragedy', *Pandora's Box* – Lulu was born. It is astounding that these two revolutionary masterpieces were written in the Victorian age. It comes as no surprise that during Wedekind's lifetime they were prosecuted and performed only in censored versions.

He was a lone wolf who became and remained throughout his life the censor's most prominent victim. The court sentences passed on him and his work fill many pages. To his contemporaries his legend was better known than his work. He did not belong to any group, follow any 'ism' or adhere to any political ideology.

His writing is paradoxically rich yet frugal, tightly woven yet translucent, and it defies all classification. In fact, Wedekind himself was quite cunning at making his work and his myth unclassifiable.

He was the terror of the German bourgeoisie, a moralist who wore the mask of an immoralist. He was loved or hated, admired or despised, praised for being an apostle or condemned for being a devil. His enemies called him a lunatic, a criminal who wrote dirty, unsavoury plays. His admirers called him an idiot with a halo, God's fool. As an actor and director he was a phenomenon, as a man he was a magician. The Viennese critic Alfred Polgar called his plays 'battlefields over which the sun rises'.

When Frank Wedekind died in March 1918 at the age of fifty-three, Bertolt Brecht, who was then twenty, wrote his obituary in the *Augsburger Neueste Nachrichten*: 'Last Saturday night we sang his songs to the guitar as we swarmed down the Lech under the star-dusted sky . . . On Sunday morning we were horrified to read that Frank Wedekind had died the day before . . . Without actually seeing him buried I cannot conceive that he is dead. Like Tolstoy and Strindberg he was one of the great educators of modern Europe. His greatest work was his personality.'

Brecht attended the funeral at the Munich Waldfriedhof. The various accounts of it read like a scene out of a Wedekind play. The long train of mourners – family, friends, artists and intellectuals – wended its way through lines of Munich's bohemians and demi-monde. After the service in the burial hall, the crowd broke up and galloped across the graves to get the best view. In the middle of it all a wild figure, waving and shouting directions, tried to film it. It was the poet Heinrich Lautensack, one of 'The Eleven Executioners', the famous Munich cabaret group, whose star performer had been Wedekind himself. After the long orations Lautensack forced his way to the grave, threw a wreath into it, broke down and cried: 'Frank Wedekind – your last pupil Lautensack!'. Then he jumped into the grave. A few days later he was shut up in a mental asylum, where he died the following year.

Brecht held a private memorial celebration. He noted in his diary:

> They stood perplexed in top hats
> As if round the carcass of a vulture. Bewildered crows.
> And though they (sweating tears) tried hard
> They couldn't bury this juggler

Wedekind remained one of Brecht's obsessions. It is recorded that he often quoted his words by heart, imitating Wedekind's style as exemplary. He called his first son Frank after him. The expressionists also found inspiration in Wedekind, and he strongly influenced two other twentieth-century playwrights, Ödön von Horvàth and Friedrich Dürrenmatt. Dürrenmatt said: 'I don't think that a writer of our time can ignore Wedekind.' Wedekind in his turn had felt himself to be indebted to Goethe, Heine and Büchner. Alban Berg based his two great operas on Büchner's *Wozzeck* and Wedekind's *Lulu*.

Wedekind was conceived in California and born in Germany on 24 July

---

* 'Frank Wedekind' in *Brecht on Theatre*, ed. John Willett, London: Methuen, 1964, pp.3–4. All further quotations by Brecht from the same source.

1864. There he was registered as stateless under the name Benjamin Franklin. He was the second of six children. His North-German father, a politically active, left-liberal doctor had emigrated to America after the failure of the 1848 revolution. In San Francisco a singer from South Germany visited his surgery as a patient. She was twenty-two and just divorced when they were married in 1862. He was forty-six. 'This fact appears to me to be not without significance', Wedekind wrote in one of his first autobiographical notes. He himself was almost forty-two when he married. His wife was twenty. Both marriages were poisoned by the husband's jealousy and clouded by their strange habits. The pattern repeated itself in the third generation. Kadidja, Wedekind's daughter, married the German expressionist playwright Carl Sternheim. He was thirty-three years older than she, twice divorced and already insane.

Wedekind's parents returned to Germany. Dr Wedekind was disgusted with Bismarck's anti-democratic politics and the outcome of the Franco-German war of 1871/72. In 1872 he purchased Castle Lenzburg near Aargau in Switzerland. Frank's childhood was not unhappy although he felt strongly the tension between his parents. This is made clear in his diaries and in a letter written to his mother in defence of his younger brother Donald, who later killed himself. He studied, not very industriously, in the local schools and soon became a partly-liked, partly-hated gangleader. In school reports he was called 'Franklin Wedekind from San Francisco'. He was already writing and performing scenes, poems and songs in the school's literary society. When he sang he accompanied himself on the guitar. His gift for friendship developed early. At home he was known as 'the thinker'. His letters are a lively and often amusing key to his personality and to the influences that helped to form him. In many of those he wrote between the ages of seventeen and nineteen he deals with the questions, problems and views that later took artistic shape in *Spring Awakening* and *Lulu*. He wrote on love, sexual desire, egotism, society, the family, the education of children, literature, music, religion and death – both seriously and humorously. All his life he remained more interested in general social conditions than in the politics to which his father was devoted.

He was surprisingly well-informed even at an early age. When he returned from America his father had retired from medical practice. In his library Frank must have found the new ideas of the time in books by Marx, Engels, Bebel and Darwin. His writings show that he was also well acquainted with the new literary names and tendencies: Zola, Ibsen, Strindberg, Wilde. At Lenzburg Dr Wedekind became more and more of a misanthrope. He shut himself in the upstairs rooms, stamping on the floor when he wanted something. The atmosphere was nightmarish. In the winters it was so cold that the water froze in the washbasins.

In those early years almost everything happened which later bore fruit in Wedekind's life as a poet and a man. There was first the intellectual influence of the 'philosophic aunt' Plümacher, a pupil of the philosopher Eduard von Hartmann and his mother's friend. With her he held endless 'pessimistic discussions'. Later she was replaced by 'the erotic aunt' Erika (Bertha Jahn), the mother of a schoolfriend.

He matriculated in 1884 and went to Lausanne University for a few months. He studied German philology and French literature. Then he went to Munich and obeyed (without much interest) his father's injunction to study law. Almost every evening he went to the theatre, concerts and (at this early time, less enthusiastically) to the opera. Opera was his mother's great passion and his sister Erika's profession. From his very first visit to the circus he became besotted with it.

His decision to become a writer brought him into serious conflict with his father who made him responsible for his own financial affairs. During a fierce row in the autumn of 1886 Frank hit him. He was very upset at having done this but it took him almost a year to apologise and make his peace. By then he was sure of his future plans. He had written his first play. He confessed to his worried mother: 'I'm convinced about my aim because I carry my aim within me . . .' The letter was posted in Zurich where he'd met the most influential poets and scientists of the 'Young Germany' movement. One of his best friends, the poet Karl Henckell, had brought him into a circle of German exiles. Until 1890 their freedom in Germany was threatened by the 'socialist law'. The leading members were Carl and Gerhart Hauptmann. But Wedekind soon fell out with these German 'Zola-ists' and their theories. Gerhart Hauptmann was outraged by Wedekind's erotic songs to guitar. He put Wedekind's private confessions about his family life into his own play The Peace Celebration (Das Friedensfest), subtitled 'A Family Catastrophe'. Wedekind's revenge was Children *and Fools*, later retitled *The World of Youth*. In this play the hero, a fanatical poet, walks through the world with a notebook and pencil. The message: when realism ends, its representatives will be earning their bread as police spies. To do Hauptmann justice, he did not take offence. Instead he defended Wedekind when his plays brought him into trouble with the public prosecutor. In his autobiography (1937) he referred to his old friendship with Wedekind and said: 'He beats me when it comes to relentless truthfulness.'

By now Wedekind had tested himself as a writer of poems, prose, sketches and plays. One of these, *The Waking of Elin (Elins Erweckung)*, dealt with some of the themes of *Spring Awakening*. He contributed articles to the *Neue Züricher Zeitung* and in 1886 he became the energetic advertising manager of the recently founded Maggi soup firm. He was proud of his next job as secretary to a travelling circus.

After his father's sudden death in 1888 Wedekind gave up study. With his inheritance of 20,000 Swiss francs he felt free enough to travel and take up writing as his profession. He became addicted to urban life and in the following decade he travelled from city to city. First he went to Berlin. In 1889 it was the centre of German intellectual life, its literary culture was dominated by naturalists and realists. He had to leave after a few weeks as he couldn't provide the original documents that would have proved his nationality. By then the fashionable literary circles had interested him in the emerging question of the emancipation of women. He returned to Munich and started *Spring Awakening: A Children's Tragedy* in October 1890. It was finished by Easter 1891. It is the only one of his plays which he did not rewrite several times. Whilst he was writing it, it was hardly mentioned in his letters and not at all in the first forty-three of his notebooks. Wedekind sent the script to a critic, stressing its moral standpoint. He was quite aware that there was no chance of getting it performed. But immediately after its publication *Spring Awakening* became well known to the younger generation.

Finally in 1906 Max Reinhardt, Germany's most famous director and producer between the early 1900s and 1933, staged it in Berlin in the Kammerspiele of the Deutsches Theater. However, crucial concessions had to be made to the censor: scenes four and six in Act Three had to be omitted and Act Two, scene three was mutilated to such an extent that Reinhardt and Wedekind decided to cut it altogether. The caricatured names of the teachers had to be replaced by inoffensive ones. This obscured the idea of seeing them from the pupils' point of view. And there were other problems: for example, young or child actors were unknown in the theatre of that time. An unexpected critic, the future commissar Leon Trotsky made this point in 1908, stressing how aesthetically unacceptable it was 'when men with shaved faces have to simulate children's breaking voices'. Nevertheless this famous production was played 615 times over a period of twenty years, with up to twenty changes in the cast. Wedekind, having written the play when he was twenty-six, was seeing it staged for the first time at the age of forty-two. He himself played the role of the Masked Man. Following this production he was at the peak of his success. Until the First World War he was the playwright most often performed in Germany, rivalled only by Gerhart Hauptmann.

But he had a long, difficult way to go before this sensational breakthrough. Between 1892 and 1895 he lived mainly in Paris, enjoying the boulevards, variétés, cafés, theatres and – again most of all – the circus. He built his philosophy of life on the idea of the circus and looked on himself as a tightrope-walker. In Paris he met friends, old and new, of many sorts. One life-long friend was Richard Weinhöppel, who later, under the pseudonym Hannes Ruch, became composer to 'The Eleven Executioners'. Wedekind's most ambiguous confidante was Willy Rudinoff, actor, opera tenor, birdsong imitator, circus clown, black-face comic, fire painter and worldwide traveller. He led the kind of life, based on following his impulses, which Wedekind greatly admired but which he only created in fantasy. Rudinoff had shown Wedekind the underside of Munich. Now he took him to the cabarets at Montmartre. There the dancers, actresses, singers and cocottes fascinated him as much as the clowns, jugglers and athletes of the circus. Through a new friend Emma, the widow of the revolutionary poet Georg Herwegh, Wedekind got an entrée into the salons of fashionable women writers.

Wedekind experienced and lived the themes of *fin de siècle* literature and art. This experience is recorded in his autobiographical notes, sketches, pantomimes and, above all, his diaries. His revealing 'Diary of an Erotic Life' ('Tagebuch eines erotischen Lebens') was translated into English in 1990. In it we see Wedekind come into his prime as man and lover, boldly involved in the social and sexual adventures of the Paris of the *belle époque*. We see how the place and the time provides the gems and incidents for *Pandora's Box*. Even the moment of its beginning is recorded. On 2 June 1892, he wrote: '. . . go into the Champs Elysées, where I get an idea for a gruesome tragedy'.

It is not a coincidence that Casanova was Wedekind's favourite writer. Wedekind had affairs and encounters with many women but he never lost sight of his quest – 'I am in search of woman'. And in the end that is what Lulu became: the essence of woman – the incarnation of 'the innocent immoralist', filtered through Nietzsche's *Beyond Good and Evil*. In one of the prologues Wedekind added to later versions of the play, the Ringmaster calls Lulu 'the true, the wild and lovely beast'. No doubt Lulu holds the real beast in her fangs – the audience. Wedekind often acted the Ringmaster himself. There is a gripping photograph of him in the role, but unfortunately no recording of his voice and no film.

The parts of the diaries which have survived and been published start in 1887 in Lenzburg. They cover the time of searching in Berlin and Munich and reach their climax in Paris. Then after a few remarks written in London and a few more in Berlin, mainly about his unpleasant dealings over contracts with Reinhardt, they dwindle almost to nothing in Munich in the year of his death 1918. The diaries had a clinical function for him. He does not dwell on the plans and processes of his work as many other writers do. When he left Paris he had finished the first four acts of the 'Monster Tragedy'. Act Five was written in London between January and June 1894. At the very time when Wedekind was writing the scene in which Jack the Ripper murders Lulu, the Ripper was still running free in Whitechapel and Wedekind might even have brushed past him one night in the street.

In 1896 Wedekind published in *Mephisto* magazine an obviously sanitised extract from his diary. It records a visit to the Middlesex Music Hall in Drury Lane and evokes Lulu's early life: 'The greatest applause is earned by a dancing-girl of about four years of age dressed in a brief white princess frock, with bare legs, short white socks and little shoes in gilded morocco leather. She sticks a monocle in her eye and sings the Monte Carlo song, showing her scanty white lace knickers up to the waist at each beat of the drum. As she withdraws into the wings, a veritable battle-cry goes up, a howl such as you might hear in a Kaffir kraal, a bawling screeching and whistling as in a menagerie when the meat appears in front of the animal cages.'

While he was in London, Wedekind was apparently secretary to the Danish painter, art dealer and congenial forger Willy Grétor. Grétor, probably the most eccentric of all his friends, helped him to survive his frequent financial crises. Wedekind found London provincial, tasteless and boring, without sun and glamour, and its women unattractive and sexless. As his day normally started at night it annoyed him that 'at twelve in the evening one is sentenced to bed by the police'. The generally unfavourable impression Wedekind got of England might have something to do with the fact that while he was there his inheritance money had begun to run out.

Grétor introduced him to his future publisher, Albert Langen, a daring but dubious character, who had opened a publishing house in Paris in 1893. Later he moved the business to Munich. Wedekind's plays and other writings never ceased to alarm and enrage the public prosecutor. Langen played a two-faced role, going behind Wedekind's back in the clashes between the prosecutor and Wedekind. This led to a parting between them. Wedekind portrayed Langen twice – in 1903 in the play *Hidalla* and in 1908 in the play *Oaha* – a key work for the circle round the satirical magazine *Simplicissimus*. It had been founded by Langen just before the turn of the century. It contained a mixture of sophisticated liberal politics and erotica. Many leading writers contributed to it, among them Knut Hamsun, Thomas and Heinrich Mann, Rilke, Schnitzler and Hofmannsthal. The illustrators included Gulbransson, Grosz, Thöny, Thomas Theodor Heine. In its first year Wedekind contributed to it more often than any other writer.

From 1897 onwards his life seems to have changed for the better. He came into contact with the forward-thinking chairman of the Leipzig Literary Society, Curt Martens, who invited him to give a reading from his works. In Germany – as elsewhere – at that time it was possible to hear and see progressive literature and theatre only in private or closed circles. In Germany these were mostly connected to working-class clubs.

The reading was followed a year later by a performance of *Earth-Spirit* in the theatre room of the Leipzig Crystal Palace. This was the first staging of a Wedekind play. It was directed by Martens' friend

Carl Heine and by Wedekind himself, hiding behind the pseudonym of his grandfather's name, Heinrich Kammerer. Wedekind also acted the part of Dr Schön (named Schöning in the original 'Monster Tragedy'). Afterwards the play toured with Heine's newly-founded 'Ibsen Theatre'. Heine and his wife Beate, with whom Wedekind exchanged affectionate letters, became his most devoted supporters. They fought many battles for him and often defended him when he was attacked.

In Munich he was engaged as dramaturg, director and actor at the Schauspielhaus where *Earth-Spirit* had its second production, again with Wedekind as Dr Schön. During the performance Wedekind was given a hint that he was going to be arrested. He had published some political poems in *Simplicissimus*. The most offensive of these concerned Kaiser Wilhelm's colonial expansionist trip to Palestine. Wedekind was then writing under the pseudonym Hieronymus Jobs. Langen had encouraged him and assured him that there would be no danger. But the Police found the handwritten originals in the Editor's office. Wedekind fled to Zurich and later to Paris. Langen had already fled before him.

In exile Wedekind roughed out the play he always thought to be his best, *The Marquis of Keith*, a masterly constructed, cynical satire about a swindler who Wedekind based on Grétor. The last sentence contains its essence: 'Life is a switchback.' As soon as he had finished it he handed himself over to the German Police. He was accused of *lèse majesté*. After six weeks imprisonment on remand the court sentenced him to a further seven months, but then commuted this to six months confinement in a fortress, a more honourable punishment than imprisonment. In Castle Königstein, near Leipzig, he wrote his best-known novel *Mine-Haha* or *The Education of Young Girls*, 'in considerable comfort'. While he was still locked up his most popular and most often performed play, *The Singer*, had its first night in Berlin. He had written it in 1897 when he was staying in Dresden with his sister Erika. She was much in demand as a concert and opera singer and was able to help him in his financial difficulties. But in *The Singer* he satirised her patronising attitude to him, disguising her as a hideously pompous Wagnerian tenor. Later the part became one of his cameo roles. Others were the Marquis of Keith and Hetmann in *Hidalla*.

He saw in the new century in his cell in Castle Königstein. When he was released in the following March he clutched at another straw, one which he had actually helped to grow. During his time in Paris he had become very interested in the new kind of literary cabaret. He passed this interest on to his friends in Berlin and Munich as early as 1895. At the turn of the century Otto Julius Bierbaum's slogan 'Life saturated with art' was being put into practice. The first German cabarets were rather naive imitations of the Montmartre originals. Soon after 'The Eleven Executioners' opened in Munich, Wedekind became their main attraction and the first important German cabaret artist. By now he was the only member not using a pseudonym. His songs protested against bureaucracy, religion and the prostitution of bourgeois marriage. His song 'Ilse' which directly refers to a girl in *Spring Awakening*, and also to the Lulu image, made the only *chansonneuse* in the group, Marya Delvard, famous overnight. Heinrich Mann recollects Wedekind's appearance on stage as puzzling and weird: 'The ribboned lute in clumsy hands, he faced the aesthetic world . . . Small steps, "I come – you shan't escape me". A strongly etched head with the profile of a Caesar, bowed in mischief, ragged short hair, offensive twitching eyes . . . Irritability and sudden sadness. Strumming as if perturbed, the performance nasal, sharp, shrilling but in pauses full of meaning, the singer twisted and hunched behind his mental barrier.' Even his enemies and fiercest critics had to admit his sheer magical, diabolical presence. In her memoirs the actress Tilla Durieux, who had played opposite him, says that Wedekind 'the dilettante, the ridiculed, was the strongest amongst us . . . Out of his heavy body his voice sounded with an abruptness and fire which only prophets have'.

He toured five years with the cabaret, wrote three more plays, another novel, many songs and several fragments. In December 1902 *Earth-Spirit* was produced at Reinhardt's Kleines Theater in Berlin. It became a success with the intellectuals but Wedekind was still not widely recognised as a major playwright. The fierce and tiring battles to get his plays staged, again and again thwarted by prejudice and stupidity, depressed him. Few people understood and encouraged him, and even fewer of these were among his colleagues in the theatres. One of the few was the actor Friedrich Kayssler, who wrote to Wedekind after he had seen him on the first night: 'You have throttled the naturalistic monster of probability and brought the element of play back to the theatre.'

This was true, and Wedekind became more and more convinced that in an age of touring actor-stars he had to become a director and train them to play in his style. When he was almost forty he took acting and dancing lessons and a postal course in make-up. About this time Brecht saw Wedekind act. He wrote:

> He was not a particularly good actor (he even kept forgetting the limp which he himself had prescribed, and couldn't remember his lines), but as the Marquis of Keith he put the professionals in the shade. He filled every corner with his personality. There he stood, ugly, brutal, dangerous, with close-cropped red hair, his hands in his trouser pockets, and one felt the devil himself couldn't shift him. He came before the curtain as Ringmaster in a red tail coat, carrying whip and revolver, and no one could forget that hard dry metallic voice, that brazen faun's head with 'eyes like a gloomy owl' set in immobile features.

Finally, in 1905, his time as a dramatist came. A cycle of his plays, with Wedekind in the leading parts was performed in Nuremberg. Germany's most influencial theatre critic, Alfred Kerr, had already praised him in Berlin. In Vienna the poet and satirist Karl Kraus, Kerr's antagonist, arranged the first production of *Pandora's Box* in a club performance. He rented a theatre for one night. Kraus played Kungu Poti, the rising actress Tilly Newes, who was then nineteen, played Lulu, and Wedekind, Jack the Ripper. Tilly Newes immediately became his idol and his ideal partner. That autumn he got her a contract to play with him in Berlin. He wrote to his mother on 7 May 1906: 'I've just gone through the most strenuous time of my life. In eight days two first nights and a wedding.'

He married Tilly on 1 May and the next day both of them played in the first performance in Nuremberg of his *Dance of Death* (later renamed *Death and Devil* to distinguish it from Strindberg's play). In Vienna Karl Kraus was not allowed to stage it even in a club performance. In an inflammatory address Kraus condemned the kind of 'imbecility' that preferred 'a badly painted palace to a well-painted gutter'.

The Wedekinds settled in Berlin and were in demand by the theatres of all the main German-speaking cities. At the end of 1906 Tilly gave birth to their first daughter Pamela, and in 1911 to a second daughter, Kadidja.

Wedekind enjoyed his fame. He wanted his wife to appear only in his plays. His courtship had been stormy and the marriage was not easy. In her honest and full autobiography, *Lulu: The Role of my Life* she tells of their difficulties, his unjust jealousy, his fear of being too old for her, the way of life he had developed as a bachelor, his working habits.

He still wrote plays, year after year, without ever reaching the greatness of his early work. He wrote at night in the popular beer and coffee houses. Then he would sleep in his room till lunchtime. Tilly was too confident of her own standing as an actress to be overawed by him. But she was loyal, appreciating his generosity and kindness. She even offered to take in his two illegitimate sons. The mother of one of these was Frida, an Austrian journalist who became Strindberg's second wife but who was by then seeking a divorce. Her affair with Wedekind had begun in Langen's office but it had already waned when the boy was born in 1897. Strindberg and Wedekind met briefly but they did not get on very well, probably because of their mutual obsession with but different outlooks on women.

Tilly said that all of Wedekind's vitality went into his work. This is underlined by the remarks of several of his contemporaries, who pointed out that his passion came from his brain. He lived by his motto 'The flesh has its own spirit'.

In 1908 the family finally settled in Munich. Wedekind loved it. He decorated the flat himself, especially his own huge study. According to Tilly, everything from the carpets and curtains to the furniture (which Wedekind painted himself) was red with a few patches of yellow. His daughters adored him, and found in him a father who treated them always as equals – as you would expect of the author of *Spring Awakening*. Much to their amusement, he invented his own coat of arms, three women's legs in different colours. Over his writing desk he hung the famous painting of Tilly as Lulu. (It was destroyed by bombs in the Second World War.) Around the walls were all the instruments he had taught himself to play: guitar, lute, mandolin, and various percussion instruments. There were many books, pieces of office equipment and props from his plays, among these a drum and a huge ball. Tilly said the whole room looked like a circus arena.

On his fiftieth birthday Wedekind received many honours. One of them was a book with contributions by leading artists and intellectuals. There were two Wedekind cycles, one in Berlin and one in Munich. There was also a celebration banquet, which was a great success and Wedekind felt flattered. Thomas Mann was one of the organisers.

In autumn he fell ill with appendicitis but the operation did not go well. The scar would not heal. Until his death almost three-and-a-half-years later he was repeatedly operated on. There is some suggestion that it might have been cancer. But he continued to perform and write. During these years of agony he controlled himself in a very disciplined way. Elisabeth Bergner who in November 1917 acted opposite him in the first performance of *Castle Wetterstein*, wasn't aware of how ill he was. A last operation took place on 2 March 1918. On 9 March he was dead. Wedekind's deathmask shows a beautiful face with a slightly mocking smile. Eight years before, Thomas Mann had stated: 'History will one day say that, in an era compounded of senility, puerility and femininity, Wedekind was the only *man*.'

When Wedekind wrote *Spring Awakening* it was the first time in his life he felt free. He remembered that he started to write the first three scenes without any overall plan. Then suddenly this strange play took shape. It broke through all the clichés of the theatre of his time, both in what he said and in how he said it. In every scene there is an element of autobiography. But there is at the same time a panorama of the growth of adolescence. The individual problems of puberty, of adapting to the adult world, of the sacrifice of the needs of childhood, of frustration and of moments of happiness in both sexes. Melchior and Moritz are the two sides of Wedekind's personality, shown trapped in the social cage he describes so brilliantly. Two of his schoolfriends had killed themselves, and even the words, 'That boy wasn't mine' were spoken by the father of one of them.

Wedekind played the Masked Man in the first production. Nine rehearsals had already taken place before he was allowed to attend: 'I found there a really horrible tragedy in the grandest dramatic style. I tried to do the most I could to bring out the sense of humour, especially in the scenes with Wendla, and in all the scenes with her mother, as well as in the last scene; I tried to develop the intellectual, the playful elements and to dampen down the passionate elements, including those in the last scene at the churchyard. I believe that the play is more gripping the more harmless, sunny, laughing the performance.' Wedekind came back to this essential point when he was writing to his teacher, the actor Fritz Basil, who took over the part of the Masked Man in Munich: 'Until Reinhardt's production the play was looked on as pure pornography. Now they've plucked up courage to see it as the driest school pedantry. But still no one's able to see humour in it.'

If people had looked closely they would have discovered that Wedekind was neither a teacher nor a preacher but a genuine educator. He had educated himself to a moral understanding and had learned the clarity which makes his plays models of their type. In *Spring Awakening* he contrasts the world of puberty with the world of bourgeois morality. Throughout his life he studied and analysed social behaviour. What his average contemporaries found so difficult to understand was the fact that he did not wallow in naturalistic details or symbolist fog. He had found a style which was as far from the usual theatre pathos as it was from the underacting which was just then becoming fashionable. As a playwright, actor and director he increasingly followed his own interpretation. In the preface to *The Singer* he asks 'the professional actor' for 'tempo, passion and intelligence'. He rejected fashionable over-designing, elaborate costumes and too many (or too few) props. Nothing should distract the audience from the words. These should have absolute priority. His wife Tilly, not always happy about his adamant views on acting, said that he actually longed for 'the trained-animal act'.

Structurally *Spring Awakening* was well ahead of its time. But it also marked a return to the techniques of Germany's best classical playwrights. There are short, tense scenes such as those found in Lenz, Grabbe, Büchner – and monologues which recall Goethe and Schiller. Following Heine he used the method of first creating and then destroying a lyrical, sentimental, poetic mood. In *Spring Awakening* he made striking use, for his time, of the mosaic-like alternation of indoor and outdoor scenes, light and darkness, bright and dim, scenes between adolescents and adults, boys and girls, boys and boys, girls and girls, mother and daughter, wife and husband, teacher and pupil. Even the smallest parts such as Wendla's sister or the locksmith are sharply etched and unforgettable. Although the sequence of events is not tightly woven, the impact gives the clear pattern of the life of a small town about 1890 with the big city, Berlin, dangerously luring, promising, in the background – its attraction embodied in Ilse and the Masked Man. The churchyard scene was truly original. On the one hand Melchior is urged by Moritz to die, as Don Giovanni was urged by the Commendatore, and on the other hand he is lured back to life by the Masked Man, as Faust was by Mephistopheles. Wedekind wanted to give life, with all its mysteries and uncertainties, priority over death. Wedekind's mother loathed the play. She was the model for Frau Gabor, Melchior's seemingly sensible, understanding mother, who in the end is also his persecutor.

The writer and director Berthold Viertel (1885–1953), who during his war-time exile in America performed Brecht in English and German, has a chapter on Wedekind in his *Writings on Theatre*. There he says: 'When we were young Frank Wedekind was the Masked Man of his (our) *Spring Awakening*. With a satanic sneer as polite as an abyss and full of cold melancholy he introduced us to the mysteries of reality which began where the views of the pacifying poets end. This was the turn of the century. Bourgeois ideas lay in their agony.'

Spring Awakening shows children growing up into the monstrous world of a highly disciplined German middle-class. In *Lulu* Wedekind moves to the word of the adult woman struggling to liberate herself socially and sexually. He deliberately sets out to shock his audience whose mock-morality he portrays. Hence the unease with which the play was, and still often is, received. The mixture of comical and tragical elements, of farce, travesty, lyricism, melodrama and Grand Guignol, drives itself – as if by the energy the mixture itself creates – to an over-life-sized blend of tragedy and comedy. It is the first play of its type and creates that type's final form. It is a classic.

Lulu does not let anyone own her – not Schöning, the man she feels closest to because he is the only one she sees as her equal, not the flawed, troubled husbands he finds her, not her lovers or the 'father' who picks her up in the gutter and sells her as a child prostitute – least of all the Countess from whom she takes everything and to whom she gives nothing. She seems even to meet her murderer as an equal – the maniac she had once dreamt of, who robs her, kills her, mutilates her and sells her sexual organs.

No writer before Wedekind had used language and subject matter in this way. His virtuosity in turning sights and sounds, language and incidents into variations which constantly probe and deepen their subject, is unmatched by his contemporaries. His use of language – words, images, phrases and rhythms – shows his fascination with music. The astonishing cascades of short one-line sentences – often lines of only one or two words – are like verbal exchanges between pistols. Themes are struck, unfold, recur, are interrupted, mixed, recalled. Soliloquies stand out like arias; conversations like ensembles. Often the other people on stage do not seem to hear what is being said. And all this is controlled with a perfect sense of shaping and timing.

Lulu's portrait as Pierrot is used in each of the five acts. In Act One it is being painted. In the next three acts its frame is changed as Lulu's social position is changed. In the last act it has been cut from its frame and is darkened and wrinkled. Then it is nailed to the attic wall in a symbolic crucifixion. It still impresses her clients and watches over the final moonlit, bloody orgy. Passing through the worlds of the bourgeois, the artist, the nouveaux riches, she ends where she started, in the gutter.

Neither Wedekind nor his contemporaries saw the play staged. He had no illusions and in fact at first called it a 'Book Drama'. But he did not even see it printed. Instead for twenty obsessed, debilitating years he struggled with the censors to save some of it – most sadly of all, becoming his own censor. He made more and more versions, defended it in prefaces and prologues, trying to make it acceptable to theatres and audiences. He cut, changed, diluted and toned down. He tore it into two separate plays and added a new act, new characters and new incidents to each of the plays. Occasionally they have been performed separately. The first is called *Earth-Spirit* and the second keeps the title of the original 'Monster Tragedy', *Pandora's Box*. Together they are known as *Lulu – A Double Tragedy*. It was only the subsequent adaptions that made the play overloaded, repetitive, confused and in a curious way bland. The only real gain Wedekind achieved in the rewriting was the incident in which Lulu dictates to Schöning his farewell letter to his fiancée – an incident Berg made into a highlight of his own reworking of the text for his opera. It was left unfinished when he died. In 1979 Friedrich Cerha completed it from Berg's sketches. It is now a milestone in the international opera repertoire.

In 1913 Wedekind made a last attempt to return to the original

'Monster Tragedy': but Jack the Ripper does not appear and Lulu only forsees her end in a vision. In the 1960s, Wedekind's daughter Kadidja made her own, truer version from the two adapted plays. This rekindled interest in the play. In the 1980s Hartmut Vinçon reconstructed the original text from the many manuscripts, fragments, drafts and notebooks which are scattered through archives in Switzerland and Germany. This reconstruction* was published in 1990, and our translation is taken from it.

The German director Peter Zadek realised the reconstructed text's importance and directed the first production in 1987 at the Hamburger Schauspielhaus. Though he updated the play to the 1950s (Lulu's picture shows her in a bathing costume and Stalin's death is announced at the end of Act Three), the production was widely acclaimed and toured in Germany and abroad.

Most of the original text is of course in German, but a large part of Act Four is in French and in Act Five Lulu's dealings with Mr Hopkins, Kungu Poti and Jack the Ripper are in English. Mr Hopkins does not speak. Kungu Poti speaks in broken English and we have kept this. Sometimes the English spoken by Lulu and Jack the Ripper is ungrammatical and slightly un-English in tone. We have corrected the grammar but otherwise kept it much as it is: it has a strange, hallucinatory effect. We have cut one of Lulu's clients, a professor called Dr Hilti. He speaks a comic Swiss-German and the point would be missed in translation into English. He is satirized for his academic silliness and social arrogance. But the main loss in cutting him is that for the whole time he is in Lulu's room the Countless sits at the back with a pistol to her head – one of her attempts at suicide. We regret the loss.

The only significant adaption we have made is to Act Four. In the original the people at the gaming table – nouveaux riches, financiers, journalists, prostitutes, pimps, etc. – are brought on stage and satirized for their lust, social ambition and greed. We have cut much of this. We

* Frank Wedekind, *Die Büchse der Pandora, Eine Monstretragödie*, Buchdrama. Historisch-kritische Ausgabe der Urfassung von 1894. Herausgegeben, kommentiert und mit einem Essay von Hartmut Vinçon. Editions – und Forschungsstelle Frank Wedekind, Darmstadt. Verlag Jürgen Häusser Darmstadt.

have also cut the letter Casti-Piani reads to Lulu: it is from a society woman he has sold to a brothel in Cairo. These cuts could be restored for a large-scale production. Apart from this we have cut a very few lines whose meaning is lost or significantly lessened. Lines which may seem too modern, for example the anarchistically comic moments in tragedy, are faithfully translated from Wedekind's German.

Wedekind is at last recognised, not as an interesting eccentric but as a founder of modern theatre and one of its most original and important playwrights.

ELISABETH BOND-PABLÉ
1992

A Note on *Spring Awakening*

Spring Awakening is partly about the misuse of authority. All the
adult men in the play work in the professions (except the locksmith
and Fastcrawler). They are members of institutions that are part of
the state, and they base their work on the state's ethos and teach its
doctrines. The judge is a verbal sadist, the doctor a quack, the head
of the reformatory an upholder of the nineteenth-century philosophy
of brutality-and-christianity, and the teachers fact-machines that
scheme but can't think. Their inefficiency as human beings and
their inefficiency as functionaries involve each other – which is why
authoritarian states are wasteful and finally collapse.

Our society is highly inefficient; the modern, scientific, industrial
state is probably the most inefficient culture that's ever existed.
Anyone who's worked in a modern office knows that office
workers spend as much of their time as they can avoiding work and
daydreaming. And when factory workers go through their minute
mechanical operations they sustain themselves not through an act of
will or pleasure but only because the conveyor belt or hopper pushes
them into activity. That's an obviously inefficient use of human
beings, and it leads to even greater inefficiency – to a breakdown
in personal and social lives. There is no human reward in such
work, only wages. That is not an acceptable recompense for a life
of industrial captivity. A modern factory puts its workers in chains.
It's designed to use machinery with the utmost possible efficiency
– in the narrowest mechanical sense – but it uses human beings
with almost total inefficiency. People are not mentally, physically or
emotionally designed to be machine watchers, least of all when the
machines belong to others. And although people can adapt to many
things, when the adaptations needed are extreme and unrewarding
they lead to irrationalism, nervousness and sickness. So factories are
constantly shut down by strikes and hampered by works-to-rule and
demarcation disputes. There isn't even any good reason to *try* to co-
operate when not only the luxuries but even the basic securities go to
the exploiters. The same irrationalism and sickness occur throughout

society and create crime and violence. These are warning signs.
When people are so organised that their culture becomes irrational
and trivial, their entertainment facile and sentimental, their politics
xenophobic and racialist, and their morality a sycophantic respect for
the law and order of self-perpetuating elites, then they are not *human*
beings. A tiger doesn't have to choose to be a tiger, but a human
being has to choose to be human or else he is only an over-efficient
animal. And that means he is an inefficient man, and dangerous to
himself and others. Our society makes it difficult to choose to be
human because we don't have a culture (in the sense I shall describe
later) but only an organisation.

The adults in *Spring Awakening* are dangerous. Obviously they
destroy or brutalise their children. But what of themselves and
their pleasures? A miserable sort of sex between unhappy women
and unfulfilled men; gloomy drinking at funerals; pride, arrogance
and isolation. The judge says 'I see the future so grey, so overcast',
and the priest calls life a cross. They are dangerous not only to
themselves but to everyone. They exist only through conflict and
their conflict doesn't come from an analytical passion but is a wish
for destruction. The teachers fight about trivialities; they are afraid
to question anything more important. Their satisfaction is associated
with their own or others' pain. Their conflict can't end because
they're each at war with themselves. They must either destroy
themselves or create new enemies. They are typical authoritarian
men: sly, cringing, mindless zombies to those over them, and
narrow, vindictive, unimaginative tyrants to those under them. And,
as they never see those under them with imagination, they don't even
really 'exist' for them! If their masters say that those under them
should be exploited more, or exterminated, the zombies carry out the
orders. They concentrate all their imagination on those over them,
and live in a rich and intricate mental world in which they either
glamorise their overlords or secretly accuse them of extravagant,
endless malice and deviousness. This is the character of the servants
of fascism. Evil is made metaphysical so that it need not be fought.
Praise and blame become the same thing, because fear has paralysed
action. The simple, brutal facts of exploitation and coercion are
ignored.

These men make wars possible. They are the means if not the

cause. The murder and suicide of children in *Spring Awakening*
shock us. But what of those who survive? If we place the play at
the turn of the century, they were killed off in the First World
War – and that was called heroism. Can a society survive having
military heroes? When Kennedy got out of the Cuba confrontation
without using nuclear weapons, some of the American military
were sorry. That's only an extreme example of the present crisis
in the relationship between force and politics. In the past a state's
security depended on its ability to control its enemy's army, now
it depends on its ability to control its own. And what of the civilian
hero? In a technological society everything depends on conformity to
routine, in work and leisure. Glamorisation of the stiff-upper-lipped,
religious, patriotic, law-abiding TV hero – the paragon of watch
committees and pro-censorship campaigners – is an incitement to
thuggery, violence and civil disorder. How else can the culturally
deprived imitate the initiative of the public hero, how else dissolve
their intellectual bewilderment in action so as to create the illusion
of a heroic solution? – except by kicking someone as innocent as
themselves. In a non-culture it's not pornography that corrupts and
produces violence – at the worst it only leads to hedonistic quietism
– but the glamorisation of public-school, clean-cut moral virtue.
An undemocratic technology creates this paradox: the closest most
members of that society can get to recreating in themselves the pose
and dynamic of a glamorised police force is by breaking the law.
Paradoxes such as this are at the heart of our cultural decay.

Many of the young people in *Spring Awakening* are already like
their elders. They have the same brash egoism, almost the same
brutality – not quite, because it is still nakedly sneering and not yet
covered with fake morality. All these boys will go to the trenches
and die with the same obedience they learned at school and were
rewarded for with exam passes. Education in that sort of society is a
preparation not for life but quite literally for death. And so is ours –
if it doesn't leave us sane and free enough to ask why human animals
who have been trained to obey like laboratory rats are sitting in front
of buttons that can begin nuclear destruction.

   This sort of discipline is synonymous with mindlessness. We
hide this by talking of 'self-discipline' and of freedom being 'the

knowledge of necessity', but in a society that is more destructive than creative that is certainly not true. Self-discipline, in this society, means coercing yourself instead of paying an official to coerce you. It isn't self-responsibility. Self-responsibility always stresses moral understanding, it defines even its certainties by questions. No *human* being can abdicate this responsibility for the sake of discipline. That doesn't mean they cannot co-operate. In fact only in this way can co-operation be efficient. The discipline imposed by authority, no matter how subtly, is inefficient. It wastes energy and stops initiative.

Disciplined people always judge by appearances, and they are educated not only to do what they are told but to believe they *want* to do it. Some children try to escape this discipline. Often the most alert and intelligent children are regarded by their teachers as the least able. Moritz isn't a fool. He sees under the surface – itself a socially undesirable thing to do. But he isn't robust. He withdraws into fantasies and dreams. These are called poetry, and it would be inhuman to deny them to a prisoner. The danger is that instead of using them as private comfort for his anguish, he fantasises reality. In Act one, scene four, it's *not* true that he's passed the exam – yet. But it *is* true that he could have run away – at least as much as Röbel or any other student. In a similar way authority corrupts art and turns it away from reality. The ineffectual pessimism which Moritz describes in the last scene – sonorous, world weary, smiling serenely over the tragedies and absurdities of the world – has great academic respectability. It's the cliché that poets write for tomorrow – about as possible as shaving in a mirror not yet made. It's Auden saying all the left-wing poetry of the thirties didn't save one Jew from the gas chambers. It can immediately be seen to be a false attitude.

Melchior is even worse than Moritz: he's normal. Only the abnormal fit into polite society. He is a threat to it. He is also another instance of the ultimate justice in human affairs: his father the judge, the defender of law and order or social injustice, has a criminal son – that is, a normal son who wishes to live in the knowledge of what he is and accept responsibility for it. But even he has been smeared over with Nietzschean melodrama. He has a philosophy of egoism that denies moral discrimination. But it is only an adolescent pose, made plausible to him because he sees the hypocrisy of public morality. In the last scene of Act one, when

he asks Wendla about charity, he doesn't attack moral differences.
The poor and unemployed would be right to hate Wendla's parents.
That would be rational. (I leave out the question of forgiveness
because that's useless in a slum.) He is only objecting to the moral
judgements of the Public God, who condemns people for doing what
they can't help doing. And there is a twist: Wendla *would* like to
visit the poor because it made her *un*happy. Discipline is joy through
misery. The paradox is another of those our society lives by. The
irony of the scene is that authoritarians must hold (as Wordsworth
did) that god created the poor for the moral education of mankind,
just as he created lepers that saints might have sores to kiss.

The play isn't out of date. It becomes more relevant as our armies
get stronger, our schools, prisons and bombs bigger, our means of
imposing discipline themselves more disciplined and more veiled,
and our self-knowledge not much greater. The aim of the education
shown in this play is to stop people asking questions. That's also a
foundation of the consumer society. Consume, and don't ask what
or where or why or anything at all except for more. There may
seem to be a great difference between Wedekind's society and ours.
There *is* a difference in technique. It's more efficient to replace
naked force with consumer rewards. But even these are backed by
force. The comfort is only apparent, the future remains insecure.
People are encouraged, but when this fails, they are still forced.
Modern technological industry offers very little security. The state
and commerce have become one inter-related machine that must
be kept running at all costs. People can't fall back on the natural
environment when their society is unacceptable to them, as drop-outs
in feudal or primitive societies could do, at least for a time. The
total-machine *is* the environment. The self-autonomy of drop-outs
in our society is really only the self-autonomy of parasites, and our
society is clearly so arranged that its parasites live off the poor not
the rich.

The only purpose of our society is to keep the total-machine
running. Human objectives are sacrificed to this mechanical
imperative. There are examples of this everywhere. Why does a
working-class father work in a factory to make bombs to drop on
other working men's children? He doesn't even have the incentive of

increasing his dividend. So has he no moral sense? That judgement is easy. What else can he do? He must take what work there is or his family will live in poverty – perhaps not in hunger and cold, but in a deeper poverty, the cultural poverty that causes crime, child battering, family violence, drunkenness, poor education, intellectual stagnation, wasted time, and social persecution and rejection. He is forced to act immorally – and rewarded for doing so – because he has no democratic responsibility for his own life. He can't ask questions because he's never allowed to choose answers. Those are left to the people who run the total-machine, and they won't provide moral answers because they are only concerned with keeping the total-machine running. So ironically the working people who are denied democratic responsibility are often the ones who insist on the total-machine being kept running at all costs – it's the only security they have. Right-wing politicians take this as proof that the working class isn't interested in moral questions. They don't see that pseudo-democracy is the political organisation that makes moral initiative impossible – at least as an integral part of the working of the state. And that really it is only another aspect of that extraordinary and optimistic truth: human emotions and mind, rationality and physical functioning, are so inter-related that only morally active people can sustain a society that is efficient, whose activity isn't just the frenzy of an explosion. Without freedom any organisation becomes sterile because there is no moral choice, no emotional commitment and no physical stability. The one leads to the other.

We live in a scientific age. We ought to educate our children well. Most children are taught lies. They are told that life has meaning and purpose, that their own actions count and so they must be careful what they do, that they must treat life as an adventure, and that they live in a democracy. But the children who go to the barrack-schools in our cities know that they will pass dull lives (the excretory metaphor is intended) in grey, ugly cities, will only be able to show initiative when they strike, and will have no democratic responsibility for the future and welfare of even their own family. So they can't learn the culture they're offered. You might as well offer them the mores of ancient Rome. Our behaviour is as absurd as if we tried to teach Latin to children who will spend their lives in industrial slums.

We *do* still teach them a dead culture, a dead religion and dead social myths.

What is culture? Human beings must have a culture, it's a biological necessity. We have mechanical, mental and emotional abilities. We see, hear, remember, we have manipulating hands and a subtle posture, we can trust, love and so on. All this creates a wide experience that pours into a child and must be organised so that it can cope with the world – that is, have a technology – and live in harmony with others; and the two together make a culture. A culture is what you live by, and it makes human living possible. But if it's going to be lived by it must be tested against reality. (This is a peculiarity of children which adults can lose by going privately mad, or by going politically mad and adopting fantasy political cultures such as fascism. This, like all attempts to live outside reality, ends in disaster.) The culture offered to children in our city barrack-schools – when they are too cowed to play truant – doesn't stand this test. So it would be irrational of children to accept it. And as the human young must have a culture, must have attitudes and beliefs, founded on experience, that enable them to form a community with the people they live with – so they are left to their own devices and develop a culture of their own. What happens in our great technological cities in this flowering of the age of science? Our children learn the culture of the outlaw. It is the only culture open to them. It is often a brutal culture, and of course this leads to calls from the law-abiding for more violence to deal with it. In this way society is doubly brutalised by its neglect. The culture of the outlaw flourishes in our cities, and – if technology hadn't made our situation dangerous and true democracy essential – that would even be a good sign, because it would show that the young are better judges of reality than the old and still reject the spurious.

Technology is a giant that must be made to work to the human scale. Factories haven't yet been designed to do this. They don't even develop the loyalty of mining communities, because there is no human pride in the work they offer, no physical or mental skill, only a few mechanical tricks. When people live and work in ways that, in spite of all the human capacity to adapt, are still unsuitable for them, when their work and entertainment make no demands on their creativity, so that their creative abilities aren't used and challenged, then they work badly and can't co-operate in a community. Why did men die so obediently in the First World War? One reason is that they were already living lingering deaths.

There will soon be a worsening of the technological crisis and more political unrest. The total-machine will stall for many reasons. Human beings aren't bits of mechanical machinery and therefore they don't fit easily into the total-machine. This activates their defensive aggression. And commercial technology not only destroys its material resources, it also stimulates rampant consumer greed and so destroys its social basis. It can only offer more and more rewards, and in a crisis its promises aren't kept and so there is still more fear and aggression. And anyway even if prosperity continued, the total-machine could still only be maintained by offering more rewards – which become more and more unrewarding, even a nuisance! Prosperity is as corroding as crisis, success as destructive as failure – another of the paradoxes that threaten us. Our system uses human beings so inefficiently that it must destroy itself either through success or failure. The usual answer to all this is force. Strikes are made illegal, the punishment of hooliganism is made harsher. But the inflationary leap-frogging of law-and-order and unrest-and-violence can't restore balance. It is itself a part of the crisis we're in. We're trapped in a cultural inflation of threat and counter-threat, and this conflict can't create its own solution. The solution, either good or bad, must be imposed from outside. And if it's good, it can't be sanctioned by our present social morality. Either way our present social system must be replaced.

Politicians will probably try to stabilise society by using technology directly against their citizens (as rewards are either no longer available or don't work). They will have the deepening crisis as a justification, and conventional morality will be on their side. Instead of creating a society in which people can live happily, which has till now been the justification for the force used in politics, they will try to create people who will fit into their society – people who are small total-machines. It's usually thought this would be done by genetics, selection, open indoctrination. Perhaps these ideas are too crude. They would require legislation that would publicly demonstrate what was going on. Our democracy could be gutted in simpler ways, even without the spoken or conscious intention of doing it. The control of ideas, information, working and living environments, entertainment, the limitation of the right to organise, and heavier penal sanctions – these are probably the only things that would be necessary. The members of the total-machine need not be tranquillised or peaceful; obedience and consent can be obtained through anger and fear. Either way, technology and science would be used to produce sycophantic loyalty, aggressive jingoism and belligerent social conformity. That is of course an irrational use of science. But science is rational only in its methods, not in its social application. The use of scientific truth has to be watched as closely as the disposal of sewage. The first responsibility lies with those who create it. We know that if society is going to work we mustn't defecate on the streets; yet scientists still defecate knowledge on the White House carpet and protest when they're called irrational. When there are no sane political controls on the use of science, what is the justification for society's decision to put scientific truth in a category higher than moral truth?

I think, anyway, that a political equilibrium created by technology would fail. I don't believe in human robots or technological ants. The only viable solution is to recreate the possibility of genuine human choice, to have a real instead of a pseudo-democracy. *Spring Awakening* doesn't go into this problem. Perhaps the Masked Man takes Melchior to an ego-land of hedonistic daydreams. But perhaps his 'doubt of having everything' is more than a *fin de siècle* pose. It could be the understanding of the inter-relatedness of living things and events, an understanding that the place where he is, and the society in which he is, are *also* man.

People used to think they had a secret soul, a centre of introspection in which god had set his tent. It might seem that the world was absurd and immorality triumphant, but every man carried the divine order in his soul and at the end of time justice would be decided there. Soul was god. In the nineteenth century god died and the soul became an empty tomb, a hole you could fall into and be lost. There was no infinite justice, only the terror of nothingness; no meaning, everything was possible. Soul was now almost the devil. We have no use for these images of soul because we can't wait for the justice of another world. We can't tolerate the injustice of this

one. But we need an image of ourselves that doesn't condemn us
to egoism or the absurd. When we talk about self-knowledge or
self-consciousness, when we consider the standard by which we judge
ourselves and others, so that we can make sense of our lives, when
we look into the hidden mirror – what do we see? Other faces. The
most intimate part of man is the most public. When we're most near
to ourselves we find other people. To use the language of earlier
times: soul is other people. My soul lives in others – but remains
mine. That shouldn't surprise us, we're social animals. But we have
to understand that if we act towards others with a lower standard
than our self-respect, so that our other-consciousness is inferior to
our self-consciousness – then that lower standard is also a form of
action or existence that we experience as part of ourselves, and must
criticise by the very act of being self-conscious. Self-consciousness
isn't merely intellectual, it's an emotional awareness of our right
to justice and autonomy. It is the standard we have for ourselves,
the judgement we make of ourselves. That is inalienable from
self-consciousness. If we try to have two standards – one for
ourselves and one for others – we *must* become self-critical, must live
in conflict with ourselves. Then no matter how much we consume
we are still feeding, clothing and entertaining someone we can't live
with. This conflict is most acute in the authoritarian man. His mind
and emotions are so well schooled in hate, that the only way he can
live with the self-hatred that results is by sacrificing himself to the
hero of destruction: the fascist leader.

Our education, social myths, economic activity, all develop this
spirit. Our culture fouls the mirror and heaps trash on it. The
class-divided consumer society can't solve this problem. We must
remain as unsatisfied as beggars till we can act towards other people
as we act towards ourselves, and till then we can't have a culture but
only an organisation. An organisation is based on class-division. It
can accommodate machines but not fulfil people or even satisfy them.
That's why it's inefficient and self-destructive. Human beings must
have a full culture in the sense I've described because, only when
they live in co-operation, mutual respect and affability with their
community, can they bear to live with themselves. Human discontent
can only be satisfied by this sort of culture, or at least the knowledge
that we're working for it. Our crisis isn't just about technology. It's

a crisis of the species. We no longer know how to live or survive. The only way to begin to solve this crisis is to look in the mirror and see other people. Did the Masked Man lead Melchior to die in the First World War, going straight from spring to winter? Our future is as doubtful. We have to understand the dangers, the opportunities and the shortage of time. Time is no longer a benign old man with a white beard, a staff and a lantern. It is a crying child tugging at our sleeve and asking to be carried.

EDWARD BOND
1974

A Note on the Language

The English version is meant to be acted, and so we have simplified
the original German in a few places. An example is the opening
of the last scene. Melchior's description of the graveyard is more
elaborate in the German. To us it sounded a bit like a description of
a Walt Disney graveyard. If we had kept *all* the original elaboration
it would have been unspeakable by contemporary performers.
Performers at the turn of the century thought and spoke in
paragraphs. For better or worse, contemporary performers think
and speak – and their audiences think and listen – in sentences.
The architectural construction of paragraphs sounds artificial to us.
It has been destroyed by the wisecrack, the retort, the exclamation.
Nevertheless the language in this translation remains elaborate and
in places consciously literary. That is because the characters use
language and imagery in a more complex way than most of us do.
The performers must *use* this complexity, and not try to sweep it
under the carpet as a nuisance. It is at the heart of the play. The
characters are afraid to use their bodies, and so their language
becomes either an embrace or a blow. It's easy to find examples
of this – the judge's verbal sadism is one. Many of the others have
the same fault. There is the children's imitation of their elders'
clichés – because these represent maturity for them. And Melchior's
mother uses style to lie to herself. How else can you describe
her extraordinary tendentiousness in her scene with Melchior and
Moritz? Later she masturbates herself with words in her letter to
Moritz; she uses morality like a coquette. And her argument with
the judge is a calculated intercourse between two rapists. When
her deceit is finally pierced the suddenness of the change shows her
emotional state. She is not slowly persuaded; it's as if her husband
suddenly knocked down a wall in her mind and revealed another
room already completely furnished and inhabited. She immediately
produces a few words as ruthless and cruel as anyone's in the play.

None of the characters can describe the things that matter or
could save them. The elders don't discuss, they make speeches.

Their voices flatten silence like drums, and their tongues beat out the rhythms like wooden drum sticks. The exception to all this is the Masked Man. He is usually drier and more ironic. Wedekind called the play a comedy – and it is very funny. But almost all the intentional jokes are made by the Masked Man. The others are too afraid to laugh, and so they can't think.

EDWARD BOND
1974

Spring Awakening: A Children's Tragedy

This translation of *Spring Awakening* was first staged on 24 May, 1974 at the National Theatre, with the following cast:

Children

MELCHIOR GABOR	Peter Firth
MORITZ STIEFEL	Michael Kitchen
HÄNSCHEN RILOW	Dai Bradley
ERNST RÖBEL	Gerard Ryder
OTTO	David Dixon
GEORG ZIRSCHNITZ	Keith Skinner
ROBERT	Martin Howells
LÄMMERMEIER	Christopher Guard
WENDLA BERGMANN	Veronica Quilligan
MARTHA BESSEL	Jane Carr
THEA	Jenny Agutter
ILSE	Patti Love

Boys in the Reformatory

DIETER	Rupert Frazer
REINHOLD	Ian Mackenzie
RUPERT	James Smith
HELMUT	Glyn Grain
GASTON	Bryan Brown

Parents

HERR GABOR	Joseph O'Conor
HERR STIEFEL	James Mellor
FRAU GABOR	Susan Engel
FRAU BERGMANN	Beryl Reid
INA MÜLLER, Wendla's sister	Judith Paris

Teachers

HEADMASTER SUNSTROKE	William Squire
PROFESSOR BONE BREAKER	Alex McCrindle
PROFESSOR GUTGRINDER	Kenneth Benda
PROFESSOR TONGUETWISTER	Stephen Williams
PROFESSOR FLYSWATTER	Peter Needham
PROFESSOR THICKSTICK	Kenneth Mackintosh
PROFESSOR APELARD	Colin Fay

Other adults

THE MASKED MAN	Cyril Cusack
DR LEMONADE	Daniel Thorndike
DR PROCRUSTES	Alan Hay
REVEREND BALDBELLY	Pitt Wilkinson
FASTCRAWLER, the school porter	Alan Hay
FRIEND GOAT	Glyn Grain
LOCKSMITH	Pitt Wilkinson
UNCLE PROBST	Peter Rocca

Directed by Bill Bryden

The action takes place in a provincial town in Germany, 1891–1892.

Act One

SCENE ONE

Living room.

WENDLA. Why have you made my dress so long, mother?

FRAU BERGMANN. You're fourteen today.

WENDLA. I'd rather not have been fourteen if I'd known you'd make my dress so long.

FRAU BERGMANN. Your dress isn't too long, Wendla. What next? Can I help it if my child is four inches taller every spring? A grown girl can't still go round dressed like a little princess.

WENDLA. At least the little princess's dress suits me better than this nightshirt. Let me wear it once more, mother. One more long summer. Fourteen or fifteen, that's still soon enough for this sackcloth. Let's keep it till my next birthday. I'd only trip over the braid and tear it.

FRAU BERGMANN. I don't know what I should say. I'd willingly keep you exactly as you are, darling. Other girls are stringy or plump at your age. You're not. Who knows what you'll be like when they're grown up?

WENDLA. Who knows – perhaps I won't be anything anymore.

FRAU BERGMANN. Child, child, where d'you get these ideas?

WENDLA. Don't, mummy. Don't be sad.

FRAU BERGMANN (*kisses her*). My precious.

WENDLA. They come to me in the evening when I can't sleep. It doesn't make me the least bit sad, and I go to sleep better then. Is it a sin to think about such things, mother?

FRAU BERGMANN. Go and hang the sackcloth in the wardrobe. Put your little princess's dress on again and God bless you. When I get a moment I'll sew a broad flounce round the bottom.

WENDLA (*hanging the dress in the wardrobe*). No, I'd rather even be twenty than that . . .!

FRAU BERGMANN. Only so that you don't catch cold! There was a time when this little dress was too long on you, but . . .

WENDLA. Now, when summer's coming? O mother, even children don't catch diphtheria in the knees! How can you be so fussy? You don't feel cold when you're my age – least of all in your knees. Would it be better if I was too hot? You ought to thank God that early one morning your precious doesn't rip the sleeves off her dress and come to you before it's still light with no shoes and stockings on! When I wear my sackcloth I'll be dressed like a fairy queen underneath. Don't be cross, mummy. No one can see it then.

SCENE TWO

Sunday evening.

MELCHIOR. It's too boring. I give up.

OTTO. Then we'll all have to stop! – Have you done your homework, Melchior?

MELCHIOR. Go on playing!

MORITZ. Where are you going?

MELCHIOR. Walking.

GEORG. It'll be dark soon!

ROBERT. Have you done your homework already?

MELCHIOR. Why shouldn't I walk in the dark?

ERNST. Central America! Louis the fifteenth! Sixty verses of Homer! Seven quadratic equations!

MELCHIOR. Damned homework!

GEORG. If only the Latin essay wasn't wanted tomorrow!

MORITZ. You can't think of anything without homework getting in the way!

OTTO. I'm going home.

GEORG. And me. Homework!

ERNST. And me, and me.

ROBERT. 'Night, Melchior.

MELCHIOR. Sleep well!

They all go except MORITZ *and* MELCHIOR.

MELCHIOR. I'd like to know exactly what we're in this world for!

MORITZ. School makes me wish I was a cart horse! What do we go to school for? To be examined! And why are we examined? So we can fail. Seven have got to fail because the next class is only big enough for sixty. – I've felt so odd since Christmas . . . O hell, if it wasn't for papa I'd pack my things tonight and sign on board a ship.

MELCHIOR. Let's talk about something else.

They walk.

MORITZ. Look at that cat with its tail poking up in the air!

MELCHIOR. D'you believe in omens?

MORITZ. Don't really know. It came from over there. It's nothing.

MELCHIOR. In my opinion that's the Charybdis people fall into when they try to rise out of the Scylla of religious superstition. Let's sit under this beech. The warm wind's blowing over the mountains. I'd like to be a little animal that's rocked and swayed in the tops of the trees the whole night.

MORITZ. Undo your waistcoat, Melchior.

MELCHIOR. O, the way the wind blows your clothes!

MORITZ. God, it's getting pitch dark, you can't see a hand stuck up in front of you. Where are you, actually? – Melchior, don't you also think that man's sense of shame is just a product of his education?

MELCHIOR. I was thinking about that the other day. It seems to me, at least, it's deeply rooted in human nature. For example, suppose you had to completely strip off in front of your best friend. You wouldn't do it, not unless he does it at the same time. – But then perhaps it's all just a question of whatever happens to be in good taste.

MORITZ. I've already decided when I have children I'll let them sleep together in the same room, in the same bed if possible – boys and girls. I'll let them help each other to dress and undress morning and night, and when it's hot the boys and the girls will both wear nothing all day except a white woollen tunic and a leather belt. I think that then when they grow up they won't be as tense as most of us are.

MELCHIOR. I'm sure of it! The only question is, what about when
the girls have babies?

MORITZ. Why have babies?

MELCHIOR. I believe in a definite instinct in these things. For
example, suppose you keep two cats – a tom and a bitch – shut
up together from when they're kittens. You keep them away
from all contact with the outside world so they've only got their
instincts left. Sooner or later the cat will become pregnant, even
though they had no example to follow.

MORITZ. With animals that must finally happen by itself.

MELCHIOR. Even more so with men I think! Listen, Moritz,
when your boys are sleeping in the same bed with your girls and
suddenly they feel their first masculine itch – I'll take a bet with
anyone that –

MORITZ. You may be right. But still.

MELCHIOR. And I'm sure it would be just the same with the girls!
Not that girls actually – obviously one can't speak definitely – but
at least you can surmise – and their natural curiosity would do
the rest!

MORITZ. By the way, I've got a question.

MELCHIOR. What?

MORITZ. But you will answer?

MELCHIOR. Of course!

MORITZ. Promise!

MELCHIOR. My hand on it. Well, Moritz?

MORITZ. Have you really done your homework?

MELCHIOR. Come on, you can tell me. There's no one else here.

MORITZ. Of course, my children will have to work all day in the
farm or the garden – or play games that are good for their bodies.
Riding, gymnastics, climbing – and certainly no sleeping on soft
beds like us. We're terribly weak. I don't believe you'd ever have
dreams if you slept on a hard bed.

MELCHIOR. From now till after the harvest I'm only going to sleep
in my hammock. I've put my bed away. It folds up . . . Last
winter I dreamed I whipped our Rufus so long he couldn't move.
That's the worst thing I've dreamed. – Why are you staring at me
like that?

MORITZ. Have you already felt it?

MELCHIOR. What?

MORITZ. How you said.

MELCHIOR. The masculine itch?

MORITZ. H-hm.

MELCHIOR. And how!

MORITZ. Me too.

MELCHIOR. I've been able to for a long time. Almost a year now.

MORITZ. It was like being struck by lightning.

MELCHIOR. Did you have a dream?

MORITZ. But only very short – some legs in bright blue ballet
tights climbing over the teacher's desk or at any rate I thought
they wanted to climb over – I only caught a glimpse.

MELCHIOR. Georg Zirnschnitz dreamed about his *mother*!

MORITZ. Did he tell you that?

MELCHIOR. Out on Hangman's Hill.

MORITZ. If you knew what I've gone through since that night!

MELCHIOR. Bad conscience?

MORITZ. Bad conscience? *Fear of death*!

MELCHIOR. My God!

MORITZ. I thought I was incurable. I believed I was suffering
from an internal defect. In the end I only quietened down when
I started to write my Memoirs. Yes, yes, Melchior, the last three
weeks have been a Golgotha to me.

MELCHIOR. I was more or less all set for it. I felt a bit ashamed.
But that was all.

MORITZ. And you're almost a whole year younger than me!

MELCHIOR. I shouldn't give it another thought, Moritz. In my
experience there isn't a set age for the first time these feelings turn
up. You know that tall Lammermeier with the blond hair and
hooked nose? He's three years older than me. Hänschen Rilow
says he still dreams about apple tart and custard.

MORITZ. Chuck it, Melchior, how can Hänschen Rilow know?

MELCHIOR. He asked him.

MORITZ. He asked him? I wouldn't dare ask anyone.

MELCHIOR. You just asked me.

MORITZ. Good Lord, yes! Perhaps Hänschen also wrote his Last
Will! The games they play with us! And we're supposed to be
grateful. I don't remember ever wanting that sort of excitement!

Why couldn't I just sleep in peace till it was all over? My poor
parents could have had a hundred better children than me. But
I came, I don't know how, and then it's my fault I didn't stay
away! Haven't you ever thought about that, Melchior, exactly how
we came into this madhouse?

MELCHIOR. You don't even know that, Moritz?

MORITZ. How should I! I see how hens lay eggs, and I hear
mother's supposed to have carried me under her heart! Is that
enough? And I remember that when I was five I was already
embarrassed when anyone turned up the Queen of Hearts with the
low-cut dress. That feeling's gone. But now I can't even speak to
a girl without something I ought to be ashamed of coming into my
head and – I swear to you, Melchior – I don't know *what*.

MELCHIOR. I'll tell you everything. I got it partly from books,
partly from illustrations, partly from looking at nature. You'll be
surprised. It turned me into an atheist. I've already told Georg
Zirnschnitz! He wanted to tell Hänschen Rilow, but he'd already
had it from his governess when he was a kid.

MORITZ. I've gone through the encyclopaedia from A to Z. Words
– nothing but words, words! Not one single straightforward
explanation. O this feeling of shame! What good is an
encyclopaedia if it doesn't answer the first questions about life?

MELCHIOR. Have you ever seen two dogs running across
the street?

MORITZ. No! You'd better not tell me now, Melchior. I've got
to face Central America and Louis the fifteenth! As well as sixty
verses of Homer, seven quadratic equations, the Latin essay – I'd
just get into hot water with everyone again tomorrow. When you
have to study like a cart horse you must be as docile and stupid as
a donkey.

MELCHIOR. Come back to my room. In three quarters of an hour
I'll do the Homer, the equations, and *two* essays. I'll decorate
yours with a few simple mistakes, and the ball's in the hole!
Mother will make us some more lemonade and we'll have a
pleasant chat about reproduction.

MORITZ. I can't. I can't have a pleasant chat about reproduction.
If you want to do me a favour give me some written instructions.
Write down all you know. Write it as simply and clearly as

possible and stick it in my book during PT tomorrow. I'll take
it home without knowing it's there. I'll come across it sometime
when I'm not expecting to. I won't be able to stop my weary eyes
running over it . . . If it's absolutely unavoidable you can go as far
as a few diagrams in the margin.

MELCHIOR. You're like a girl. Well, have it your own way! It'll be
rather interesting homework. One thing, Moritz.

MORITZ. Hn?

MELCHIOR. Have you seen a girl?

MORITZ. Yes!

MELCHIOR. Everything?

MORITZ. The lot.

MELCHIOR. And me! So you won't need many diagrams.

MORITZ. At the fair. In the cubicle at the back of the wax works. If
I'd been caught I'd have been chased out of school! So beautiful –
and o! as clear as daylight.

MELCHIOR. Last summer I was with mama at Frankfurt . . . Are
you going already, Moritz?

MORITZ. Homework. 'Night.

MELCHIOR. Good night.

SCENE THREE

THEA, WENDLA *and* MARTHA *come along the street arm in arm.*

MARTHA. How the water gets into your shoes!

WENDLA. How the wind blows in your face!

THEA. How your heart thumps!

WENDLA. Let's go to the bridge. Ilse said the river's full of trees
and bushes. The boys have taken a raft out on the water. They
say Melchior Gabor was nearly drowned last night.

THEA. O, he can swim!

MARTHA. Of course he can, brat!

WENDLA. If he couldn't swim he could easily have been drowned!

THEA. Your plait's coming undone, Martha! Your plait's coming
undone!

MARTHA. O – let it come undone! It annoys me day and night. I
    mustn't have short hair like you, I mustn't have natural hair like
    Wendla, I mustn't have a fringe, I even have to go round the
    house with it done up – all to please my aunts!
WENDLA. Tomorrow I'll bring some scissors to Bible class. While
    you recite 'Blessed is the man who walks not in the counsel of the
    wicked' I'll cut it off.
MARTHA. For God's sake, Wendla! Papa beats me till I'm crippled
    and mama locks me up in the coal cellar for three nights at a time.
WENDLA. What does he beat you with, Martha?
MARTHA. Sometimes I think they'd miss something if they didn't
    have a disgraceful brat like me!
THEA. But, Martha!
WENDLA. And they wouldn't let you thread a bright blue ribbon
    through the top of your petticoat like us?
THEA. Pink satin! Mama insists pink satin goes with my pitch
    black eyes.
MARTHA. Blue looked so well on me! Mama pulled me out of my
    bed by my plait. Well – I fell head first flat on the floor. You see,
    mother comes up to pray with us every evening . . .
WENDLA. If I was you I'd have run far away long ago.
MARTHA. 'There you are, see what it'll come to! Yes, there you
    are! But she'll learn – O, she'll soon learn! At least I'll never be
    able to blame my mother when anything goes wrong – '
THEA. Hoo hoo!
MARTHA. D'you know what my mother meant by that, Thea?
THEA. No. Do you, Wendla?
WENDLA. I'd have asked her.
MARTHA. I lay on the floor and screamed and roared. Then papa
    comes. Rip – petticoat down. I'm out through the door. 'There
    you are! Now I want to go out on the street like that! – '
WENDLA. But that wasn't true, Martha!
MARTHA. I was freezing. I'd got the street door open. I had to
    sleep in a sack all night.
THEA. I couldn't sleep in a sack to save my life!
WENDLA. I'd like to sleep in your sack for you once.
MARTHA. If only they wouldn't beat me.
THEA. But you'd suffocate in it!

MARTHA. Your head's free. They tie it under your chin.

THEA. And then they beat you?

MARTHA. No. Only when it's something special.

WENDLA. What do they beat you with, Martha?

MARTHA. O, whatever they lay their hands on. Does *your* mother maintain it's indecent to eat bread in bed?

WENDLA. No, no.

MARTHA. I always think, they have their pleasure – even though they never talk about it. When I have children I'll let them grow up like the weeds in our rose garden. No one looks after them but they grow tall and strong – and the roses get weaker every summer and hang down on their stems.

THEA. When I have children I'll dress them all in pink – pink hats, little pink dresses, pink shoes. Only the stockings – stockings pitch black. When I go for a walk I'll let them all trot along in front of me. What about you, Wendla?

WENDLA. D'you already know you'll get some?

THEA. Why shouldn't we get some?

MARTHA. Aunt Euphemia hasn't got any.

THEA. Goose! Because she's not *married*!

WENDLA. Aunt Bauer was married three times – and she hasn't got even one.

MARTHA. If you do get some, Wendla, what d'you want: boys or girls?

WENDLA. Boys! Boys!

THEA. And boys for me!

MARTHA. And me. I'd rather have twenty boys than three girls.

THEA. Girls are boring.

MARTHA. If I wasn't already a girl I know I wouldn't want to become one.

WENDLA. That's a matter of taste, Martha. I'm happy because I'm a girl. Believe me I wouldn't change places with a king's son. – But I still only want boys!

THEA. That's stupid, so stupid, Wendla!

WENDLA. But surely, child, it must be a thousand times more ennobling to be loved by a man than a girl!

THEA. You're not claiming that Herr Pfalle the Junior Afforestation Officer loves Melli more than she loves him?

WENDLA. Of course I do, Thea. Pfalle has pride. He's proud of being a Junior Afforestation Officer – because that's all he's got! But Melli has *bliss* – because she's got a million times more than she had when she was on her own!

MARTHA. Aren't you proud of yourself, Wendla?

WENDLA. That would be silly.

THEA. Watch how she walks – how she looks – how she holds herself, Martha! If that's not pride!

WENDLA. But why? I'm just so happy at being a girl. If I wasn't a girl I'd kill myself so that next time . . .

    MELCHIOR *passes and greets them.*

THEA. He's got such a wonderful head.

MARTHA. He makes me think of the young Alexander going to school with Aristotle.

THEA. O God, Greek history! All I remember is that Socrates lay in a barrel while Alexander sold him a donkey's shadow.

WENDLA. I heard he's third in his class.

THEA. Professor Bonebreaker says he could be first if he wanted.

MARTHA. He's got a beautiful forehead, but his friend's got soulful eyes.

THEA. Moritz Stiefel? That dormouse, always asleep.

MARTHA. I've always found him very interesting company.

THEA. He puts you in a compromising situation everytime you meet. At the Rilows' Children's Ball he offered me some chocolates. Imagine, Wendla, they were warm and soft. Isn't that –? He said they'd been in his trousers too long.

WENDLA. What d'you think: Melchior Gabor once told me he didn't believe in anything – not in God, the afterworld – hardly in anything in this world!

SCENE FOUR

Park in front of the Grammar School.

MELCHIOR, OTTO, GEORG, ROBERT, HÄNSCHEN RILOW, LÄMMERMEIER.

MELCHIOR. D'you know where Moritz Stiefel's got to?

GEORG. He'll catch it! O, he'll catch it!

OTTO. He goes too far, he'll trip up one day!

LÄMMERMEIER. God knows I wouldn't like to be in his shoes now!

ROBERT. Impertinence! Disgraceful!

MELCHIOR. What – what is it?

GEORG. What is it? I'll tell you what it is . . .

LÄMMERMEIER. I don't want to be involved.

OTTO. Nor me – God, no.

MELCHIOR. If you don't tell me immediately . . .

ROBERT. It's very simple, Moritz Stiefel is burglaring the staff room.

MELCHIOR. The staff room!

OTTO. The staff room. Straight after Latin.

GEORG. He was last. He stayed behind on purpose.

LÄMMERMEIER. When I went down the corridor I saw him open the door.

MELCHIOR. I'll be damned!

LÄMMERMEIER. No – he'll be!

GEORG. They probably forgot the key.

ROBERT. Or Moritz carries a skeleton key.

OTTO. I wouldn't put that past him!

LÄMMERMEIER. He'll be lucky if all he gets is detention.

ROBERT. It'll go on his report.

OTTO. If the governors don't just kick him out.

HÄNSCHEN. There he is.

MELCHIOR. White as a sheet.

   MORITZ *comes in in frantic excitement.*

LÄMMERMEIER. Moritz, Moritz, what have you done now!

MORITZ. Nothing – nothing . . .

ROBERT. You're shaking.

MORITZ. With excitement – with happiness – with luck.

OTTO. Were you copped?

MORITZ. I've passed! Melchior, I've passed! O now the world can go to hell! I've passed! Who thought I'd pass? I still can't believe it! I read it twenty times! I couldn't believe it! O God it was

still there! Still there! *I've passed*! (*Smiles*.) I don't know – it's
so funny – the floor's going round – Melchior, Melchior, if you
knew what it was like!

HÄNSCHEN. Congratulations, Moritz. Just be grateful you
got away.

MORITZ. You can't know, Hänschen, you can't imagine the risk!
For three weeks I crept by that door as if it was the gates of hell.
And today a crack, the door was open. I think if someone had
offered me a fortune – nothing, o nothing could have stopped
me! I stood in the middle of the room. I pulled the files open –
tore through the pages – there it is! – and the whole time . . . I'm
shuddering.

MELCHIOR. And the whole time . . .?

MORITZ. The whole time the door was wide open behind me. How
I got out – how I got down the stairs I'll never know.

HÄNSCHEN. Has Ernst Röbel passed?

MORITZ. O yes, Hänschen! Ernst Röbel passed too!

ROBERT. Then you didn't read it right. If you don't count the
dunces, then we and you and Röbel make sixty-one, and the next
class only holds sixty.

MORITZ. I read it perfectly clearly. Ernst Röbel goes up as well as
me – of course at the moment we're both only provisional. Next
term they'll decide which of us has to give way. Poor Röbel! God
knows I'm not worried about myself now. I've been too near the
abyss already.

OTTO. I bet five marks you have to give way.

MORITZ. You haven't got it. I don't want to clean you out.
O Lord, I'll work like a slave after this. I can tell you now
– I don't care if you believe me – it doesn't matter anymore
– I – I know how true it is: if I hadn't passed I'd have shot
myself.

ROBERT. With a peashooter!

GEORG. Yellow belly!

OTTO. I'd like to see you shoot!

LÄMMERMEIER. Clip his ear and see what he does!

MELCHIOR (*hits* LÄMMERMEIER). Come on, Moritz. Let's go to
the forester's hut.

GEORG. You don't believe that rubbish!

MELCHIOR. Would it bother you? Let them chatter, Moritz, we'll go – out of this town!

PROFESSORS GUTGRINDER *and* BONEBREAKER *go by*.

BONEBREAKER. Beyond my comprehension, my dear fellow, how my best student can feel himself drawn towards precisely my very worst.

GUTGRINDER. Beyond mine too, my dear chap.

SCENE FIVE

A sunny afternoon.

MELCHIOR *and* WENDLA *meet each other in the forest.*

MELCHIOR. Is it really you, Wendla? What are you doing up here on your own? I've been wandering through the forest for three hours without meeting a soul, and now suddenly you come towards me out of the trees.

WENDLA. Yes, it's me.

MELCHIOR. If I didn't know you were Wendla Bergmann I'd think you were a wood nymph that's fallen out of the branches.

WENDLA. No, no, I'm Wendla Bergmann. Where have you come from?

MELCHIOR. I've been thinking.

WENDLA. I'm collecting woodruff. Mama uses them for spring wine. She *was* coming with me but Aunt Bauer turned up at the last moment. She doesn't like climbing so I came on my own.

MELCHIOR. Have you got the woodruff?

WENDLA. A whole basket full! It's as thick as clover over there under the beeches. Now I'm trying to find a path. I seem to have gone wrong. Perhaps you could tell me what time it is?

MELCHIOR. Just after half past three. When are you expected?

WENDLA. I thought it was later. I lay down quite a while on the moss by the stream and dreamed. Time went so quickly. I was afraid evening was already coming.

MELCHIOR. If you're not expected, let's stay here a little bit longer. My favourite spot's under the oak. If you lean your head

back against the trunk and stare through the branches up at the
sky, it hypnotises you. The ground's still warm from the sun this
morning. – I've wanted to ask you something for weeks, Wendla.

WENDLA. But I must be home by five.

MELCHIOR. We'll go together. I'll carry the basket and we'll go
along the river bed and be on the bridge in ten minutes. When
you lie like this with your head propped in your hands you have
the strangest ideas . . .

Both are lying under the oak.

WENDLA. What did you want to ask me, Melchior?

MELCHIOR. I know you often visit the poor, Wendla, and take
them food and clothes and money. D'you go because you want to
or does your mother send you?

WENDLA. Mostly mother sends me. They're poor working-class
families with too many children. Often the man can't find work so
they're cold and hungry. We've got a lot of left-over things lying
about in cupboards and drawers, we'll never use them now. What
made you think of that?

MELCHIOR. Are you pleased when your mother sends you?

WENDLA. O very pleased! How can you ask!

MELCHIOR. But the children are dirty, the women are sick, the
rooms are crowded with filth, the men hate you because you don't
have to work . . .

WENDLA. That's not true, Melchior. And if it were true I'd go
even more.

MELCHIOR. Why even more, Wendla?

WENDLA. I'd go to them even more. It would give me far more
happiness to be able to help them.

MELCHIOR. So you go to the poor to make yourself happy?

WENDLA. I go to them because they're poor.

MELCHIOR. And if it didn't make you happy you wouldn't go?

WENDLA. Can I help it if it makes me happy?

MELCHIOR. And for that you go to heaven! I was right, I've been
going over this for a month! Can a miser help it if visiting dirty,
sick children doesn't make him happy?

WENDLA. O, I'm sure it would make you very happy!

MELCHIOR. And yet because of that he suffers eternal

damnation! I'll write an essay and send it to the Reverend
Baldbelly. He put all this in my head! Why does he drivel on
at us about the joys of sacrificing yourself for others? If he can't
answer, I'm not going to any more confirmation classes and I
won't be confirmed.

WENDLA. Don't make your poor parents miserable over that! Let
them confirm you. They don't cut your head off. If it wasn't for
our dreadful white dresses and your baggy trousers we might even
get some fun out of it.

MELCHIOR. There is no self-sacrifice! There is no selflessness! I
watch the good enjoying themselves while the bad tremble and
groan – I watch you shaking your curls and laughing, Wendla
Bergmann, and it all makes me feel as lost as an outcast –
Wendla, what did you dream about when you were on the grass
by the stream?

WENDLA. Nonsense – silly things . . .

MELCHIOR. With your eyes open?

WENDLA. I dreamed I was a poor, poor beggar girl. I was sent
out on the streets every morning before five. I had to beg from
brutal, heartless people, all day in the storm and rain. And when
I came home at night, shivering with hunger and cold, and when
I didn't have all the money my father wanted, I was beaten . . .
beaten . . .

MELCHIOR. I understand, Wendla. You get that from silly
children's books. I promise you there aren't brutal people like that
any more.

WENDLA. O no, Melchior, you're wrong. Martha Bessel is beaten
night after night and you can see the weals next day. O what she
must suffer! It makes me hot when she tells us about it. I pity
her so much. I often have to cry in my pillow in the middle of
the night. I've been thinking for months how I can help her. I'd
happily take her place just for one week.

MELCHIOR. The father should be reported immediately. Then
they'd take the child away.

WENDLA. I haven't been hit in my whole life, Melchior – not even
once. I can hardly imagine what it's like to be beaten. I've beaten
myself to find out what it does to you. It must be a horrifying
feeling.

MELCHIOR. I don't believe it ever makes a child better.

WENDLA. What?

MELCHIOR. Being beaten.

WENDLA. With this switch for example. Ugh, how springy and thin.

MELCHIOR. That would draw blood.

WENDLA. Would you like to beat me with it once?

MELCHIOR. Who?

WENDLA. Me.

MELCHIOR. What's the matter, Wendla?

WENDLA. There's no harm in it.

MELCHIOR. O be quiet! I won't beat you.

WENDLA. But if I let you do it!

MELCHIOR. No, Wendla.

WENDLA. But if I ask you for it, Melchior!

MELCHIOR. Are you out of your mind?

WENDLA. I've never been beaten in my whole life!

MELCHIOR. If you can ask for something like that . . .

WENDLA. Please, please!

MELCHIOR. I'll teach you to ask! (*He hits her.*)

WENDLA. O God – I don't feel it at all . . .

MELCHIOR. Of course not – through all your skirts.

WENDLA. Then beat my legs!

MELCHIOR. Wendla! (*He hits her harder.*)

WENDLA. You're only stroking me! Stroking me!

MELCHIOR. You wait, you bitch, I'll thrash the devil out of you!

> *He throws the stick away and hits out at her with his fists. She bursts into a terrible scream. He takes no notice and punches at her in fury. Heavy tears stream down his face. He jumps up, grips his head and runs into the wood sobbing with misery.*

Act Two

SCENE ONE

Evening in Melchior's study.

The window is open, the lamp burns on the table. MELCHIOR *and* MORITZ *sit on the sofa.*

MORITZ. I'm quite lively again now, just a bit on edge. But I slept all through Greek. I'm surprised old Tonguetwister didn't twist my ears. I just scraped in on time this morning. My first thought when I woke up was irregular verbs. Damnation-hell-and-fireworks, I conjugated all through breakfast and all the way to school, till everything was green in front of my eyes . . . I must have gone blank about three. The pen made one more blot in my book. When Mathilde woke me up the lamp was smoking and the blackbirds were singing their hearts out in the lilac under the window – suddenly I felt so completely miserable again. I fastened my collar and put a brush through my hair. – But you feel satisfied when you've forced something out of yourself.

MELCHIOR. May I roll you a cigarette?

MORITZ. Thanks, I'm not smoking. – If I can only keep it up! I'll work and work till my eyes drop out. Ernst Röbel's already failed six times since the holidays: three times in Greek, twice with Bonebreaker, the last time in literary history. I've only been in that pitiful condition five times, and and it's definitely not happening again! Röbel won't shoot himself! Röbel's parents didn't sacrifice everything for him. He can become a mercenary whenever he likes, or a cowboy or a sailor. If *I* fail my father will have a heart attack and my mother go into a madhouse. I'd never survive it. Before the exams I prayed like Christ in the garden, I implored God to let me catch consumption so that this bitter cup would pass. It passed – but I'm still afraid to look up day or night. The halo that floats over it is winking at me from the

distance. Well now I've got the bull by the horns I'm going to
climb on its back. Then if I fall I have an infallible guarantee that
I'll break my neck.

MELCHIOR. Life is always unexpectedly mean. I rather incline to
hanging myself from a tree. What's keeping mama with the tea?

MORITZ. Tea will do me good. I'm actually shaking, Melchior! I
feel so strangely disembodied. Please touch me. I see – I hear
– I feel much more clearly – and yet it's all in a dream – o, so
strange. The garden's lying down there in the moonlight, so
still and deep, as if it's lying in eternity. There are veiled figures
coming out of the ground under the bushes. They hurry over the
clearings – busy and breathless – and vanish in the dusk. It's as
if a meeting's gathering under the chestnut trees. Shouldn't we go
down, Melchior?

MELCHIOR. After tea.

MORITZ. The leaves are rustling like little insects! It's as if my
dead grandmother was telling me the story of 'The Queen with
No Head'. There was a beautiful queen, as beautiful as the sun,
more beautiful than all the other girls. But unfortunately she came
into the world with no head. She couldn't eat, or drink, or see,
or laugh, or even kiss. She could only make the court understand
her by her soft little hands, and she tapped out declarations of war
and death sentences with her pretty little feet. One day she was
defeated by a king who happened to have two heads. They got in
each other's hair all the time and quarrelled so much that neither
of them could get a word in. The top wizard took the smaller
head and put it on the queen. There, it fits marvellously. So the
king married the queen, and instead of getting in each other's hair
they kissed: on their foreheads, their cheeks, their mouths – and
lived happily ever after. All rubbish! Since the holidays I can't get
the headless queen out of my mind. When I see a beautiful girl, I
see her with no head – and I keep suddenly seeing myself with no
head . . . Perhaps one day someone will put a head on me.

FRAU GABOR *brings tea and puts it on the table in front of*
MORITZ *and* MELCHIOR.

FRAU GABOR. There, boys, drink your tea. Good evening, Herr
Stiefel, how are you?

MORITZ. Thank you, Frau Gabor. – I'm watching the dance down there.

FRAU GABOR. You don't look too well. D'you feel all right?

MORITZ. It's nothing. I've been going to bed a bit late the last few nights.

MELCHIOR. Imagine, he worked through the whole night.

FRAU GABOR. You shouldn't, Herr Stiefel. You must look after yourself. Think of your health. School can't give you your health back again. Brisk walks in the fresh air. That's worth more at your age than perfect grammar.

MORITZ. Yes – brisk walks! While you're walking you can work in your head! Why didn't I think of that? – But I'd still have to do the written work indoors.

MELCHIOR. Do the written stuff with me. That'll make it easier for both of us. Mother, you know Max von Trenk went down with nervous exhaustion? Well, Hänschen Rilow came straight from Trenk's deathbed lunch-time today and told the Head Trenk had just died in his presence. The Head said 'Indeed. Haven't you still got two hours detention owing from last week? Here's a note for your Form Master. Get it sorted out. The whole class will assist at his funeral'. Hänschen could hardly move.

FRAU GABOR. What's your book, Melchior?

MELCHIOR. *Faust.*

FRAU GABOR. Have you read it?

MELCHIOR. Not all of it.

MORITZ. We're just in the Walpurgis Night.

FRAU GABOR. If I were you I'd have waited a year or two for that.

MELCHIOR. I haven't come across any other book that I think is so beautiful, mother. Why shouldn't I read it?

FRAU GABOR. Because you don't understand it.

MELCHIOR. You can't know that, mother. Of course, I know I don't understand its deepest meaning . . .

MORITZ. We always read together. That makes it incredibly easier to understand.

FRAU GABOR. You're old enough to know what's good for you and what's bad for you, Melchior. Do whatever you feel able to answer for to your own conscience. I shall be the first to acknowledge it if you never give me any cause to forbid you anything. I only want to make you aware that even the best can work harm when one lacks the maturity to know how to use it. But I shall always put my trust in you, rather than in some vague doctrine of education. If you need anything else, boys, come and call me, Melchior. I'm in my bedroom. (*Goes.*)

MORITZ. Your mother meant the business with Gretchen and the baby.

MELCHIOR. Did we even pause over it?

MORITZ. Faust couldn't have treated it more cold-bloodedly!

MELCHIOR. A common little scandal like that can't be the summit of such a masterpiece! Suppose Faust had just promised to marry her and then walked off? That would have been just as bad. There'd have been no baby – but Gretchen could still have died of a broken heart. When you see how frantically they all pounce on that one incident you'd think the whole world revolved round penis and vagina.

MORITZ. Frankly, Melchior, since reading your essay I feel it does. It fell out on the floor when I was reading a history book. I bolted the door and went through your lines like an owl flying through a burning wood. I think I read most of it with my eyes shut. It was like listening to your own forgotten memories – a song you hummed to yourself when you played as a child, and then hearing it again when you're lying down to die, coming out of someone else's mouth and breaking your heart. What moved me most was the part you wrote about the girl. I can't get it out of my mind. Honestly, Melchior, I'd rather suffer wrong than do wrong. To have to be overpowered by such a gentle force, and still be innocent – that seems the greatest sort of happiness to me.

MELCHIOR. I don't want to be given happiness like a beggar!

MORITZ. Why not?

MELCHIOR. I don't want anything I didn't have to fight for!

MORITZ. But would that still be happiness, Melchior? Melchior, the girl enjoys it like someone in heaven. It's a girl's nature to protect herself, to keep herself free from all bitterness till the last moment – so that she can feel all heaven falling on her at once. A girl is afraid of hell even at the moment she steps into paradise. Her feelings are as fresh as a stream when it breaks from the rocks. The girl lifts up a chalice that no earthly mouth has touched, a cup of flaming sparkling nectar and gulps it down – I think the satisfaction a man gets out of it must be cold and flat.

MELCHIOR. Think what you like but shut up. I don't like to think about it . . .

SCENE TWO

FRAU BERGMANN *wearing a hat and cape, and with a beaming face, comes through the middle door. She carries a basket on her arm.*

FRAU BERGMANN. Wendla! Wendla!

WENDLA *appears in petticoat and stays at the side door right.*

WENDLA. What is it, mother?

FRAU BERGMANN. You're up already, precious? What a good girl!

WENDLA. You've been out this early?

FRAU BERGMANN. Get dressed quickly. You must go down to Ina. You must take her this basket.

WENDLA (*gets fully dressed during the following*). You've been to Ina's? How was Ina? Won't she ever get better?

FRAU BERGMANN. You'll never guess, Wendla, last night the stork was with her and brought her a little boy.

WENDLA. A boy! A boy! O that's wonderful! That's what her chronic influenza was!

FRAU BERGMANN. A perfect boy!

WENDLA. I must see him, mother! Now I'm an aunt three times – aunt to one girl and two boys!

FRAU BERGMANN. And what boys! That's what happens when you live so close to the stork! It's only two years since she walked up the aisle in her white dress.

WENDLA. Were you there when he brought him?

FRAU BERGMANN. He'd just flown off again. Don't you want to pin on a rose?

WENDLA. Why didn't you get there a bit sooner, mother?

FRAU BERGMANN. I believe he might have brought you
something too – a brooch perhaps.

WENDLA. It's such a pity.

FRAU BERGMANN. Now I told you he brought you a brooch.

WENDLA. I've got enough brooches.

FRAU BERGMANN. Then be contented, child. What more do
you want?

WENDLA. I would very much like to have known whether he flew
in through the window or down the chimney.

FRAU BERGMANN. You must ask Ina. O yes, you must ask Ina
that, precious. Ina will tell you exactly. Ina spoke to him for a
good half hour.

WENDLA. I shall ask Ina when I get there.

FRAU BERGMANN. And don't forget, precious. I shall be very
interested myself to know if he came in through the window or
the chimney.

WENDLA. Or perhaps I'd better ask the chimney-sweep. The
chimney-sweep's bound to know if he used the chimney.

FRAU BERGMANN. Not the chimney-sweep, dear. Not the
chimney-sweep. What does the chimney-sweep know about
storks? He'll tell you all sorts of nonsense he doesn't believe
himself. What – what are you staring at in the street?

WENDLA. Mother, a man – as big as three horses, with feet like
paddle-steamers!

FRAU BERGMANN (*running to the window*). I don't believe it! I
don't believe it!

WENDLA (*at the same time*). He's holding a bed-stead under his
chin and playing 'Watch on the Rhine' on it – he's just gone
round the corner.

FRAU BERGMANN. You'll always be a child! Frightening your
silly old mother. Go and get your hat. I sometimes wonder if
you'll ever get any sense in your head. I've given up hope.

WENDLA. So have I, mother, so have I. There's not much hope
for my head. I've got a sister who's been married two and a half
years, and I'm an aunt three times, and I've no idea how it all
happens . . . Don't be cross, mummy, don't be cross! Who in the
world should I ask but you? Please, mummy, tell me. Tell me,
dear. I feel ashamed of myself. Do tell me, mummy! Don't scold

me for asking such things. Answer me – what is it? – how does it happen? You can't really insist that now I'm fourteen I still have to believe in the stork?

FRAU BERGMANN. But good lord, child, how funny you are! What ideas you get! I really cannot do such a thing.

WENDLA. Why not, mother? Why not? It can't be anything ugly if it makes you all so happy.

FRAU BERGMANN. O – O God help me! I would deserve to be . . . Go and get dressed, Wendla. Get dressed.

WENDLA. I'll go . . . and what if your child goes to the chimney-sweep to ask?

FRAU BERGMANN. But this will send me out of my mind! Come here, Wendla, come to me. I'll tell you! I'll tell you everything! O Almighty Father! – Only not now, Wendla. Tomorrow, the day after tomorrow, next week – whenever you like, my precious.

WENDLA. Tell me today, mother! Tell me now! This moment. I can never stop asking now I've seen you so frightened.

FRAU BERGMANN. I can't Wendla.

WENDLA. O why can't you, Mummy? I'll kneel at your feet and lay my head in your lap. Put your apron over my head and talk and talk as if you were sitting alone in your room. I won't flinch or cry out. I'll be patient and bear it whatever it is.

FRAU BERGMANN. Heaven knows none of this is my fault. Wendla! Heaven sees into my heart. I'll put myself into God's hands, Wendla – and tell you how you came into this world. Now listen to me, Wendla.

WENDLA (*under the apron*). I'm listening.

FRAU BERGMANN (*ecstatically*). But I can't, child! I can't be responsible! I'd deserve to be put in prison – to have you taken away from me . . .

WENDLA (*under the apron*). Be brave, mother!

FRAU BERGMANN. Well, listen!

WENDLA (*under the apron, trembling*). O God, o God!

FRAU BERGMANN. To have a child – you understand me, Wendla?

WENDLA. Quickly, mother – I can't bear it anymore.

FRAU BERGMANN. To have a child – the man – to whom you're married – you must – *love* – love, you see – as you can only love your husband. You must love him *very much with your whole heart* – in a way that can't be put into words! You must *love* him, Wendla, in a way that you certainly can't love at your age . . . Now you know.

WENDLA (*getting up*). Well, good heavens!

FRAU BERGMANN. Now you know what a testing time lies before you!

WENDLA. And that's all?

FRAU BERGMANN. As God is my witness! Now take that basket and go to Ina. She'll give you some chocolate to drink, and some cake too. Come on, let me look at you once more – boots laced up, silk gloves, sailor suit, rose in your hair . . . your little skirt really is getting too short for you, Wendla!

WENDLA. Have you bought the meat for lunch, mummy?

FRAU BERGMANN. God bless you. I must sew a broad flounce round the bottom.

SCENE THREE

HÄNSCHEN RILOW (*with a light in his hand, he bolts the door behind him and lifts the lid*). Have you prayed tonight Desdemona?

> *He takes a reproduction of the Venus of Palma Vecchio from the inside pocket of his jacket.*

You don't look like the Lord's Prayer, darling – contemplating the coming moments, the lovely moments of coming ecstasy – still just as when I first saw you lying in the window of that little corner shop, just as alluring with those smooth limbs, this soft curve of the hips, these young, tense breasts – o, how drunk the Great Master must have been when the fourteen-year-old original lay stretched out before him on the studio couch!

Will you come to me in my dreams now and then? I'll welcome you with outstretched arms and kiss your breath away. You'll take me over like an heiress moving back into her deserted palace. Gates and doors fly open with unseen hands, and down below in the park the fountain begins to splash happily . . .

It is the cause! It is the cause! The terrible hammering in my

breast proves I'm not murdering you for a whim! My throat goes
dry when I think of the lonely nights ahead. And I swear to you,
woman, it's not the disgust that comes from over-indulgence!
Who'd flatter himself by being disgusted with you? No – you
suck the marrow from my bones, bend my back, take the sparkle
from my young eyes. Your inhuman modesty is too demanding,
your motionless limbs too exhausting! It's me or you! And
I've won!

If I counted them all – all the others I fought this battle with
on this same spot! Rubens' Venus – bequeathed to me by that
waspish-thin governess Miss Hatherley-Brown, the rattle-snake
in my nursery paradise! Correggio's Io. Titian's Galatea. J van
Beer's Ada. Cupid by Bouguereau – the Cupid I abducted from
the secret drawer in papa's desk and locked up in my harem.
A quivering, trembling Leda by Makart I came across in my
brother's exercise books. *Seven*, o, lovely candidate for death,
have gone before you down the path to Tartarus. Let that
console you and don't make my torments unbearable with those
imploring looks!

You don't die for *your* sins but *mine*! With a bleeding heart I've
murdered seven wives in self-defence. There's something tragic in
the role of Bluebeard. All his wives put together didn't suffer as
much when he strangled them as he did each time!

But my conscience will be at peace, my body will get stronger
when you no longer dwell in the red silk cushions of my jewelry
box. Now I shall open my opulent pleasure dome to portraits of
The Puritan Maid, Mary Magdalen, The Respectable Farmer's
Wife – and then I'll get over you sooner. Perhaps in another three
months, my angel, your naked flesh-pot would have started to
gnaw my brains like the sun melting butter pudding. It's time we
were granted a decree!

Ugh, I feel a Heliogabalus rising in me! Moritura me salutat!
Girl, girl why d'you press your knees together – even now
when you stand before eternity? *One* tremble, and I'll set
you free! *One* feminine wriggle, *one* flicker of lust, of pity,
woman! I'd let you lie in a gold frame over my bed! Don't
you know it's your respectability that drives me to my
debaucheries? Alas, alas, so much inhumanity! One always

notices her sort had a good upbringing! It's exactly the same with me!

Have you prayed tonight, Desdemona?

My heart breaks. Rot! Even St. Agnes had to die for her virginity, and she wasn't half as naked as you! One last kiss on your blooming body, your girlish, budding breasts, your sweet curved – your cruel knees . . .

It is the cause, it is the cause, my soul! Let me not name it to you, you chaste stars! It is the cause!

The picture falls into the depths. He shuts the lid.

SCENE FOUR

A hayloft.

MELCHIOR *lies on his back in fresh hay.* WENDLA *comes up the ladder.*

WENDLA. *Here's* where you've crept to! They're all looking for you. The hay wagon's gone out again. You've got to help. There's a storm coming.

MELCHIOR. Go away. Go away.

WENDLA. What is it? Why are you hiding your face?

MELCHIOR. Get out! I'll throw you down on the threshing floor!

WENDLA. Now I certainly won't go. (*Kneels beside him.*) Come out in the fields with me, Melchior? It's sticky and gloomy here. It doesn't matter to us if we get soaked!

MELCHIOR. The hay smells so good. The sky outside must be as dark as the grave. All I can see is the bright poppy on your breast – I can hear your heartbeat . . .

WENDLA. Don't kiss me, Melchior! Don't kiss me!

MELCHIOR. Your heart – listen to it beating.

WENDLA. You love each other – when you kiss – no, no!

MELCHIOR. O, believe me, there's no such thing as *love*! It's all self, all ego. I don't love you anymore than you love me.

WENDLA. Don't! Don't, Melchior!

MELCHIOR. Wendla!

WENDLA. O, Melchior! Don't, don't.

SCENE FIVE

FRAU GABOR *sits and writes.*

FRAU GABOR. Dear Herr Stiefel,

After twenty-four hours of thinking and thinking over what
you have written to me, I take up my pen with a heavy heart. I
cannot, I give you my solemn word, obtain the cost of a passage
to America for you. Firstly, I do not have that much at my
disposal, and secondly, if I had, it would be the greatest possible
sin to put into your hands the means of carrying out a recklessness
so fraught with consequence. You would do me a grave injustice,
Herr Stiefel, if you found in this refusal a sign of any lack of
love on my part. On the contrary, it would be a grave offence to
my duty as a motherly friend if I also were to lose my head and,
influenced by your momentary desperation, abandon myself to
first impulses. I will gladly, should you so wish, write to your
parents and try to persuade them that throughout this term you
have done all that lay in your power, and exhausted your strength
– so much so that any rigorous condemnation of your failure
would not only be unjust but might very well be detrimental to
your physical and spiritual health.

The threat hinted at in your letter – that if your escape were
not made possible you would take your life – does to be frank,
Herr Stiefel, somewhat surprise me. Be a misfortune never so
undeserved, one should not allow oneself to stoop to underhand
methods. The method by which you seek to make me, who have
always been kind to you, responsible for any ensuing tragedy,
smacks somewhat of that which in the eyes of ill-disposed persons
might well be taken as an attempt at extortion. I must own that,
least of all from you, who otherwise know so well the respect one
owes oneself, was the above mentioned to be expected. However,
I am convinced that you were still suffering from the effects of
first shock and therefore unable to understand the nature of your
conduct. And so I confidently trust that these my words will reach
you in an already more composed frame of mind. Take things for
what they are. In my opinion it is quite wrong to judge a young
man by his examination results. We have too many instances

before us of bad scholars who became remarkable men, and, contrariwise, of splendid scholars who did not especially prove themselves in later life. Be that as it may, I give you my assurance that, so far as lies within my power, your misfortune shall in no way alter your relations with Melchior. It will always afford me joy to watch my son's intercourse with a young man who, let the world judge him how it may, will always be able to command my fullest sympathy. And therefore, head up, Herr Stiefel. These crises come to us all in one form or another and must be seen through. If we immediately resort to dagger and poison there will very soon be no one left in the world. Let me hear a line from you before long. The very best wishes of your staunch devoted motherly friend Fanny G.

SCENE SIX

The BERGMANNS' *garden in morning sunlight.*

WENDLA. Why did you slip out of the room? To pick violets! Because mother sees me smiling. Why can't you close your lips anymore? I don't know. I really don't know, I don't know the words . . .
The path's like a soft carpet. No stones, no thorns. My feet don't touch the ground . . . O how I slept last night!
They were here. I feel as solemn as a nun at communion. These beautiful violets! Hush, mother, I'll wear my sackcloth. O God, if only someone could come and I could throw my arms round his neck and tell!

SCENE SEVEN

Evening, dusk.

The sky is lightly clouded, the path winds between low bushes and reeds. The river is heard a little way off.

MORITZ. The sooner the better. I don't belong here. Let them kick each other to bits. I'll shut the door behind me and walk away

into freedom. Why should I let them push me about? I didn't
force myself on them. Why should I force myself on them now?
I haven't got a contract with God. Look at it from any angle you
like, they forced me. I don't blame my parents. Still, they were
old enough to know what they were doing. I was a baby when
I came in the world – or I'd have had enough sense to come as
someone else!
I'd have to be off my head: someone gives me a mad dog, and
when he won't take his mad dog back *I* play the gentleman
and . . .
I'd have to be off my head!
You're born by pure chance and after mature reconsideration you
mustn't . . .? I could die laughing! At least the weather cares. It
looked like rain all day and now it's cleared. The strange stillness
everywhere. Nothing harsh or loud. The whole world like a fine
cobweb. Everything so calm and still. The landscape is a beautiful
lullabye. 'Sleep, little prince, go to sleep.' Fräulein Hectorina's
song. A pity she holds her elbows awkwardly! The last time I
danced it was the feast of St. Cecilia. Hectorina only dances
with young toffs. Her dress was cut so low at the back and the
front. Down to the hips at the back, and in front down to – you
mustn't think about it. She couldn't have had a bodice on . . .
That might keep me here. More out of curiosity. It must be a
strange sensation – like being dragged over maelstroms. I won't
tell anyone I've come back half-cocked. I'll behave as if I've done
everything. It's shameful to have been a man and not known the
most human thing. You come from *Egypt*, dear sir, and you've
never seen the pyramids?
I don't want to cry anymore. Or think about my funeral.
Melchior will lay a wreath on my coffin. Reverend Baldbelly will
console my parents. The Head will cite examples from history.
I don't suppose I'll get a tombstone. I'd have liked a snow-white
marble urn on a black syenite column – luckily I won't miss
it. Monuments are for the living not the dead. It would take at
least a year to go through everyone in my head and say goodbye.
I don't want to cry now. I'm glad I can look back without
bitterness. The beautiful evenings with Melchior! – under the
willows, the forester's hut, the old battleground with the five lime

trees, the quiet ruins of the castle. When the moment comes I'll
think with my whole being of whipped cream. Whipped cream
won't stop me. It leaves behind a pleasant aftertaste, it doesn't
end up in your trousers . . . And then I've always thought people
were worse than they are. I've never met one who didn't try his
best. I felt sorry for them because they had me to deal with.
I go to the altar like an ancient Etruscan youth. His death rattles
bring his brothers prosperity for the year ahead. Drop by drop I
drink the dregs. The secret shudders of crossing over. I weep with
the sadness of my lot. Life gave me the cold shoulder. From the
other side solemn, friendly faces beckon me: the headless queen,
the headless queen – compassion, waiting for me, with open arms
. . . The laws of this world are for children, I've earned my pass.
The balance sinks, the butterfly rises and flies away. The painted
veil no longer blinds me. Why should I play this mad game with
Illusion? The mists part! Life is a question of taste.

> ILSE, *in torn clothes and with a coloured scarf on her head, taps
> his shoulder from behind.*

ILSE. What have you lost?
MORITZ. Ilse?
ILSE. What are you looking for?
MORITZ. Why did you frighten me?
ILSE. What are you looking for? What have you lost?
MORITZ. Why did you frighten me like that?
ILSE. I've just come from town. I'm going home.
MORITZ. I don't know what I've lost.
ILSE. No use looking for it then.
MORITZ. Blast! Blast!
ILSE. I haven't been home for four days.
MORITZ. Creeping about like a cat.
ILSE. I've got my dancing shoes on. Mother's eyes will pop out.
   Walk back to our house with me.
MORITZ. Where have you been this time?
ILSE. With the Phallustics!
MORITZ. Phallustics!
ILSE. With Nohl, Karl, Paganini, Schiller, Rank, Dostoevsky – with
   anyone I could! O, mother will jump!

MORITZ. Do you sit for them?

ILSE. Karl's painting me as an eremite. I stand on a Corinthian
column. Karl's off his head, believe me. Last time I trod on his
tube of paint. He wiped his brush in my hair. I boxed his ears.
He threw his palette at me. I knock the easel down. He chases
me with his paint stick over the divan, tables, chairs, round
and round the studio. There's a drawing by the fire. Behave or
I'll tear it! He says he'll behave and then ends up kissing me
terribly-terribly, believe me.

MORITZ. Where d'you spend the nights when you're in town?

ILSE. Yesterday at Nohl's – the day before at El Greco's – Sunday
with Bojokewitsch. We had champagne at Paganini's. Velazquez
sold his Plague Sufferer. Adolar drank out of the ashtray. Schiller
sang 'The Mother who Murdered her Child' and Adolar beat
hell out of the guitar. I was so drunk they had to put me to bed.
You're still at school, Moritz?

MORITZ. No, no – this is my last term.

ILSE. That's right. O, time passes much better when you're earning.
D'you remember how we played bandits? Wendla Bergmann
and you and me and the others. You all came to our place in the
evenings and drank the goat's milk while it was still warm. What's
Wendla up to? Last time I saw her was at the flood. What does
Melchior Gabor do? Does he still look so solemn? We used to
stand opposite each other in music.

MORITZ. He's a philosopher.

ILSE. Wendla was at our place a while back and brought mother
some stewed fruit. I was sitting for Isidor Landauer then. He
wants me for the Virgin Mary, the mother of God with the baby
Jesus. He's an idiot and disgusting. Ugh, never settles. Have you
got a hangover?

MORITZ. From last night. We knocked it back like
hippopotamuses. I staggered home at five.

ILSE. You've only got to look at you! Were there any girls?

MORITZ. Arabella. We drank beer out of her slipper. She's
Spanish, you know. The landlord left us alone with her the
whole night.

ILSE. You've only got to look at you, Moritz! I don't know what a
hangover is! Last carnival I didn't go to bed or get out of my

clothes for three days and nights! From fancy dress balls to the
cafés, lunch on the lake, cellar revues in the evenings, nights back
to the Fancy Dress Balls. Lena was with me and that fat Viola.
Heinrich found me on the third night.

MORITZ. Was he looking for you?

ILSE. He tripped over my arm. I was lying unconscious on the street
in the snow. Afterwards I went back to his place. I couldn't get
away for two weeks – that was a terrible time! Every morning I
had to pose in his Persian dressing gown, and every evening walk
round his rooms in a black page-boy tunic. White lace, cuffs,
collar and knees. He photographed me in a different way every
day – once as Ariadne on the arm of the sofa, once as Leda, once
as Ganymede, and once on all fours as a female Nobobycanesor.
He was always squirming on about murder, shooting, suicide,
drugs and fumes. He brought a pistol in bed every morning,
loaded it with shot, and pushed it into my breast: one twitch
and I press. O, he would have pressed, Moritz, he would have
pressed. Then he put the thing in his mouth like a pea-shooter.
It's supposed to be good for the self-preservation instinct. Ugh –
the bullet would have gone through my spine!

MORITZ. Is Heinrich still alive?

ILSE. How should I know? There was a big mirror in the ceiling
over the bed. The little room looked as tall as a tower, as bright
as an opera house. You saw yourself hanging down alive from the
sky. I had terrible dreams. God, o God, if only the day would
come. Good night, Ilse. When you're asleep you're so beautiful I
could murder you.

MORITZ. Is this Heinrich still alive?

ILSE. No, please God. One day he was fetching absinthe and I threw
my coat on and slipped out in the street. The carnival was over.
The police picked me up. What was I doing in men's clothes?
They took me to the station. Then Nohl, Karl, Paganini, Schiller
and El Greco, all the Phallustics, came and stood bail for me.
They carried me home in a posh cab. Since then I've stuck to the
crowd. Karl's an ape, Nohl's a pig, Berlioz's a goat, Dostoevsky's a
hyena, El Greco's a bear – but I love them, all of them together,
and I wouldn't trust anyone else even if the world was full of
saints and millionaires.

MORITZ. I must go home, Ilse.

ILSE. Come back to my place.

MORITZ. Why? Why . . .?

ILSE. To drink warm goat's milk. I'll curl your hair and hang a bell round your neck. Or there's a rocking-horse you can play on.

MORITZ. I must go home. I've still got the Sassanids, the sermon on the mount, and the Parallelepipedon on my conscience. Good night, Ilse.

ILSE. Sleep tight! D'you still play in the wigwam where Melchior Gabor buried my tomahawk? Ugh! Before you're ready I'll be in the dustbin. (*She hurries away.*)

MORITZ (*alone*). One word! That's all it needed! (*Calls.*) Ilse! Ilse! Thank God she can't hear.

I'm not in the mood. You have to be clear-headed and relaxed for that. Pity, pity – a wasted chance.

I'll say I had huge crystal mirrors over my beds and reared an untamed colt and let it prance round me on carpets in long black silk stockings and shiny black boots and long black kid gloves and black velvet round its throat and in an insane frenzy I took the pillow and smothered it – I will smile when they talk of lust – I will – scream! – Scream! To be you, Ilse! Phallic! Unselfconscious! That's what takes my strength away! That happy child, that child of nature – that little whore on my path of misery!

(*In the bushes on the bank.*) I've come here again without knowing it . . . the grass bank. The rods of the bulrushes look taller since yesterday. The view through the willows is the same. The river passes as slowly as melted lead. I mustn't forget . . . (*He takes* FRAU GABOR's *letter from his pocket, and burns it.*) How the sparks float . . . here and there, round and round – souls! Shooting stars!

Before I made the flame I could see the rushes and a line on the horizon. Now it's dark. I shan't go home now.

Act Three

SCENE ONE

Staff room.

Portraits of Pestalozzi and J.J. Rousseau. Gas-lamps burn over a green table. At the table sit PROFESSORS APELARD, THICKSTICK, GUTGRINDER, BONEBREAKER, TONGUETWISTER and FLYSWATTER. HEADMASTER SUNSTROKE sits at the head of the table on a raised chair. The School Porter FASTCRAWLER huddles by the door.

SUNSTROKE. Would any gentleman care to add any further remarks? Gentlemen! We cannot for the gravest of reasons abstain from asking the Minister of State for Cultural Affairs for the expulsion of our guilt-laden student. We cannot abstain so as to atone for the disaster that has already befallen us, and no less we cannot so as to secure our Institution against similar blows. We cannot abstain so as to chastise our guilt-laden student for the demoralising influence he has borne over his fellow students, and no less we cannot so as to prevent the further bearing of that demoralising influence. We cannot abstain – and here, gentlemen, might lie our most compelling reason, whereby whatsoever objections that are raised may be utterly crushed – so as to protect our Institution from the devastation of a suicide epidemic which has already come to pass in other Institutions and which has rendered, until now, our scholarly task of uniting our scholars by means of the fruits of scholarly instruction to the fruition of the life of scholarship, ridiculous. Would any gentlemen care to add any further remarks?

THICKSTICK. I can no longer close my mind to the conviction that the time has come when the opening of a window should be permitted somewhere.

TONGUETWISTER. The at-atmosphere here is dom-dominated by a resemblance to the subterranean cat-catacombs of a medieval a-a-a-ssize!

SUNSTROKE. Fastcrawler!

FASTCRAWLER. Present, sir!

SUNSTROKE. Open a window. Thanks to God we have sufficient atmosphere outside. Would any gentlemen care to add any further remarks?

FLYSWATTER. Should any of my colleagues wish to permit the opening of a window I for my part raise no objection. I would merely request that the window permitted to be open is not immediately in the back of my neck!

SUNSTROKE. Fastcrawler!

FASTCRAWLER. Present, sir!

SUNSTROKE. Open the other window. Would any gentlemen care to add any further remarks?

GUTGRINDER. Without in any way wishing to complicate the issue I would ask you to recall that since the long holidays the other window has been bricked up.

SUNSTROKE. Fastcrawler!

FASTCRAWLER. Present, sir!

SUNSTROKE. Let the other window be shut. I see myself forced, gentlemen, to put the matter to a vote. I call upon those colleagues who are in favour of permitting the opening of the only window that now comes into question, to rise from their seats. (*He counts.*) One, two, three. Fastcrawler!

FASTCRAWLER. Present, sir!

SUNSTROKE. Leave the other window shut as well. For my part I hold to my conviction that the atmosphere here leaves nothing to be desired. Would any gentlemen care to add any further remarks? Gentlemen! Let us suppose that we were to abstain from requesting the Minister of State for Cultural Affaires for the expulsion of our guilt-laden student – then we would be held responsible for the disaster that has befallen us. Of the various schools plagued by suicide epidemics the Minister has already shut down those in which the devastation has claimed a sacrifice of twenty-five percent. It is our duty as guardians and defenders of our Institution to defend it against so shattering a blow. It deeply

pains us, my dear colleagues, that we find ourselves in no position
to take into account the mitigating features presented by our guilt-
laden student. An indulgent approach that left us blameless in our
handling of our guilt-laden student would not leave us blameless
in our handling of the at present highly probable threat to the
existence of our Institution. We see ourselves forced to judge the
guilty so as not to be judged guilty ourselves! Fastcrawler!

FASTCRAWLER. Present, sir!

SUNSTROKE. Fetch him up.

   FASTCRAWLER *goes.*

TONGUETWISTER. If the dom-dominating at-at-atmosphere
   officially leaves nothing to be desired might I then pro-propose
   the motion that the other window also be bricked u-u-u-u-u-u-u-
   u-u-u-u-u-up?

FLYSWATTER. Should it appear to our respected colleague that
   our room is not sufficiently ventilated, might I propose the motion
   that he has a ventilator bored in the top of his head?

TONGUETWISTER. I do-do-don't have to put up with that! I
   do-do-don't have to put up with rudeness! I'm in possession of all
   my f-f-f-f-five senses!

SUNSTROKE. I must call upon our colleagues Flyswatter and
   Tonguetwister for a show of decorum. Our guilt-laden student
   stands at the door.

   FASTCRAWLER *opens the door, and* MELCHIOR *steps in
   front of the meeting. He is pale but composed.*

SUNSTROKE. Step closer to the table. After the respectable
   landlord Herr Stiefel had been informed of his late son's unseemly
   misconduct, that bewildered father searched, in the hope that
   he might come across the cause of this disgusting crime, in
   the remaining effects of his son Moritz and found, in an at the
   moment irrelevant place, a handwritten document which, without
   in any way making this disgusting crime at all comprehensible,
   does afford us an, alas, all too clear insight into the criminal's
   state of moral chaos. I refer to a handwritten document in
   dialogue-form entitled '*On Copulation*', replete with life-size
   illustrations, and crammed with obscenities so shameless that

they might well satisfy the utmost demands for depravity that a degenerate lecher could make on obscene literature.

MELCHIOR. I have . . .

SUNSTROKE. You have to be silent. After Herr Stiefel had put the document in question into our hands and we had given the bewildered father our solemn word to at all costs ascertain its author, the handwriting was compared with the handwriting of every fellow student of the deceased malpractiser and matched, according to the unanimous verdict of the whole faculty and in complete agreement with the expert opinion of our honoured colleague the Professor of Calligraphy, yours.

MELCHIOR. I have . . .

SUNSTROKE. You have to be silent. Notwithstanding the overwhelming evidence of this identification, acceded to by such unimpeachable authorities, we believe ourselves able to refrain from precipitate action for the moment, and to instead impartially interrogate you about the crime against morality of which you stand accused and which served as an incitement to self-destruction.

MELCHIOR. I have . . .

SUNSTROKE. You have to answer the precisely phrased questions, which I shall put to you one after the other, with a simple and respectful yes or no. Fastcrawler!

FASTCRAWLER. Present, sir!

SUNSTROKE. The file. I request our secretary, Herr Flyswatter, to take down the protocol from now on word for word as exactly as possible. (*To* MELCHIOR.) Do you know this document?

MELCHIOR. Yes.

SUNSTROKE. Do you know what this document contains?

MELCHIOR. Yes.

SUNSTROKE. Is the handwriting in this document yours?

MELCHIOR. Yes.

SUNSTROKE. Does this obscene document owe its manufacture to you?

MELCHIOR. Yes. Sir, I ask you to show me one obscenity in it.

SUNSTROKE. You have to answer the precisely phrased questions, which I shall put to you, with a simple and respectful yes or no.

MELCHIOR. I've written no more and no less than everyone of you knows to be a fact.

SUNSTROKE. This insolent puppy!

MELCHIOR. I ask you to show me one offence against morality in that paper!

SUNSTROKE. Do you imagine that I will stand here and let myself become the butt of your jests? Fastcrawler!

MELCHIOR. I have . . .

SUNSTROKE. You have as little respect for the dignity of your assembled masters as you have for mankind's sense of shame when confronted with the moral order of the universe. Fastcrawler!

FASTCRAWLER. Present, sir!

SUNSTROKE. This is the definitive text on how to learn Esperanto in three easy months without a master!

MELCHIOR. I have . . .

SUNSTROKE. I call upon our secretary to close the protocol.

MELCHIOR. I have . . .

SUNSTROKE. You have to be silent. Fastcrawler!

FASTCRAWLER. Present, sir!

SUNSTROKE. Put him down.

SCENE TWO

Churchyard in pouring rain.

REVEREND BALDBELLY *stands in front of the open grave with an umbrella in his hand. On his right* HERR STIEFEL, FRIEND GOAT *and* UNCLE PROBST. *On the left* HEADMASTER SUNSTROKE *and* PROFESSOR BONEBREAKER. STUDENTS *make up the rest of a circle. Some distance off* MARTHA *and* ILSE *stand by a half-fallen grave stone.*

BALDBELLY. Whosoever spurns the grace with which the Eternal Father blesses all who are born in sin, he shall die the death of the spirit. And whosoever in flesh and pride denies the worship owed to God and lives and serves evil, he shall die the death of the body. But whosoever sacrilegiously casts aside the cross with which the Almighty inflicts this life of sin, verily, verily I say unto you, he shall die the eternal death. (*He throws a shovel of earth into the grave.*) But we who go forth on the path of thorns, let us praise the Lord, the All Merciful, and thank him for his unsearchable gift of predestination. For as surely as this died the three-fold death, as surely will Lord God lead the righteous to salvation and eternal life. Amen.

HERR STIEFEL (*with tear-choked voice as he throws a shovel of earth into the grave*). That boy wasn't mine. That boy wasn't mine. I had my doubts about that boy since he was a tot.

SUNSTROKE (*throws a shovel of earth into the grave*). While suicide is the greatest conceivable offence against the moral order of the universe, it is at the same time the greatest conceivable proof of the moral order of the universe, in that the suicide spares the moral order of the universe the necessity of pronouncing its verdict and so confirms its existence.

BONEBREAKER (*throws a shovel of earth into the grave*). Dilatory – dissipated – debauched – dissolute – and dirty!

UNCLE PROBST (*throws a shovel of earth into the grave*). I would not have believed my own mother if she'd told me a child would treat its parents so basely.

FRIEND GOAT (*throws a shovel of earth into the grave*). To do that to a father who for twenty years cherished no other thought from morning till night than the welfare of his son!

BALDBELLY (*shaking HERR STIEFEL's hand*). We know that they who love God make all things serve the best. Corinthians I, 14:12. Think of the comfortless mother and try to replace her loss by redoubled love.

SUNSTROKE (*shaking HERR STIEFEL's hand*). And after all it's clear that we might well not have been able to promote him anyway.

BONEBREAKER (*shaking HERR STIEFEL's hand*). And if we had promoted him he'd certainly have been left standing next spring.

UNCLE PROBST (*shaking HERR STIEFEL's hand*). It's your duty to think of yourself before everything else now. You are head of a family . . .

FRIEND GOAT (*shaking HERR STIEFEL's hand*). Take my arm. Cats-and-dogs weather, enough to wring the bowels. If we don't all immediately perform the vanishing trick with a glass of hot punch we'll catch a heart condition!

HERR STIEFEL (*blowing his nose*). That boy wasn't mine. That boy wasn't mine.

> HERR STIEFEL *is led away by* PASTOR BALDBELLY, HEADMASTER SUNSTROKE, PROFESSOR BONE-BREAKER, UNCLE PROBST *and* FRIEND GOAT. *The rain lessens.*

HÄNSCHEN (*throws a shovel of earth into the grave*). Rest in peace, poor sod. Give my regards to my dead brides – and put in a word for me to God, you poor fool. You're so innocent they'll have to put something on your grave to scare the birds off.

GEORG. Did they find the pistol?

ROBERT. There's no point in looking for a pistol.

ERNST. Did you see him, Robert?

ROBERT. Rotten, blasted swizz! Who saw him? Anyone?

OTTO. That's the mystery! They threw a cloth over him.

GEORG. Did his tongue hang out?

ROBERT. The eyes! That's why they threw the cloth over him.

OTTO. Horrible!

HÄNSCHEN. Are you sure he hanged himself?

ERNST. They say he's got no head now.

OTTO. Rubbish! All talk!

ROBERT. I had the rope in my hand. They always cover up a hanged man.

GEORG. He couldn't have chosen a more small-minded way of going off.

HÄNSCHEN. What the hell, hanging's supposed to be fun!

OTTO. The fact is, he still owes me five marks. We had a bet. He swore he'd be promoted.

HÄNSCHEN. It's your fault he's down there. You said he was bragging.

OTTO. Rot! I have to slave through the nights too. If he'd learned his Greek history he wouldn't have had to hang himself.

ERNST. Have you done your essay, Otto?

OTTO. Only the start.

ERNST. I don't know what we're supposed to write about.

GEORG. Weren't you there when Apelard gave it out?

HÄNSCHEN. I'll stick together some bits of Democrites.

ERNST. I'll get something out of the reference library.

OTTO. Have you done tomorrow's Virgil?

The STUDENTS *go.* MARTHA *and* ILSE *come to the grave.*

ILSE. Quick, quick! The gravediggers are coming over there.

MARTHA. Shouldn't we wait?

ILSE. What for? We'll bring fresh ones. Always fresh, fresh! They grow everywhere!

MARTHA. That's right, Ilse. (*She throws an ivy wreath into the grave.* ILSE *opens her apron and lets a stream of fresh anemones fall onto the coffin.*) I'll dig up our roses. I get beaten anyway. They'll grow so well here.

ILSE. I'll water them every time I go by. I'll bring forget-me-nots from the brook and irises from home.

MARTHA. It'll become a marvel!

ILSE. I'd already crossed the bridge when I heard the bang.

MARTHA. Poor thing.

ILSE. And I know why, Martha.

MARTHA. Did he tell you something?

ILSE. He was on parallelepipedon! Don't tell.

MARTHA. Cross my heart.

ILSE. Here's the pistol.

MARTHA. That's why they couldn't find it.

ILSE. I took it straight out of his hand when I went by.

MARTHA. Let's have it, Ilse! Let's have it, please!

ILSE. No, it's my keepsake.

MARTHA. Ilse, is it true he's down there with no head?

ILSE. He must have loaded it with water. His blood was spattered round and round on the bulrushes. His brains were hanging all over the willows.

SCENE THREE

HERR *and* FRAU GABOR.

FRAU GABOR. . . . . They needed a scapegoat. The accusations were getting louder and they couldn't wait for them to die down. And because Melchior had the misfortune to cross those pedants just at this moment, shall I, his mother, help the hangmen to finish their work? God keep me from such a thing!

HERR GABOR. For fourteen years I've silently observed your imaginative methods of rearing children. They contradicted my own convictions. I have always lived by the conviction that a child isn't a toy. A child has a right to our solemn seriousness. But I told myself, if spirit and grace can replace serious principles, then they might be preferable to serious principles. I'm not blaming you, Fanny. But don't stand in my way when I try to make amends for the wrong you and I have done the boy.

FRAU GABOR. I'll stand in your way as long as there's a drop of human blood in me! My child would be lost in a reformatory. A natural criminal might be made better in such an institution. I don't know. But a decent nature will be made criminal just as a plant dies when it's taken from the light. I'm not aware of any wrong. I thank God now, as I always have, for showing me how to make my child decent and honest. What has he done that's so terrible? It would never enter my head to make excuses for him – but it's not his fault he's been hounded out of school! And if it had been his fault he's certainly paid for it! You may understand these things better than I do. Theoretically you may be perfectly right. But I will not allow my son to be brutally hounded to his death!

HERR GABOR. That doesn't depend on us, Fanny, that's the risk that went with our happiness. He who's too weak falls by the wayside. And in the end it's not the worst if the inevitable comes on time. May heaven spare us that! Our duty now is to strengthen the waverer, so long as reason shows us how. It's not his fault they hounded him out of school. If they hadn't hounded him out that wouldn't be his fault either! You're too easy going. You see minor peccadillos when we are faced with fundamental defects of character. Women aren't called on to judge these things. Whoever can write what Melchior wrote must be contaminated in his innermost core. The marrow as affected. Even a nature only half-sound couldn't bring itself to that! None of us are saints, we all stray from the way. But his document is grounded in Principle. It doesn't suggest one accidental false step, it documents with terrifying clarity an openly cherished talent, a natural propensity, for the Immoral for the sake of the Immoral. It shows that rare spiritual corruption we lawyers call 'moral insanity'. Whether anything can be done about his condition, it's not for me to say. If we wish to preserve one glimmer of hope, and above all keep our consciences unsullied as the parents of the culprit, then we must act with resolution and determination. Don't let's quarrel anymore, Fanny! I know how hard this is for you. You worship him because he matches your own generous nature so well. Rise above yourself! For once act unselfishly in your relations with your son.

FRAU GABOR. O God – how can one fight against it! Only a man can talk like that. Only a man can be so blinded by the dead letter he can't see what's staring him in the face! I've handled Melchior responsibly and carefully from the beginning. Are we to blame for this coincidence? Tomorrow a tile could fall on your head and your friend comes – your father, and instead of tending your wounds he treads on you! I will not let my child be taken out and murdered in front of my eyes. That's what his mother's for! – I cannot understand it. It's beyond belief. What in the world has he written? Isn't it the clearest proof of his harmlessness, his silliness, his child-like innocence, that he *can* write something like that? You don't need to know much about people – you must be an utterly soulless bureaucrat or totally shrivelled up, to see moral corruption in that! Say what you like. When you put Melchior in a reformatory, I shall divorce you! And then I shall see if somewhere in the world I can't find help to save my son from destruction.

HERR GABOR. You will have to give in – if not today then tomorrow. It's not easy for any of us to discount our misfortunes. I shall stand by you when your courage fails, I shall begrudge no effort or sacrifice to lighten your burden. I see the future so grey, so overcast – it only needs you to be lost to me now.

FRAU GABOR. I'll never see him again. I'll never see him again. He can't bear vulgarity. He can't live with filth. He'll lose all restraints – that terrible example is before his eyes! And if I

saw him again – O God, God, that heart full of spring – that
bright laughter – all, all – his young determination to fight
for everything that's good and just – as bright and fresh as the
morning sky – that boy I cherished as my highest good! Take me
if his crime cries out for retribution! Take me! Do what you want
with me! Let me bear the guilt! But keep your terrible hand away
from my child.

HERR GABOR. He has offended!

FRAU GABOR. *He has not offended*!

HERR GABOR. *He has* offended! I would have given anything
to spare your boundless love for him. This morning a woman
came to me, like a ghost, hardly able to speak, with *this* letter in
her hand – a letter to her fifteen-year-old daughter. Out of silly
curiosity she'd opened it – her daughter was not at home. In
the letter Melchior explains to the fifteen-year-old child that his
conduct gives him no peace, he has wronged her etcetera etcetera.
She is not to worry, even if she suspects consequences. He is
already taking steps to find help, his expulsion makes that easier.
The earlier wrong may yet lead to their happiness – and more of
the same meaningless chatter.

FRAU GABOR. I don't believe it!

HERR GABOR. The letter is forged. It's an attack. Someone trying
to use an expulsion that's already known to the whole town. I
haven't yet spoken to the boy – but kindly look at the hand. Look
at the writing.

FRAU GABOR. An unheard of, shameless infamy!

HERR GABOR. I fear so!

FRAU GABOR. No, no – never.

HERR GABOR. Then all the better for us. The woman stood
wringing her hands and asking me what she should do. I told her
not to let her fifteen-year-old daughter climb about in haylofts. As
luck would have it she left the letter with me. If we send Melchior
away to another school, where he wouldn't even be under parental
supervision, we'll have another incident within three weeks –
another expulsion – his spring-like heart is already getting used to
it. Tell me, Fanny, where shall I put the boy?

FRAU GABOR. In the reformatory.

HERR GABOR. The . . .?

FRAU GABOR. Reformatory.

HERR GABOR. Above all, he'll find there what he was unjustly
denied at home: iron discipline, principles and a moral force
under which he must at all times subordinate himself. By the
way, the reformatory isn't the chamber of horrors you imagine.
It lays its main emphasis on developing Christian thinking and
sensibility. There the boy will finally learn to put the good
before the interesting, and to act not according to his nature
but according to the rules. Half an hour ago I had a telegramme
from my brother, which confirms the deposition of that woman.
Melchior has confided in him and asked for money for their flight
to England . . .

FRAU GABOR (covers her face). God have mercy on us!

SCENE FOUR

Reformatory. A corridor.

DIETER, REINHOLD, RUPERT, HELMUT, GASTON *and*
MELCHIOR.

DIETER. Here's a coin.

REINHOLD. What for?

DIETER. Drop it on the floor. Spread yourselves out. The one who
hits it, keeps it.

RUPERT. Coming in, Melchior.

MELCHIOR. No thanks.

HELMUT. Git!

GASTON. He can't anymore. He's here for the rest cure.

MELCHIOR (*to himself*). It's not clever to stay out. They're all
watching me. I'll join in – or I've had it. Being shut up makes
them suicidal. If you break your neck it's all right! If you get out
it's all right! You can only win! Rupert looks friendly, he'll show
me round. I'll teach him about the Bible – how Lot got drunk
and slept with his daughters and offered them to other men,
how David was a Peeping Tom who slept with a soldier's wife
and warmed his bed with a beautiful virgin called Abishay the
Shunnamite. He's got the unluckiest face in my squad.

RUPERT. Coming!

HELMUT. I'm coming too.

GASTON. Day after tomorrow if you're lucky!

HELMUT. Hold on! Now! Jesus – Jesus.

ALL. Altogether now! – Ten out of ten!

RUPERT (*taking the coin*). Ta, very much.

HELMUT. That's mine, pig!

RUPERT. Animal!

HELMUT. They'll top you!

RUPERT (*hits him in the face*). For that? (*Turns and runs away.*)

HELMUT (*chasing him*). I'll kick your head off!

THE OTHERS (*chasing them*). Get him, after him! Get him! Get him! Get him!

MELCHIOR (*alone, turns to the window*). That's where the lightning conductor goes down. You'd have to wrap a handkerchief round . . . When I think of her the blood goes to my head, and Moritz is like a chain round my feet. I'll try the newspapers. Become a hack. They pay by the hundred lines. News, gossip, articles – ethics – psychology. You can't starve now! Soup kitchens, hostels. – This building is sixty feet high and the plaster's falling off . . . She hates me – I took her freedom away. Whatever I do now, it's still rape. But later on perhaps she'll . . . I must hope. The new moon in eight days. I'll grease the hinges. Find out who has the key. On Sunday night I'll have a fit in the chapel. I hope to God no one else is ill! I'll slip over the sill – swing – grab – but you must wrap a handkerchief round . . . Here comes the Grand Inquisitor. (*Goes off left*).

DR. PROCRUSTES *comes on right with a* LOCKSMITH.

PROCRUSTES. Undoubtedly the windows are on the fourth floor, and I've planted stinging nettles underneath. But what are stinging nettles to degenerates? Last winter one of them climbed out of the skylight. We had all the fuss of fetching, carrying, interning . . .

LOCKSMITH. Would you like the grating in wrought iron?

PROCRUSTES. Wrought iron – and since you can't build it into the wall, rivet it.

SCENE FIVE

A bedroom.

FRAU BERGMANN, INA MÜLLER *and* DR. LEMONADE.
WENDLA *in bed.*

DR. LEMONADE. How old are you actually?

WENDLA. Fourteen and a half.

DR. LEMONADE. I've prescribed purgative pills for fifteen years
and in a large number of cases witnessed the most dazzling
success. I place them above codliver oil and iron tonic. Start
with three or four pills a day and increase the dosage just as fast
as you can tolerate them. I advised Fräulein Elfriede Baroness
von Witzleben to increase the dose by one pill every third day.
The baroness misunderstood me and increased the dose by three
pills every day. After barely three weeks the baroness could
already proceed with her lady mother to an exclusive spa in the
mountains. I excuse you from all fatiguing walks and special
diets. But you must promise me, dear child, to keep moving and
not be too shy to ask for food as soon as the desire for it returns.
Then this wind round the heart will go away, and the headaches,
the shivering, the dizzyness – and our terrible indigestion. Only
eight days after starting the cure Fräulein Elfriede Baroness von
Witzleben could already eat a whole roast chicken with new boiled
potatoes for breakfast.

FRAU BERGMANN. May I offer you a glass of wine, Doctor?

DR. LEMONADE. Thank you kindly, dear Frau Bergmann. My
patients await me. Don't take it too much to heart. In a few weeks
our charming little patient will once more be as fresh and lively as
a sprite. Rest assured. Good day, Frau Bergmann. Good day, dear
child. Good day, ladies. Good day.

  FRAU BERGMANN *goes to show him out.*

INA (*at the window*). The leaves on your plane-trees are changing
colour. Can you see it from the bed? They come and go, a short
glory, hardly worth being happy about. I must go too. Herr
Müller's meeting me at the post office, and before that I have
to go to the dressmaker. Mucki's getting his first trousers, and
Karl's going to get a new jersey suit for the winter.

WENDLA. Sometimes I'm so happy – there's so much joy and the sunshine is so bright. I want to go out, and walk over the fields when it's dusk, and look for primroses and sit and dream by the river. And then this *toothache* starts, and I think that tomorrow is the day I shall die. I feel hot and cold, everything goes dark, and the monster flutters in . . . Whenever I wake up mother's crying. O that hurts so much . . . I can't tell you, Ina.

INA. Shall I lift your pillow?

FRAU BERGMANN *comes back.*

FRAU BERGMANN. He thinks the vomiting will stop and then it will be safe for you to get up. I think you should get up soon, too, Wendla.

INA. Perhaps next time I come to see you you'll be jumping round the house again. Bless you, mother. I really must go to the dressmaker. God bless you, Wendla, dear. (*Kisses her.*) Soon, soon better!

WENDLA. Thank you, Ina. Bring me some primroses next time you come. Goodbye. Say hello to the boys for me.

INA *goes.*

WENDLA. What did he say outside, mother?

FRAU BERGMANN. Nothing. He said Fräulein von Witzleben also tended to faint. Evidently it almost always happens with anemia.

WENDLA. Did he say I have anemia, mother?

FRAU BERGMANN. When your appetite returns you're to drink milk and eat fresh vegetables.

WENDLA. O mother, mother, I don't think I have anemia.

FRAU BERGMANN. You have anemia child. Be quiet, Wendla, be quiet. You have anemia.

WENDLA. No, mother, no! I know it! I can feel it! I haven't got anemia. I've got dropsy.

FRAU BERGMANN. You have anemia. He said you have anemia. Be quiet, Wendla. It will get better.

WENDLA. It won't get better. I have dropsy. I'm going to die, mother. O mother, I'm going to die.

FRAU BERGMANN. You won't have to die, Wendla. You won't have to die . . . Merciful heaven, you won't have to die.

WENDLA. Then why d'you cry so much?

FRAU BERGMANN. You won't have to die, child! You haven't got dropsy. You have a baby, Wendla! You have a baby! O, why have you done this to me?

WENDLA. I haven't done anything to you . . .

FRAU BERGMANN. O don't keep lying, Wendla! I know everything. I couldn't say it before. Wendla, Wendla . . .

WENDLA. But it's just not possible, mother. I'm not even married.

FRAU BERGMANN. God in heaven – that's just it, you're not married! That's what's so terrible! Wendla, Wendla, Wendla, what have you done?

WENDLA. O God, I don't know anymore. We were lying in the hay – I've never loved anyone in the world except you, you, mother!

FRAU BERGMANN. My precious!

WENDLA. O mother, why didn't you tell me everything?

FRAU BERGMANN. Child, child, don't let's make each other more unhappy. Keep calm. Don't give up hope, my dear! Tell that to a fourteen year-old girl? No, I'd sooner have believed the sun could go out! I did nothing to you my dear mother hadn't done to me! O let us put our trust in the dear lord, Wendla. Let us hope in his mercy, and do our part. Look, so far nothing's happened. And if only we don't become timid now – God's love will not abandon us. *Be brave, be brave, Wendla* . . . Once before I sat with my hands in my lap and stared out of the window, and in the end everything turned out well – and now suddenly the world falls to pieces and my heart breaks . . . why are you shaking?

WENDLA. Someone knocked.

FRAU BERGMANN. I didn't hear anything, my precious. (*Goes to the door and opens it.*)

WENDLA. O I heard it so clearly. Who's outside?

FRAU BERGMANN. No one. Mr. Schmidt's mother from Garden Street. You're just on time, Mrs. Schmidt.

SCENE SIX

MEN *and* WOMEN *working in a hillside vineyard.*

The sun sets behind the mountains. The clear-toned notes of bells come up from the valley. HÄNSCHEN RILOW *and* ERNST RÖBEL *loll in the dry grass at the top of the vineyard, under over-hanging rocks.*

ERNST. I've worked too hard.

HÄNSCHEN. We mustn't be sad. Time passes so quickly.

ERNST. The grapes hang there. You can't even reach out for them. And tomorrow they're crushed.

HÄNSCHEN. Being tired is as bad as being hungry.

ERNST. O no more.

HÄNSCHEN. That big one.

ERNST. I can't stretch.

HÄNSCHEN. I could bend the branch till it swings between our mouths. We needn't move. Just bite the grapes and let the branch swing back.

ERNST. You only have to make up your mind – and all your old energy gushes up.

HÄNSCHEN. And the flaming sky – the evening bells – I don't hope for much more out of life.

ERNST. Sometimes I already see myself as a dignified parson – a cheerful little housewife, big library, all sorts of honours and decorations. Six days shalt thou labour and on the seventh open your mouth. When you're out walking school-children greet you politely, and when you get home the coffee's steaming, there's home-made cake on the table, and the girls are bringing in the apples through the garden door. Can anything be better?

HÄNSCHEN. Half-shut eyelashes, half-open mouths, and Turkish pillows. I don't believe in the Sentimental. You know, the old people wear dignified faces to hide their stupidity. Among themselves they call each other fools just as we do. I know it. When I'm a millionaire I'll erect a great monument to God. Think of the future as bread and milk and sugar. Some people drop it and howl, others stir it till they sweat. Why not just cream off the top? Or don't you think you can?

ERNST. Let's cream off the top.

HÄNSCHEN. And throw the rest to the chickens. I've already slipped my head out of so many nooses.

ERNST. Let's cream off the top. Why are you laughing?

HÄNSCHEN. You're off again!

ERNST. Someone's got to start!

HÄNSCHEN. In thirty years when we look back to this evening, I
suppose it could seem incredibly beautiful.

ERNST. And now it just happens!

HÄNSCHEN. Why not?

ERNST. If I was on my own – I might even cry.

HÄNSCHEN. We mustn't be sad. (*Kisses his mouth.*)

ERNST (*kissing him*). When I left home I only meant to speak to you
and then go back.

HÄNSCHEN. I was waiting for you. Virtue looks good but it only
suits imposing figures.

ERNST. It's several sizes too big for us. I'd have been on edge if I
hadn't met you. I love you, Hänschen, I've never loved anyone
like this –

HÄNSCHEN. We musn't be sad! Perhaps when we look back in
thirty years we'll jeer – but now everything is beautiful. Glowing
mountains, grapes hanging down in our mouths, the evening wind
stroking the rocks like a little kitten playing . . .

SCENE SEVEN

Bright November night.

*Dry leaves rustle on bushes and trees. Torn clouds chase each other over
the moon.* MELCHIOR *climbs over the churchyard wall.*

MELCHIOR(*jumping down inside*). That pack won't follow me here.
While they search the brothels, I'll get my breath and sort myself
out . . . Jacket in shreds, pockets empty. I couldn't defend myself
against a child. I'll keep moving through the woods during the
day . . . I knocked a cross down – the frost's killed all the flowers
anyway. Everything's bare! The kingdom of death!
This is worse than climbing out of the skylight! Like falling
and falling and falling into nothing! I wasn't prepared for this! I
should have stayed where I was!
Why her and not me? Why not the guilty? Providence or a riddle?
I'd break stones, starve – how can I even walk upright? One

crime leads to another: I'll sink in a swamp. I haven't got the
strength to finish it . . . It was not wrong! It was not wrong! It
was not wrong!

No one's ever walked over graves and been so full of envy. No –
I wouldn't have the courage! O, if I could go mad – tonight! The
new ones are over there. The wind whistles on each gravestone in
a different key – listen, the voices of pain! The wreaths are rotting
on the marble crosses. They fall to pieces and jog up and down on
their long strings. There's a forest of scarecrows over the graves.
Taller than houses. Even the devil would run away. The gold
letters flash so coldly. That's a willow tree groaning. Its branches
are like a giant's fingers feeling over the epitaphs. A stone angel.
A tablet.

That cloud's thrown its shadow on everything. How it races and
howls! Like an army rushing up to the east! And no stars. There's
evergreen round this one. Evergreen? A girl.

> Here rests in God
> Wendla Bergmann
> Born 5 May 1878
> Died of anemia
> 27 October 1892
> Blessed are the pure in heart

And I murdered her. I am her murderer. Now there's nothing. I
mustn't cry here. I must go away. I must go.

> MORITZ STIEFEL, *with his head under his arm, comes
> stamping across the graves.*

MORITZ. One moment, Melchior! This chance won't come again so
soon. You can't know how much depends on time and place . . .

MELCHIOR. Where have you come from?

MORITZ. Over there by the wall. You knocked my cross down. I lie
by the wall. Give me your hand, Melchior.

MELCHIOR. You are *not* Moritz Stiefel!

MORITZ. Give me your hand. I know you'll be grateful. It will
never be so easy for you again. This is a very lucky meeting. I
came up especially . . .

MELCHIOR. Don't you sleep?

MORITZ. Not what you call sleep. We sit on church towers, on the roofs of houses – wherever we like . . .

MELCHIOR. At peace?

MORITZ. For pleasure. We ride on the wooden horses at fairs, and float round empty churches. We fly over great assemblies of people, over scenes of disaster, gardens, festivals. We crouch in the corners of people's houses, and wait by their beds. Give me your hand. The dead are alone, we don't go with each other, but we see and hear everything that happens in the world. We know that it's all vanity, the things men do and strive after, and we laugh at it.

MELCHIOR. What help is that?

MORITZ. What use is help? Nothing touches us now, for good or bad. We stand high above earthly things – each alone for himself. We don't go with each other because it's boring. None of us has anything it would hurt him to lose. We are infinitely above all despair and rejoicing. We are content with ourselves, and that is all. We despise the living so much we can hardly pity them. They amuse us with their pretensions – and if they will live they don't deserve to be pitied. We smile at their tragedies – each to himself – and watch. Give me your hand! When you give me your hand you'll fall over laughing at what happens then –

MELCHIOR. Doesn't that disgust you?

MORITZ. We stand too high for that. We smile! At my funeral I stood among the mourners. I quite enjoyed myself. That is serenity, Melchior, the sublime! I howled more than anyone and tottered to the wall holding my belly with laughing. Our serenity is simply the attitude that allows us to swallow the dregs. They laughed at me too, before I raised myself up to their height.

MELCHIOR. I don't want to laugh at myself.

MORITZ. The living are the last who deserve to be pitied! I admit I'd never have thought it. But now I don't know how men can be so naïve. I see through the fraud so clearly and no more doubts are left. How can you still hesitate, Melchior? Give me your hand! In less time than it takes to twist a chicken's neck you'll rise high over yourself. Your life is a sin of omission –

MELCHIOR. Can you forget?

MORITZ. We can do anything. Give me your hand! We can sorrow
for youth because it takes its anxieties for ideals, and old age
because stoical resolution breaks its heart. We see the emperor
quake with fear at the street ballad, and the clown at the last
trumpet. We see through the comedian's make-up, and watch
the poet put on his mask in the dark. We look at the satisfied in
all their destitution, and the capitalists toiling and groaning. We
watch lovers blush before each other, when they already know
they'll betray and be betrayed. We see parents bringing children
into the world to be able to shout at them: how lucky you are
to have such parents – and we see the children go off and do the
same. We know about the innocent in their lonely passions, and
we hear Schiller in the mouth of a ten-minute whore. We see
God and the devil exposing themselves to ridicule in front of each
other, and hold in us the unshakable conviction that they're both
drunk . . . Peace, rest, Melchior! Just give me your little finger.
You can be as white as snow before this moment comes again.

MELCHIOR. If I throw in my lot with you, Moritz, I do it out of
self-disgust. I'm a pariah. Everything that gave me courage is in
the grave. I'm incapable of any ideals – and I can see nothing,
nothing that can stand in my path to the bottom. I think I'm the
most disgusting creature in creation . . .

MORITZ. Why hesitate?

A MASKED MAN *comes in.*

MASKED MAN (*to* MELCHIOR). You're shivering with hunger.
You're certainly in no state to decide anything. (*To* MORITZ.)
Get out!

MELCHIOR. Who are you?

MASKED MAN. That will be made clear. (*To* MORITZ.) Hop it!
What are you up to? Why aren't you wearing your head?

MORITZ. I shot myself.

MASKED MAN. Then stay where you belong. You're finished!
Don't pester us with the stench of your grave. Incredible – look at
your fingers! Filthy brute! It's already rotting.

MORITZ. Please, don't send me away –

MELCHIOR. Who are you?

MORITZ. Don't send me away. Please. Let me stay with

you a little longer. I won't contradict you. It's terrible
under there.

MASKED MAN. Then why all this bragging about serenity and
the sublime? You know very well that's humbug – sour grapes.
Why must you lie so persistently? – you – you wraith! If it means
so much to you, stay as far as I'm concerned. But stop all this
huffing and puffing, young man – and please don't stick your
rotting thumb in my pie!

MELCHIOR. Will you tell me who you are?

MASKED MAN. No. I'll make you a proposition: put yourself in
my hands. For a start, I'll do something about your present mess.

MELCHIOR. You're my father!

MASKED MAN. Wouldn't you know your dear father from
his voice?

MELCHIOR. No.

MASKED MAN. Your father is at this moment seeking comfort in
the strong arms of your mother. I'll open the world for you. Your
temporary despair is caused by your miserable condition. With a
hot dinner inside you you'll joke about it.

MELCHIOR (*to himself*). Only *one* of them can be the devil!
(*Aloud.*) After the things I've done, a hot dinner won't give me
peace again!

MASKED MAN. It depends on the dinner. One thing I will tell
you, your little girl would have given birth marvellously. She
was built ideally. Unfortunately, she was put down – entirely
by Mother Schmidt's abortion methods. I'll take you out into
the world. I'll give you the chance to widen your horizon in
astonishing ways. I'll introduce you to every single interesting
thing in the world.

MELCHIOR. Who are you? Who are you? I can't put myself in the
hands of someone I don't know!

MASKED MAN. You only learn to know me *by* putting yourself in
my hands.

MELCHIOR. Is that true?

MASKED MAN. It's a fact. And by the way, you have no choice.

MELCHIOR. I can give my hand to my friend whenever I like.

MASKED MAN. Your friend is a charlatan. No one smiles
while he's still got a penny to spend in his pocket. The

sublime humorist is the most miserable, pitiful creature in creation.

MELCHIOR. The humorist can be what he likes! Tell me who you are, or I'll give him my hand.

MASKED MAN. Now?

MORITZ. He's right, Melchior. I was trying it on. Take his invitation, and get everything you can out of him. It doesn't matter how well he's masked – at least he's *something*!

MELCHIOR. Do you believe in God?

MASKED MAN. Depends.

MELCHIOR. Well, tell me who invented gunpowder.

MASKED MAN. Berthold Schwarz – a Franciscan monk at Freiburg in Breisgau about 1330.

MORITZ. What wouldn't I give if he hadn't!

MASKED MAN. You'd only have hanged yourself.

MELCHIOR. What are your views on morality?

MASKED MAN. Son – am I a schoolboy?

MELCHIOR. How do I know what you are!

MORITZ. Don't quarrel. Please, don't quarrel. What's the use of that? Why sit here in the churchyard – two living and one dead – at two o'clock in the morning, if all we can do is quarrel like drunks? It will be a pleasure for me to be present at these discussions. If you want to quarrel, I'll take my head and go.

MELCHIOR. You're still the same old drag!

MASKED MAN. The ghost isn't wrong. One should never lose one's dignity. By morality I understand the real product of two imaginary forces. The imaginary forces are *should* and *would*. The product is called Morality, and no one is allowed to forget that's real.

MORITZ. If only you told me that before! My morality hounded me to death. I used the murder weapon because of my dear parents. 'Honour thy father and mother and thy days shall be long.' The Bible certainly came unstuck over me.

MASKED MAN. You shouldn't be carried away by appearances, my boy. Your parents would no more have died than you needed to. Looked at clinically, they'd have raged and stormed simply for the good of their health.

MELCHIOR. That might be true. But I can certainly tell you that if

I'd given my hand to Moritz just now, sir, that would have been
purely and simply because of my morality!

MASKED MAN. And that's exactly where you're not Moritz!

MORITZ. I don't think there's much difference – not so much
that you shouldn't have been allowed to pop up for me. I walked
slowly enough along that alder plantation with the pistol in my
pocket.

MASKED MAN. Then you don't remember me? Even in your
last moments you were still standing undecided between life and
death. But I think this is really not the best place to prolong such
a profound discussion.

MORITZ. It's certainly getting chilly. They dressed me up in my
Sunday suit but they didn't put anything on underneath.

MELCHIOR. Goodbye, Moritz. I don't know where this man will
take me. But *he* is alive . . .

MORITZ. Don't hold it against me for trying to kill you, Melchior.
It was only my old devotion. I'd spend a whole lifetime of tears
and misery, if I could walk by your side again.

MASKED MAN. In the end everyone has his part – *you* the
comforting knowledge of having nothing – *you* the tormenting
doubt of everything. Goodbye.

MELCHIOR. Goodbye, Moritz. Thank you for coming back once
more. The happy, good times we had together in those fourteen
years! I promise you whatever happens in the years to come, if I
change ten times, and go up or down, I'll never forget you . . .

MORITZ. Thank you, thank you. You were my only friend.

MELCHIOR. . . . and one day if I'm old and my hair's grey,
perhaps then you'll be closer to me again than all the people who
share my life.

MORITZ. Thank you. Good luck on the journey, gentlemen. Don't
let me keep you any longer.

MASKED MAN. Come on, young man. (*He takes* MELCHIOR's
arm and disappears with him over the graves.)

MORITZ (*alone*). I sit here with my head in my arm. The moon
covers its face, the veil falls away, and it doesn't look any wiser.
So I go back to my place. I straighten my cross after that clumsy
idiot's kicked it over, and when everything's in order I lie down
on my back again, warm myself in my rotting decay and smile.

Using *Lulu*

Lulu is a play about sex and money. Goll and Schöning are rich and die. Schwarz is poor, becomes rich and dies. Alwa lives off his father's money, becomes rich and dies. Schigolch was poor, became rich – and moments after he appears calls himself a cadaver. Jack the Ripper is poor – he even borrows his bus fare from his victim. But he survives. Why?

Lulu comes from the gutter, lives in mansions and ends on the street. When she was a child she was sold for sex even 'before she could feel it'. She murders Rodrigo because she wants money. She pays the murderer in sex. When she is threatened with desertion she does not speak of love or even jealousy: she says she will not be made poor again. She also says that she won't become a prostitute – she calls it being 'turned into money' – to feed her family. In the end Jack the Ripper cuts out her womb to sell it – turns her body into cash. Why?

The original play lasts some six or seven hours. It begins in Berlin when it was becoming a major capitalist city. It moves to Paris, which was still synonymous with the financial sleaze of the Second Empire. It ends in London, then the capital of capitalism. In the original text a great deal of the Paris act is in French and the London act in English. Lulu barters with her customers in English. The play shows an African speaking it. It is becoming the world language – English is the language of capitalism. The first audiences would have been presumed cosmopolitan enough to understand the three languages. The impression is strangely modern, like a multi-language film with subtitles. When the play was written Europe was obsessed with sex and money and fascinated by the recent murders of Jack the Ripper. The murders combined sex with money and violence, occurred in East end slums and the victims were poor prostitutes.

Folklore immediately associated the killer with the aristocracy. He was even said to be the Prince of Wales. The language, the length, the amalgam of farce and tragedy are there because the play is struggling to deal with a contemporary crisis. The play is 'faction' before that form was invented.

No one would produce the original play. It was not even printed. Wedekind made various versions of it so that at least not all of it would be wasted. The versions are confused and pretentious. The original manuscripts were dispersed in several archives. A few years ago they were collected and the original play reconstructed and published in Germany.

Before starting to translate the play I read the existing English versions. Their triviality dismayed me. How could the writer of *Spring Awakening* write so trivially? This was not the translators' fault. They were translating the mutilated versions. Then I read the reconstructed original. I read with increasing interest and then with awe. I shall remember turning the pages of the play as I read it – especially the pages of the great last act. Surely on the next page the writer would cop out, the vision and honesty would not be maintained? Most other writers would have hidden in cliché or sentiment.

I was reading the first modern play. More modern than *Woyzeck* because it did not need Büchner's romanticism to combine the characters' sufferings with an explanation of why people suffer. More modern than Ibsen because it did not seek significance in empty idealism – Jack the Ripper is mad but a realist. More modern than Chekhov, whose plays never get far beyond middle-class apprehension of the future – Wedekind shows the future. More modern than Jarry, because the farce is more serious and so more funny – and unlike *Ubu*, *Lulu* goes beyond iconoclasm to analysis. More modern than surrealism, because its vision is based on social realism not psychological mysticism. More modern than Brecht, because it joins objective politics with subjective realism and so creates a theatre of reason not rationalism. (Though it should be said that Brecht's plays are closer to Wedekind than his theory. *Lulu* and *Mother Courage* are of the same family – one sells goods and the other sells herself, but both invoke violence.)

Lulu joins social realism with individual psychology and this makes it a truly political play: the solutions are seen to be social and not personal, just as they are in Shakespeare and the Greeks. And because it is a play of political realism it is a tragedy. It cancels out the trivia of the theatre of the absurd. Schigolch creates that theatre but goes beyond it. The absurd is seen not as the absence of meaning but as the meaning of a particular time and situation. Part of the play could be called 'Waiting for Jack the Ripper'. But Jack the Ripper comes.

The strongest argument against censorship is that even if it prevents something bad, the good it prevents always outweighs the bad. If the original *Lulu* had been seen soon after it was written, it would not have been fully understood. But that is all the more reason why it should have been seen. It is enough to see through a glass darkly. Most of the time we live in a world of brightly-lit trivialities, or comfortably move about in bleary daylight; and in a crisis the lies flood us with their neon-light. When the truth is revealed we are like the blind when they first see – we see what darkness is. Truth teaches us to grope.

If the play had been staged a century ago we would now understand ourselves better. Perhaps some of the horrors would have been prevented and our society would not be as destructive as it is. We might not have the mechanical violence of TV – a sort of military training for civilians. Or a Press (serious and gutter) that corrupts our democracy. Or a government that degrades education to training. Or a former Prime Minister who sells her services to a tobacco company: among all the grosser enormities, that piece of political harlotry seems to encapsulate our moral destitution.

I will try to explain why *Lulu* is the first modern play. Here I can do it only schematically but still it is worth doing. If, as I said, the play prophetically illuminated what was to come – now that it has come and is past, the facts are already 'against it'. It is not just history that gets rewritten, we rewrite the present – we 'explain away' the facts even as they happen, so that they *can* happen. That is the power of ideology. This makes it even more important to understand the play: because it is still prophesying our and our children's future.

Sexuality is an instinctive drive that reproduces the species. But because our physiology and circumstances are complex, we cannot choose to procreate as we choose to make a chair. That is why the sex drive must be prior to reason. It requires, in the act and generally, that we abandon ourselves to it. That is how it serves us. So if we are not to become its slaves it is necessary that it has limits. And it does – to pregnancy and sexual capacity, and even (usually) to sexual interest. Yet *Lulu* portrays an unlimited sexuality. Lulu seems amoral. For instance, in each act she provokes one or more Oedipal confrontations between a 'father' and a 'son'. When she does this – as for instance between Schöning and Alwa in Act Three – she is not distressed. She behaves like a Jocasta who laughs at the misery of Laius and Oedipus – worse, she simpers. There is a totality about her that brings to mind de Sade's remark 'It is necessary for philosophy to say everything'. That is a very modern remark. It presages, for example, Nietzsche's murder of god.

Sexuality is constant in humans. We do not have rutting seasons. That does not mean that sex has no natural limits, that it has to do everything. It has to do more than puritans allow because it has to do with human bonding, making humans human. Sex is powerful, not just in order to continue the species – a rutting season could do that – but because of the highly developed human brain. We need a society of bonded adults to nurture our young while their brain learns to work. Sex bonds and humanizes us. But still this does not make it a totality. De Sade invented sexual ghettos and envisaged the world as one brothel. Sex did not create and nurture but destroy. That is Total Sex in the sense of Total War. It is said that there are no trees in de Sade. That is not quite true, but there is very little nature. His sex belongs to a mechanical world. Human sex becomes Total Sex only in the age of machines. The age of machines is also the age of capitalism. And the play's thesis is that the combination of sex and capitalism is destructive, that it creates the age of violence.

Sex breeds desire but it is not a total, whole system of life. Money breeds itself – and capitalism removes the restraints on money to breed. Money grows exponentially when it is lent on interest. It does this without limits. Capitalism distributes debt and so generates social activity. We can think of machines as capitalism's sexual offspring. Capitalism breeds machines as frogs breed tadpoles. Most tadpoles do not survive. Machines do. It seems odd to connect money and technology with human biology, they seem worlds apart. But money is a strange pseudo-magic connecting them.

If you believe in god, god exists – for you. If society believes in money, money works for it. But money depends on faith as much as religion does. Loss of faith leads to runs on banks and collapsing stockmarkets. But faith is blind: it changes how you think of the world and how you behave – it changes what you are. Money forges a connection between itself and all desire, not just sexual desire. We are as imprisoned in our money system as believers in their faith or madmen in their illusions. Capitalism is Total Money and it takes over all things.

There are two constraints on the breeding and expansion of money. One, the clear ecological limits to technology. Two, some human characteristics – for example, the fear that aggravates slumps. But money is more ruthless than instinct in overcoming its limitations. Money subordinates even our instincts to its needs. It does this, of course, not by repressing them in a Freudian way, but by unleashing them. It takes them over. It charges the whole of society with its own blind, objectless, limitless potency. It is a monstrous abnormality.

All peoples live in a culture. Cultures combine technology with desire and reason. Reason explains a culture to itself in a way which justifies it, and the justification is the way the members are humanised. The justification organises the three elements (reason, desire, technology) so that each supports the others. Historically, our cultures' success in doing this has meant the increasing humanisation of our species. We depend on our culture for our humanness. Money disturbs the balance that is culture. Money has no limits and destroys the limits of the other social elements.

Capitalism – Total Money – subordinates all things to the market's needs. This profoundly changes society. In fact Western society is the first society not to create culture – it is merely a system. We do not live to create a culture but exist to maintain a system. Doing this does not increase humanisation in the way creating a culture does. Capitalism dehumanises us not because it is not susceptible to moral persuasion, but for structural reasons. Money must take precedence over other social elements, and so we give society and ourselves new meanings. We move from the traditional cultures of the 'fathers' Goll and Schöning, through the experimental, transitory cultures of the 'sons' Alwa and Schwarz – to the figure of Jack the Ripper. He is the Negative Superman, the great engineer and entrepreneur that is the wizened heart of capitalism.

Total Money metamorphoses the human psyche in order to maintain itself: all parts of the psyche become aspects of the system. But money attaches itself particularly to sex because sex is fundamental and protean. Even nature took a risk when it evolved sex. Freud found symbolic connections between money and sex, but he saw money as passive and sex as dynamic. In capitalism the dynamic of money is added to the dynamic of sex and so sex becomes over-determined. Its objects (which are limited even when they are the search for pleasure) are colonised by money's dynamic. Sex loses its objective limits and becomes Total Sex. This creates a vacuum, an objectless behaviour. The vacuum consumes the whole of psyche and society. The emptiness is not characteristic of sex itself, it is the characteristic of sex under capitalism: indeed, of all desire under capitalism – it turns fulfilment into emptiness. This is not a matter of individual behaviour, attitudes or emotions. It is a social reality. Just as we turn with the turning earth but are not directly aware of it, so we become part of the social dynamic which is also a vacuum. We become the meaning by which the system maintains itself.

Capitalism's dynamic needs to make sex a consumer product. It cannot do this because consumerism has no limits, but sex always seeks a limit in acknowledging to itself its own humanness: it is, after all, why sex is associated with love and happiness and unhappiness. But the dynamic of money exceeds, swamps, the dynamic of sex, and so in order to assert itself sex becomes pathological. Always what makes sex pathological (destructive) is not that it corrupts – it is its desire to assert and experience its own humanness. So *Lulu* is both a farce and a tragedy.

There are two main arguments against capitalism. One is ecological: capitalism is organised looting. Two is that capitalism is the only real perversion – capitalism is an acid-semen. Yet we see it becoming the world system.

Lulu is capitalism's prophetic history. It shows sex as the victim not the aggressor. Wedekind wrote within the old culture and could not understand all he showed. It is as if he mocks us by showing us his fears – like a child, using its weaknesses as strengths. But that is because he understood so much of the future. He saw Western culture changing into a system, that we were losing control. We see that Western 'capitalist culture' is destroying other cultures. It destroys them in the way that simpler forms of life destroy higher forms. The simpler forms have fewer entanglements. Cultures use energy to humanise their members. A system does not humanise its members – that is its lack of entanglement, and what makes its impact so ruthless. But because we purloin the artefacts and customs of the cultures we destroy – and market them as products and 'lifestyles' – we can pretend for a while that we are culturally strong. Really we are only a system, and more and more we consume to satisfy the desires of money and to fill the appetites of our machines. And out of this emptiness comes 'Jack the Ripper'.

EDWARD BOND
1992

Three *Lulu* poems
by Edward Bond

Wedekind's Cuffs

When I try to see the writer
I see his cuffs: white – hard – harsh
Two hands stretched from a hole in ice
Or are they handcuffs and the collar leaves a hangman's mark?
The generation wore the white and grey or black of prisoners
All his life he wrote in prisons
And there he saw in the white window of his cell
The map of humankind
But others wore their manacles as honourable wages
And loved the streets – even the dust they trod
And whores and housewifes
Cheered men marched to Mills Bombs and the Gattling guns
Modern machines in medieval armour
And skeletons using bones as flails
To thresh the young seed on the threshing floor
The husks were winnowed by the blasts of war
And baked bread for the dead

Lulu

At seven she was sent to the streets
To keep her family
The cracks between the paving stones – the wind
Each time there was danger – often they used their fists
In her small hand she clutched the coins as she was raped
The weak learn to survive among the strong
Later she was rich
But now there must be danger all the time
The street – the cracks between the paving stones – the wind
A door to be kicked down
And death to enter
Men sense it in her too
She can only be taken in the wrong place at the wrong time by the
    wrong man
The door is broken down – death comes
And everywhere it is the same
The poor learn to be hungry
The banker trades – men labour – death makes war
And the weak learn to desire
She searches the streets
The cracks between the paving stones – the wind
Till Jack the Ripper comes
He also searches: he is dead
The door is opened to him
He takes the money from her hand
For the last time she is a virgin with a bowl of water
Then with his knife he turns her body
Into cash
And makes his departure on a city omnibus

22 December 1892

On this day in a shuttered room in Paris
Frank Wedekind stood before
A naked man and naked woman
The grunts and groans of twisting bodies
Only the woman's shoulders shone white
In the dark room
Till suddenly a trembling waiter sprang
Turned up the taps
And in the gaslight's glare
The playwright saw the act of love
Accomplished on the floor
That in that place served for a bed
Because he knew that all desire to see the moment they are made
It is the amulet against the wind reeds wear
And that we do not own the tears we shed
But strangers use our eyes to weep in
And he said
Let there be light

Lulu: A Monster Tragedy

This translation of *Lulu: A Monster Tragedy* was toured in Britain in 1992 by Cambridge Theatre Company, with the following cast:

DR SCHÖNING, an editor	Fred Pearson
ALWA SCHÖNING, his son, a playwright	Jonathan Wrather
DR GOLL	Jimmy Gardner
EDVARD SCHWARZ, a painter	John Baxter
SCHIGOLCH	Jimmy Gardner
DR BERNSTEIN	Jimmy Gardner
RODRIGO QUAST, Strong Man at the Belle Union Circus	Ewen Cummins
PUNTSCHUH, a banker	Fred Pearson
GENDARME	John Baxter
FERDINAND, a stable boy	John Baxter
CASTI-PIANI	John Baxter
MR HOPKINS	John Baxter
KUNGU POTI	Ewen Cummins
JACK	Fred Pearson
LULU	Susan Lynch
COUNTESS MARTHA GESCHWITZ	Melanie Jessop
HENRIETTE, a maid	Melanie Jessop

Director Nick Philippou
Designer Stewart Laing
Lighting Designer Stephen McManus
Sound Designer John A Leonard

Act One: Berlin
Act Two: Berlin
Act Three: Berlin
Act Four: Paris
Act Five: London

Time: the 1890s

Act One

Berlin.

A spacious studio. Back left, the main entrance. Down left, a side door to the bedroom. In the middle, back and slightly left, a platform. Behind the platform a folding screen. In front of the platform a Smyrna carpet. Down right, two easels. On the one further back, in a working frame, a pastel portrait of a forty-year-old woman in evening gown. An unframed canvas is leaning, showing its back, against the other easel. In front of the easels an ottoman with Turkish cushions. Over it a tiger skin. At the back a high step-ladder. The studio window is presumed to be at the front of the stage. Late morning.

EDUARD SCHWARZ, FRANZ SCHÖNING.

SCHÖNING (*a photograph in his hand. Studies the pastel portrait*) . . . I can't tell you what it is. I miss the very thing I wanted you to paint. It's a woman in a ball dress, I don't deny. But I see nothing of the wife I looked up to with respect – like a shy child – for half my life.

SCHWARZ. Working from a photograph isn't as easy as licking the back of a stamp.

SCHÖNING. You know nothing would have made her sit for you. She was too high-minded for that. She thought that was frivolous – honouring her unimportant, transitory side. She was too much the good wife and mother to understand that sort of homage. You show nothing of this . . .

SCHWARZ. D'you see it in the photograph?

SCHÖNING. It's suggested – certainly. I drew it to your attention. – To be fair, perhaps my mind's still haunted by her memory.

SCHWARZ. I treated every word you told me as if it were sacred.

I ran through the streets looking for a woman who'd come closer
to how I imagined her, so at least I'd have something to grasp in
reality.

SCHÖNING. Perhaps it is good. I don't know. I told you, I'm the
last person to judge. People who didn't know my wife closely
would recognise her at a glance.

SCHWARZ. D'you like the hair?

SCHÖNING. Good. Good. How well you've brought the left hand
out from the material! You've altered the light.

SCHWARZ. I stole that from a little dancer at the Odeon.

SCHÖNING (*indicating the photograph*). Look at this gaze – under
this brow. Imagine she's speaking to you – the eyebrows rise – the
lowered head – the candid gaze: then you have a dignity that can't
be touched by anything common or trivial. That's what's lacking.
It's in the eyes, in this indefinable calmness of her closed mouth.

SCHWARZ. Please step back as far as you can.

SCHÖNING (*goes slowly backwards and knocks over the canvas leaning
against the other easel*). Sorry . . .

SCHWARZ (*picking up the canvas*). No please . . .

SCHÖNING (*recognising the portrait*). What – what . . .

SCHWARZ. You know her?

SCHÖNING. No. She sits for you?

SCHWARZ. Since Christmas.

> *He lifts the picture onto the easel. It shows a woman dressed as
> Pierrot. In her hand she holds a long shepherd's crook.*

SCHWARZ. It still misses so much.

SCHÖNING. And – in this costume?

SCHWARZ. That surprises you? – And she's out of the top drawer.

SCHÖNING (*with a glance* at SCHWARZ). Well – I congratulate you.

SCHWARZ. Oh Christ . . .

SCHÖNING. Ah.

SCHWARZ. How would you feel? Her husband drives up with her,
and for two hours I have the pleasure of talking to the old buffoon
– about art of course, just to complete my luck.

SCHÖNING. How did you get into it?

SCHWARZ. How? Her husband suddenly turns up in my studio,

a fat tottering old midget, would I paint his wife? Of course,
for God's sake! – even if she's as ugly as sin. Ten o'clock next
morning the door opens and this over-fed pig drives this vision
in front of him. I had to hold onto the easel. Behind them there's
a servant in green uniform with a parcel under his arm. Where's
the changing room? – What shall I do? I open my bedroom
door – luckily the bed was already made. The sweet little thing
disappears inside and the old man posts himself like barbed-wire
in front of it. Two minutes later she steps out as this Pierrot . . .
(*Takes a deep breath.*) A fairy-tale come to life! From head to
toe every bit of her belongs to this absurd costume – as if she was
born in it! And such grace! The way she lifts her feet, buries her
elbows in the pockets, tosses her little head to the side – all so
naturally – sometimes the blood shoots to my head . . .
SCHÖNING. You should harden yourself against such attacks.
SCHWARZ (*shakes his head*). You should see her! Tell me what I'm
not hardened against! It disgusts me even when a girl uncovers
her breasts. I find it almost repulsive.
SCHÖNING. This is more than nakedness.
SCHWARZ. If you like. Perhaps less.
SCHÖNING. To see that the gaze goes deeper. But you need a steady
hand. The soul evaporates in the heat and falls back on the body
as sweat. The spirit lives in the figleaf.
SCHWARZ. I'll show you! (*He goes out left.*)
SCHÖNING (*alone*). He should get outside these four walls for once.
SCHWARZ (*comes back with a white satin costume*). She's supposed to
have worn it at a Freemason's ball.
SCHÖNING (*admiringly*). Hmmm.
SCHWARZ (*unfolding the costume*). Cut low front and back.
SCHÖNING. The huge pompons.
SCHWARZ (*feeling the pompons*). Black silk thread.
SCHÖNING. Crows in snow.
SCHWARZ (*lifting the costume by the shoulder straps*). She doesn't
wear anything underneath.
SCHÖNING. All in one piece.
SCHWARZ. Waist and legs.
SCHÖNING. And no buttons.
SCHWARZ. She doesn't need them.

SCHÖNING. How does she get in?

SCHWARTZ. Through the top.

SCHÖNING. Of course.

SCHWARZ. She has nothing else on her body.

SCHÖNING. If that slipped from her shoulders.

SCHWARZ. Don't be silly.

SCHÖNING. It can't possibly stay in place!

SCHWARZ. She sticks her right arm in the air.

SCHÖNING. But the legs.

SCHWARZ. Why do they bother you?

SCHÖNING. They're too long.

SCHWARZ. She hitches the left one up.

SCHÖNING. Yes.

SCHWARZ. That's the pose. She holds it with her hand above the knee.

SCHÖNING. As if she's just rucked it up.

SCHWARZ. She does it beautifully.

SCHÖNING. The right leg falls over her foot.

SCHWARZ. To the tip of her toes.

SCHÖNING. And white satin shoes.

SCHWARZ. And black silk stockings.

SCHÖNING. Transparent of course!

SCHWARZ (*with a sigh*). And that has to be painted!

SCHÖNING. Only death is gratis.

SCHWARZ. And on top of it she flirts.

SCHÖNING. Marvellous!

SCHWARZ. You don't believe it!

SCHÖNING. I see it!

SCHWARZ (*turning to the picture*). Just look at that arm.

SCHÖNING. The elegant way she stretches.

SCHWARZ. She holds the rod as high up as she can.

SCHÖNING. It lifts her figure.

SCHWARZ. And exposes her armpits.

SCHÖNING. Yes.

SCHWARZ. No one else does that so naturally.

SCHÖNING. Is that flirting?

SCHWARZ. You wait. The arm is a jewel – every curve accentuated – the hollow inside the elbow stretched taut –

the bright blue veins – the soft shimmer over it – flickering
light . . .!

SCHÖNING. I can imagine – though there's not much of it to
see yet.

SCHWARZ. And then the armpit . . .!

SCHÖNING. Yes.

SCHWARZ. There – in the middle of the fullest matt flesh tone –
she shows you two coal-black little locks!

SCHÖNING. They're also missing.

SCHWARZ. Dyed of course.

SCHÖNING. Where did you get that nasty idea?

SCHWARZ. Where did I get it? – they're darker than her hair –
darker than her eyebrows – but her body hair . . .

SCHÖNING. Go on.

SCHWARZ (folding the costume). Anyway she certainly pays careful
attention to it.

SCHÖNING. What I want to say . . .

SCHWARZ. Please . . .

SCHÖNING. And the old man stands guard?

SCHWARZ. Our sort, you know . . . after all . . . (He takes the
costume back to his bedroom.)

SCHÖNING (alone to himself). Our sort.

SCHWARZ (coming back, looks at the clock). By the way if you want
to meet her.

SCHÖNING. No.

SCHWARZ. They must be here any moment.

SCHÖNING. I'll satisfy myself with the counterfeit. (Turning to the
pastel portrait.) I'd be grateful if you'd design the frame.

SCHWARZ. If you like. A few immortelles . . .

SCHÖNING. I leave it to your taste. As I said, the picture has all
one could reasonably ask. Come and see me soon.

SCHWARZ (accompanying him). Thank you.

SCHÖNING. Please don't trouble.

> Goes upstage left and in the doorway runs into DR. GOLL and
> LULU.

Oh God.

SCHWARZ (bustling up). May I introduce –

GOLL (*measuring* SCHÖNING *with a look*). What are you up to here?

SCHÖNING (*holding out his hand to* LULU). Mrs Goll.

LULU. But this is wonderful!

SCHÖNING (*giving* GOLL *his hand*). I came to look at my wife's portrait.

LULU. You don't want to go already?

SCHÖNING. I thought your sitting would begin now.

LULU. That's exactly why!

GOLL. It doesn't matter. You might as well stay.

SCHÖNING. You can't expect me to say no.

GOLL (*putting down his hat and stick*). It so happens I have something to say to you . . .

LULU (*gives her hat and coat to* SCHWARZ). We saw the Duchess of Villa-Franca sweep by in her coach!

GOLL (*looking at the pastel portrait*). She should have lived more! Lived more! – She had a good heart. (*As he lights a cigarette.*) Perhaps she lacked some impulse –

SCHÖNING. Who doesn't lack it?

GOLL. You certainly don't!

SCHÖNING. One doesn't go looking for it. That's what's lacking. One is too lazy to take a holiday.

GOLL. Elly, go. Change!

LULU. It's my turn now.

GOLL. Why else did we come here! Mr Schwarz is already licking his brush.

LULU. Everyone has a turn. I imagined it would be more amusing.

SCHÖNING. At least you have the satisfaction of amusing others.

LULU (*going left*). Wait and you'll see.

SCHWARZ (*opening the door to his bedroom for her*). If Mrs Goll would be so kind . . . (*Shuts the door behind her.*)

GOLL. I've christened her Elly.

SCHÖNING. Why didn't you call her Mignon?

GOLL. That would have been a possibility. In love, you know, the 'unformed' – the 'awkward' – that can't do without a fatherly figure . . .

SCHÖNING (*lighting a cigarette*). And therefore doesn't demand to be taken seriously –

GOLL. At least then it doesn't take one over –

SCHÖNING. And the advantages stay the same –

GOLL. – rather the contrary.

SCHÖNING. What a pity it takes so long to learn that!
Unfortunately, doctor, all one can do is remind oneself to
feel well.

GOLL. Every minute of the mortal day I battle with the Grim
Reaper, that bore, and – as you know – I have no children. But
there are certain needs one can't wean oneself off, however much
one's brains are turning to chalk. (*To* SCHWARZ.) What's your
little dancer up to?

SCHWARZ. She only sat as a favour. I met her on an outing with a
local glee club.

GOLL (*to* SCHÖNING). I think there'll be a change in the weather.

SCHWARZ. Obviously Mrs Goll has some difficulties in changing.

GOLL. The undressing isn't as bad as the dressing. It's the buttons
down the back. I have to be the lady's maid.

SCHÖNING. Invent some new healthier style of clothing.

GOLL. The unhealthy ones are too interesting. (*Calls.*) Nelly . . .

SCHWARZ (*hurries to the door and calls through the keyhole*).
Mrs Goll.

LULU (*in the bedroom*). Coming, coming.

GOLL (*to* SCHÖNING). I can't understand these cold fish.

SCHÖNING (*While* SCHWARZ *looks through the keyhole*). I envy
them. They have their 'ego' – the one inexhaustible source of
pleasure. At night they lie at peace in their own arms. How can
you pass judgement on a man who's had to scrape by on his
doodlings since he was a lad? Take him in hand – make him! It's
just an exercise in mathematics. I can't raise the moral energy
to do it! For me it would be the same sort of schoolboy prank as
discovering America: one day everything will be lit by electricity!
And why should I bother with that? Not the sort of thing that's
easy to digest . . .

LULU (*coming from the bedroom as Pierrot*). Here I am.

SCHÖNING (*staring at her*). It's infernal!

LULU (*coming closer*). Well?

SCHÖNING. Almost overwhelming.

LULU. How d'you like me?

SCHÖNING. I'm lost for words.

LULU. Aren't you!

SCHÖNING. I mean it.

GOLL. Something worth seeing! Something worth seeing!

SCHÖNING. Certainly.

LULU. And don't I know it!

SCHÖNING. Then you might have a bit more consideration!

LULU. I only do what's expected of me.

SCHÖNING. You've been painting yourself.

LULU. What an idea! – Do I really look sunburnt?

SCHÖNING. On the contrary.

LULU. Under the whiteness of the wig?

SCHÖNING. You're more dazzling than ever.

GOLL. She has exceptionally white skin. I've told our artist to do as little as possible on the skin. I don't get excited over this heavy modern daubing.

SCHÖNING. It depends on the dauber.

GOLL. It might do for a piece of meat in the slaughterhouse.

SCHWARZ (*busy at the easel*). At least the Impressionists solved more interesting problems than the sugary romantics ever did.

SCHÖNING. There are two sides to everything.

SCHWARZ. So you say.

SCHÖNING (*to* SCHWARZ). Even to narrow-mindedness.

GOLL (*to* LULU *as she embraces and kisses him*). Your petticoat's showing. Pull it down. He's capable of painting it.

LULU. I should have left it off altogether. It only gets in the way. (*She steps onto the platform.*) What would you say, Mr Schöning, if you had to stand like a pole for two hours?

SCHÖNING. I? I'd give my salvation to be a little creation like you.

GOLL (*sitting left*). Come here. From here she's even more beautiful.

LULU (*taking up her pose*). I'm just as beautiful from everywhere . . . (*Bending her head backwards.*) Now please have a little pity!

SCHWARZ. Right knee forward – fine. The satin settles gently – but every time in a different way. At least the light's tolerable today.

GOLL. Dash her down with more brio. Hold your brush further up. Bigger strokes. She doesn't lend herself to a heavy hand. There's nothing statuesque about her.

SCHWARZ. I'm trying to concentrate all her expression into one
fleeting moment.

SCHÖNING. Treat her as a still life.

SCHWARZ. Exactly.

SCHÖNING. Paint snow on ice. If you try to go deeper nature
beats you.

SCHWARZ. Exactly, exactly.

SCHÖNING. Think of the background as a salver she's served up
on.

GOLL. Art, you know, should at least present people so that you can
enjoy their spiritual side. Go to any exhibition, it's full of pictures
that – faced with them the best thing you can do is castrate
yourself.

SCHÖNING. Little Miss O'Murphy is making her debut at the
Empire.

GOLL. As a Peruvian Pearl-fisher. Prince Polossow took me there.

SCHÖNING. At least she fished up the biggest pearl. She'll fleece
him and spend it on her Anton.

GOLL. Or her clown . . . What swines.

SCHÖNING. Well I've never seen her. I'm still in mourning.

SCHWARZ (*from time to time stepping back as he paints*). Last autumn
I could've rented another studio. The moving frightened me off.
When the sun shines the courtyard sends in warm reflections.

GOLL (*to LULU*). Why are you rummaging in your pockets?

LULU. They're empty.

SCHÖNING. You thought your handkerchief was there?

SCHWARZ. What's more the heating's not what it might be. In
winter the air's so dry it gives you a headache by the afternoon.

GOLL. Open a window! Poor man! There's nothing healthier than
a blazing fire with open windows! (*To* SCHÖNING.) The opera's
just had a hit. Go and see it. I prescribe it for you.

SCHÖNING. I take chloral hydrate instead.

GOLL. Forget the chloral hydrate. Go and see it. It doesn't ruin
your stomach or go out of fashion so quickly.

LULU. I think someone knocked . . .

SCHWARZ. Excuse me. (*He goes to the door and opens
it.*)

GOLL (*to* LULU). It's safe to make your smile a little more

friendly. It doesn't disturb him. What's your sugar-snout for? I
have to listen to his complaints.

ALWA (*still behind the screen*). May a friend of the arts push in?

SCHÖNING. You . . .?

GOLL. Show yourself!

LULU. That's Alwa Schöning.

ALWA (*coming forward, reaching his hand to* GOLL). How are you
doctor?

GOLL. Don't be astonished –

LULU. Mr Alwa has been looking at very different models.

ALWA (*has turned round quickly*). Ah!

LULU. You recognise me?

ALWA. Who could forget you – once they'd admired you dressed
like that! (*To* SCHÖNING.) How are things?

SCHÖNING. Fine. And you?

ALWA. I wanted to ask you to my dress rehearsal.

SCHÖNING. Today? So soon?

LULU. It opens on Sunday.

GOLL. So? How do you know?

LULU. But you read it out to me!

GOLL (*to* ALWA). Tell me my boy – what d'you call your play?

ALWA. Zarathustra.

GOLL. Zarathustra? –

SCHÖNING. What shall I do there?

GOLL. – I thought he was in a madhouse.

ALWA. You mean Nietzsche.

GOLL. Exactly. I get them mixed up.

ALWA. Well I did get the material from his books.

SCHÖNING. You'll need a special beat for the lame cripple's dance.

GOLL. It's a dance drama?

ALWA. But Nietzsche – forgive me – is the holiest genius of the
dance the world has known!

GOLL. Then I must mean someone else.

ALWA. Oh God spare me.

GOLL. I thought he was a philosopher.

SCHÖNING. He believed the rest of the world was limping – and
that made him dance for joy.

ALWA. You've read him then?

SCHÖNING. He repels me. The spectacle of him hopping round on his crutches is nauseating. I'd never make a ballet out of it.

GOLL. I don't see why not.

ALWA. I've based the whole of the second act on his 'Song of the Dance' – young girls in a clearing in the wood – Eros sleeps by a well – Zarathustra and his disciples step from the bushes – the dew falls –

GOLL. Imagine! Who wrote the music?

ALWA. Me. Me. The first act's set in the City of the Painted Cow – you see the Tightrope Dancer – the Matrons and Virgins –

GOLL. Not bad – hm –

ALWA. The Wild Dogs – the Twisted Potentate – the Little Girls –

GOLL. The Little Girls . . .

ALWA. You see the Last Man, the Red Judge, the Grunting Hog, the Pale Criminal, the Famous Sages, the Daughters of the Desert, the Watchmen of the Night . . .

GOLL. It must be the most sublime ballet that's ever been put on the boards.

ALWA. And you see – see Zarathustra as night falls bury the blood-drenched Tightrope Dancer in the market place.

GOLL. That won't worry us, you know – we're all realists now. Congratulations!

ALWA. The best scene is the Fire Hound spewed out of the Fire Mountain with the Dwarfs – the Dwarfs are hidden in black sacks from the waist up – all you see are legs.

GOLL. Legs – legs – one sees the stage genius in that.

ALWA. In the last act they come on reversed.

GOLL. One must never waste one's talents.

ALWA. Fourth Act. Zarathustra's Homecoming – quick scene change – he pulls the snake out of the shepherd's throat – the birth of the Superman! – Corticelli dances the Superman –

GOLL. She was always a bit superhuman.

SCHÖNING. La Corticelli?

GOLL. The music of the spheres.

SCHÖNING. And she's lived a little. While her mother was still around she danced with her legs. When she was free she danced with her brains. Now she dances where her heart takes her.

GOLL (to ALWA). I hope you haven't thrown a sack over her!

ALWA. Over the Superman! The skimpy bit of stuff she wraps
  round herself – blame that on the police.

GOLL. Thank God.

ALWA. But that's not what makes her the Superman.

GOLL. Hm . . .

ALWA. The Superman, you see Dr Goll, is represented by curly
  hair pulled out into two wings and a huge ruff – and under
  the ruff is the innermost soul, that strives ever forwards, ever
  beyond. And how shall I put that on stage!

SCHÖNING. My son, my son – save yourself from the madhouse.

GOLL. Hm – is Corticelli rehearsing too?

ALWA. Do come Dr Goll – in the last act you see Zarathustra before
  his cave, the Two Kings, the Ancient Pope. They're all rehearsing
  – the Mad Dogs, the Little Girls . . . with cleavage down to the
  innermost soul – the Grunting Hog –

GOLL. Good man!

ALWA. Then come and join us.

GOLL. Impossible.

SCHÖNING. And anyway we haven't got that much time to lose.

GOLL. I'd only be there for the Superman.

ALWA. Then come – you'll like the Feast of Asses – it's the
  last scene.

GOLL. I can't – I can't.

ALWA. Why not? Afterwards we're dropping in at Peter's. You can
  give vent to your admiration there.

GOLL. She's going – to Peter's?

ALWA. The whole show!

GOLL. Don't push me any further – I beg you.

ALWA. You won't miss anything here.

GOLL. When I come back *that* ass will have botched up my picture.
  Next time gentlemen.

ALWA (*takes his arm*). The Daughters of the Desert are getting into
  their tights.

GOLL. Damned daubing – it doesn't do, you see – if you don't
  explain every brush stroke to these people.

ALWA. Goodbye Mrs Goll.

LULU. Tell us afterwards!

GOLL. At least take my cab.

SCHÖNING. We'll send it back.

GOLL (*to* ALWA). And pay my respects to the Daughters of the Desert!

ALWA. They'll be cross. We'll be told off for not bringing you. Allons!

GOLL (*to* LULU). I'll be back in five minutes.

ALWA. The desert is spreading.

GOLL (*taking his hat and stick*). I probably won't come to Peter's.

SCHÖNING (*to* LULU). Goodbye.

ALWA. Be a good girl and don't move (*Forcing* GOLL *and* SCHONING *to the exit.*) – the desert is spreading – woe to him who hides the desert in his soul!

   LULU *is left alone with* SCHWARZ.

LULU. He doesn't normally leave me alone for a minute.

SCHWARZ (*painting*). Wouldn't you like a little rest?

LULU. I'm afraid . . .

SCHWARZ. Hm. For us it's either the everlasting skies of lead – hardly once in a lifetime the thunder breaks through – or over there – in the bright sun – always the same reek of decay.

LULU. I'd never have dreamt it.

SCHWARZ. The choice would be difficult.

LULU. It's better if there is no choice.

SCHWARZ. What would you never have dreamt?

LULU. That he'd go with them.

SCHWARZ. Sour grapes.

LULU. Just paint!

SCHWARZ. Left side straighter – enough.

LULU. I could stand here for half a lifetime.

SCHWARZ (*painting*). I'm working on your hip.

LULU. Their Corticelli must be very good at something.

SCHWARZ. Huh! She's like the rest!

LULU. You know her?

SCHWARZ. God Forbid! She has the enormous talent of being able to fill a theatre from a hundred yards – simply by her gyrations. So her enormous salary. For every step that sends her little skirt flapping up, she gets more than I get for a picture I've worked on for three quarters of a year.

LULU. I feel – I don't really know . . .

SCHWARZ. What is it? Are you faint?

LULU. It's the first time he's left me alone with a stranger.

SCHWARZ. But the doctor goes out on his rounds?

LULU. That's why Lisa's there. I don't know where she's from.
She's looked after his housekeeping for fifty years.

SCHWARZ. But you do help now and then?

LULU. No. She puts me to bed at night and dresses me in the
morning. She bathes me and does my hair, and the rest of the day
drinks absinthe.

SCHWARZ. Phew!

LULU. And if I even pour myself a teeny glass she boxes
my ears.

SCHWARZ. Your husband puts up with it?

LULU. He takes her side.

SCHWARZ. And you can tolerate such an existence?

LULU. I read to myself – mostly in French.

SCHWARZ. Throw the bitch out on the street. The wife's entitled
to!

LULU. And then?

SCHWARZ. Then? Then –

LULU. I'm lost without her. Who'd choose my dresses for the
dancing lessons?

SCHWARZ. Surely you can do that yourself.

LULU. I don't know myself well enough for that.

SCHWARZ. What does she dress you in?

LULU. As little as possible.

SCHWARZ. God above!

LULU. And I don't have the inspiration to choose.

SCHWARZ. Who gives you the dancing lessons?

LULU. Him.

SCHWARZ *lets his brush sink.*

LULU. Paint.

SCHWARZ. I'd like to see him showing you the steps.

LULU. He knows all the dances – Czardas – Samaqueca – Shimmy
– Russian – Hornpipe –

SCHWARZ. I'd fall over laughing!

LULU. He only tells me how to dance. I dance on my own. He plays the violin for me.

SCHWARZ. And you dance in costumes?

LULU. I have two rooms full of costumes.

SCHWARZ (*drawing his breath*). The world's certainly got some strange corners in it.

LULU. That's why I'm happy.

SCHWARZ. When do you dance?

LULU. After we've dined.

SCHWARZ. Every evening?

LULU. Yes.

SCHWARZ. Tell me – the painting goes better when you talk.

LULU. Last winter we were in Paris. We saw a different dancer every evening – and I'm supposed to be able to do it the moment we get home. It was terrible.

SCHWARZ. Yes there's a lot of misery in Paris.

LULU. We only went out at night. He spent the whole day at the Ecole de Medicine and I slept at home – or sat in front of the fireplace.

SCHWARZ. Then you haven't seen much of the real Paris?

LULU. My legs were still aching six months later.

SCHWARZ. What costumes have you got?

LULU. I've got one as a Fisherboy – then I dance in heavy clogs. A rough linen shirt – front totally open – with short white sleeves – and little shorts – but wide – made of rough wool.

SCHWARZ. And the old boy sits in front of you while you do it?

LULU. You can't see anything.

SCHWARZ. Doesn't it disgust you?

LULU. Why . . .

SCHWARZ. Is that a marriage?

LULU. Every Thursday Mr Schöning comes. Once Prince Polossow came. I was Eve.

SCHWARZ. Well well . . .

LULU. Long red laced boots – violet stockings – and my hair in a Greek knot – with a red ribbon round it.

SCHWARZ (*sinking back*). I can't do any more.

LULU. Paint.

SCHWARZ. My arm's stiff.

LULU. It never got stiff before.

SCHWARZ. And the light's changed.

LULU. You only have to adjust the curtains.

SCHWARZ. Anything I do now – the moment you're gone I'll scratch it out again.

LULU. You've never taken a rest before.

SCHWARZ. This is just misery! That won't make the picture better! What I'll never understand is how you put up with it!

LULU. I have it easy.

SCHWARZ. At any rate in that costume – why don't you freeze?

LULU. You should see me at home.

SCHWARZ. When you dance?

LULU. During the day – when he's working at home – all I usually have on is a petticoat.

SCHWARZ. Just a petticoat.

LULU. The house is warm. And I'm used to it now.

SCHWARZ. We learn something new every day.

LULU. I let my hair down in a loop. Yesterday I had a dark green vest – with my white ballroom shoes – a pink bow in my hair – and garters pale, pale pink.

SCHWARZ. That's pure brothel!

LULU. It's so comfortable – especially in winter when the rooms are nice and warm – you can breathe.

SCHWARZ. You can do that anyway.

LULU. In this costume too – I feel so good –

SCHWARZ. So?

LULU (*breathing*). Look . . .

SCHWARZ. Stop that! (*Jumps up and throws aside the palette and brush and goes up and down in excitement.*) The boot-boy only has to bother with her feet – and the paints don't eat up his money. Tomorrow when I can't afford dinner – no woman will ask me if I know how to eat oysters!

LULU (*pleading*). Please paint.

SCHWARZ. What drove the oaf off to his rehearsal?

LULU. He won't be away long. I prefer it when there's three too!

SCHWARZ (*back at his easel, paints*). But it peels off! It peels off! it peels off!

LULU. I'm not responsible for the costume. He thought it up and the wardrobe mistress at the theatre cut it so low. I didn't want to offend you.

SCHWARZ. This is soul destroying. (*Lets the brush sink.*) I can't! I can't!

LULU. Paint – I beg you!

SCHWARZ. When the colours are dancing in front of my eyes!

LULU. Then just pretend!

SCHWARZ. I'm seeing sparks.

LULU. He'll be back in a moment. For your own sake – paint!

SCHWARZ (*begins again*). Of course! What else can I do? Suppose tomorrow I'm branded immoral! Only the medical profession can allow itself that luxury! (*He paints.*)

LULU (*breathing deeply*). Thank God.

SCHWARZ. No, an artist must be a martyr to his profession – that's made very clear! If you could manage to hold the left trouser leg a little higher.

LULU. Even higher?

SCHWARZ. A touch.

LULU. I can't. You'd see –

SCHWARZ (*going to the platform*). Allow me.

LULU (*bending away*). I can't.

SCHWARZ. Why not?

LULU. My stockings aren't long enough.

SCHWARZ (*taking her hand*). I'll show you where.

LULU (*throws the shepherd's crook in his face*). Leave me alone! (*Hurries to the door.*)

SCHWARZ. Where are you trying to go –

LULU. It'll be a long time before you get me.

SCHWARZ. You can't understand a joke. (*Forces her into the corner, left.*)

LULU (*escaping to the right*). Oh yes – I understand jokes – I understand everything. Just leave me alone. You don't get anything from me by force.

SCHWARZ (*stepping back*). Please . . .

LULU (*going back to the platform*). Go back to work. You have no right to pester me.

SCHWARZ (*coming closer to her*). Stay in your pose.

LULU. Stay at your easel first. (*She flees as he tries to grab her from behind the ottoman*).

SCHWARZ (*trying to go round the ottoman*). Not till I've punished you!

LULU. You'll have to catch me first!

SCHWARZ (*trying to catch her from the left*). You'll soon see that all right!

LULU (*evading him – going right*). Sure? (*Teasing him.*) Chook-chook!

SCHWARZ. If it costs me my life! (*Groping right, round the ottoman.*)

LULU (*avoiding him*). Here – here – here – here!

SCHWARZ (*at the top end*). You'll pay me for that!

LULU (*opposite him, straightening up*). Go back to your work. You won't catch me. I promise you.

SCHWARZ (*feigning moves backwards and forwards*). One more little moment . . .

LULU. If I was wearing a long dress I'd never be able to protect myself –

SCHWARZ. You're a child!

LULU. – but in this thing!

SCHWARZ. You just wait.

LULU. And I'm only wearing a little thing underneath.

SCHWARZ (*throws himself over the ottoman*). Got you!

LULU (*throws the tiger skin over his head*). There! (*Jumps across the stage and clatters up the step-ladder.*) I blaze – I blaze – like the sun – I see far out over all the cities –

SCHWARZ (*unwrapping himself from the cover*). This pelt!

LULU (*supporting herself with her left hand, the right raised aloft*). I catch the clouds – I stick the stars in my hair –

SCHWARZ (*clattering after her*). I'll shake till you fall!

LULU (*climbing higher*). If you don't stop I'll knock the ladder over!

SCHWARZ. You're beautiful!

LULU. I'll kick your head in!

SCHWARZ (*shaking the ladder*). Lightning strikes!

LULU. Get your claws off my legs!

SCHWARZ. Don't kick – or I'll rip you to bits!

LULU. God save Poland!

She topples the ladder over, is flung onto the platform and throws the screen over SCHWARZ's head as he groans and struggles to his feet.

The Children of Heaven race over the field!

By the easel, right following SCHWARZ's movements.

Didn't I tell you – you wouldn't get me –

SCHWARZ (*freeing himself*). Mind the picture!

LULU. I want to rush like the wind with a pack of hounds!

SCHWARZ (*coming closer*). If you can – (*Tries to grab her.*)

LULU. Keep away from my body – or – (*As SCHWARZ makes a grab at her*) – that's what happens!

She throws the easel with the pastel portrait at him, the picture crashes to the ground.

SCHWARZ. God no!

LULU (*back right*). You made the hole yourself!

SCHWARZ. My rent for the studio! My trip! My trip to Norway!

LULU. Why did you chase me?

SCHWARZ. Nothing matters now! (*Lunges after her.*)

LULU (*jumps over the ottoman, over the fallen step-ladder, runs in front of the platform and does a somersault on the carpet*). A ditch! – A ditch! – don't fall! (*Jumps up, stamps through the pastel portrait and falls.*)

SCHWARZ (*falling on top of her*). Got you!

LULU (*twists free and escapes*). You squashed my body!

SCHWARZ *gets up and follows her.*

LULU (*at the back*). Now let me alone. I feel sick.

SCHWARZ (*stumbling over the screen*). I won't forgive you for this!

LULU (*out of breath, coming forward*). I feel . . . oh . . . I feel . . . I feel . . . oh God. (*Sinks on the ottoman.*)

SCHWARZ (*gasping for breath.*) Oh God – this woman. (*Goes to the back and bolts the door. Coming back.*) This world's dirty . . . I'm supposed to think of a salver she's served on . . . words are easy. (*Lies beside her.*)

LULU (*opening her eyes*). I'm falling down . . .

SCHWARZ. The world's – dirty.
LULU. Deep down.
SCHWARZ. How d'you feel?
LULU. Storm.
SCHWARZ (*kisses her bare arm*). Take your clothes off.
LULU. It's too cold.
SCHWARZ. Please. (*Tries to pull down her dress.*)
LULU. Don't.
SCHWARZ. Then come.
LULU. Where?
SCHWARZ. In the bedroom.
LULU. He might come back.
SCHWARZ. Just for a minute.
LULU. Why?
SCHWARZ. I love you.
LULU (*shudders*). Oh.
SCHWARZ (*pulling up her trouser legs*). Darling.
LULU (*stopping his hand*). Don't.
SCHWARZ (*kissing her*). Then come.
LULU. Better here.
SCHWARZ. Here.
LULU. If you like.
SCHWARZ. Then let me undress you.
LULU. Why?
SCHWARZ. So I can love you.
LULU. I'm yours!
SCHWARZ. Oh God.
LULU. If you want.
SCHWARZ. You're cruel.
LULU. Why don't you want me?
SCHWARZ. Please sweetheart.
LULU. I'm yours.
SCHWARZ. Be nice.
LULU. I want to be nice.
SCHWARZ. Then take it off.
LULU. But why?
SCHWARZ. Your costume.
LULU. But I'm yours.

SCHWARZ. Nelly.

LULU. What's wrong with my costume?

SCHWARZ. Nelly – Nelly –

LULU. But I'm not Nelly.

SCHWARZ. Your costume.

LULU. I'm Lulu.

SCHWARZ. I'd call you Eve.

LULU. If you like.

SCHWARZ. Then be nice.

LULU. If you like.

SCHWARZ. Eve.

LULU. What shall I do?

SCHWARZ. Take your clothes off.

LULU. Why?

SCHWARZ. You're playing with me.

LULU. You don't want to.

SCHWARZ. I . . .

LULU. I'm yours.

SCHWARZ. But Eve.

LULU. Then why not?

SCHWARZ. Please.

LULU. You don't like me.

SCHWARZ. God above.

LULU. Try.

SCHWARZ. Eve – Eve.

LULU. All right – then don't.

SCHWARZ. You . . . (*Sits up, jumps to his feet, confused, out of his mind.*). Oh God . . . Oh God, oh God . . . Oh God in Heaven!

LULU (*shouts*). Don't kill me.

SCHWARZ. It happens! – Everything happens.

LULU (*half raising herself*). I think – you've never – made love!

SCHWARZ (*spins round on her, blushing deep red*). Nor have you –

LULU. Me?

SCHWARZ. How old are you?

LULU. Eighteen – and you?

SCHWARZ. Twenty-eight – It sounds mad – it sounds mad – I know – it sounds insane – but everything happens.

GOLL (*outside*). Open!

LULU (*has leapt up*). Hide me! Oh God – hide me!

GOLL (*pounding on the door*). Open!

SCHWARZ. God in Heaven. (*Goes towards the door.*)

LULU (*holds him by the arm*). You can't –

GOLL (*pounding on the door*). Open!

LULU (*has sunk in front of SCHWARZ and clings to his knees.*) He'll beat me to death – hide me.

SCHWARZ. Where – where –

> *The door crashes into the studio.*

GOLL (*crimson faced, bloodshot eyes, throws himself on SCHWARZ with a raised stick*). You cur – you cur – you – (*He crashes forwards on the floor*).

> SCHWARZ *stands shaking, swaying at the knees.* LULU *has fled to the door. Pause.*

SCHWARZ (*stepping towards GOLL*). Dr – Dr – Goll.

LULU (*in the doorway*). Quick, straighten the studio.

SCHWARZ. Be quiet! (*Pause.*)

LULU (*risks coming back*). Surely he's not –

SCHWARZ (*lifts his head*). Dr Goll . . . (*Steps back.*) He's bleeding.

LULU. He must have smashed his nose.

SCHWARZ. Help me to lay him on the couch.

LULU (*steps back*). No – no –

SCHWARZ (*trying to turn him*). Mr Goll . . . Dr Goll . . .

LULU (*motionless*). He's kicked the bucket.

SCHWARZ. A stroke – it could be a stroke. At least help me a bit . . .

LULU. Even the two of us couldn't lift him.

SCHWARZ (*standing up*). Oh this could turn out very nice!

LULU. He's incredibly heavy.

SCHWARZ. We must get a doctor. (*Takes his hat.*) Please be kind enough to straighten the place up a little. (*Going.*) Now I suppose I've had it with the other picture too!

> SCHWARZ *goes.* LULU *is alone.*

LULU (*staying some way off*). Suddenly – he'll jump up. (*Whisper.*)

Kissie-kissie – (*Holding both hands to her temples.*) . . . He's not giving himself away – (*Circles round him.*) He's split his trousers – and – doesn't feel it. (*Standing behind him.*) Kissie-kissie. (*Touches him with the tip of her toe.*) Piglet! . . . (*Drawing back.*) He really means it. (*Staring in front of her.*) . . . No more lessons. I've lost my trainer. (*Goes right, deep in thought.*) He's had enough of me – what shall I do? I had some clothes. (*Turning to the bedroom.*) – I can't dress myself. Undress myself – I can do that. (*Comes forward and bends low.*) Face of a total stranger – if he walked in now like that – ha – (*As she straightens up.*) – and there's no one – to close his eyes –

SCHWARZ (*hurrying on*). Not come round yet . . .?

LULU (*coming from left*). What'll become of me?

SCHWARZ (*bent over GOLL*). Dr Goll.

LULU. I don't think he'll come round.

SCHWARZ. Dr Goll.

LULU. He's done a runner.

SCHWARZ. Talk decently!

LULU. He never dreamt of this.

SCHWARZ (*tries to sit him up*). He weighs two hundred weight.

LULU. And before he knows it he's stone cold.

SCHWARZ (*rolling GOLL onto his back*). Please Mr Goll – Dr . . . (*To LULU, indicating the ottoman.*) Get that cushion.

LULU (*handing the cushion to SCHWARZ*). Perhaps if I did the hornpipe?

SCHWARZ (*gliding the cushion under GOLL's head*). The doctor'll be here in a couple of shakes.

LULU. He must find me alone with him.

SCHWARZ. I sent the caretaker.

LULU. He's beyond pills.

SCHWARZ. We must do what we can.

LULU. He didn't believe in them.

SCHWARZ. Shouldn't you change at least?

LULU. If there was anyone there – to help me.

SCHWARZ. You can manage that for yourself for God's sake!

LULU. No . . .

SCHWARZ. If I can be of use . . .

LULU. After you've closed his eyes.

SCHWARZ. Dear God – you think he's really –
LULU. Mm.
SCHWARZ. I don't know.
LULU. If not –
SCHWARZ. I've never seen anyone die.
LULU. – then not.
SCHWARZ. You're a monster.
LULU. And you?

> SCHWARZ *stares wide-eyed at her.*

It'll be my turn one day.
SCHWARZ. Why can't you shut up!
LULU. And yours.
SCHWARZ. You don't have to tell me!
LULU. Do it!
SCHWARZ. What?
LULU. Before it's too late.
SCHWARZ. It's your job.
LULU. Me? Hm – ah!
SCHWARZ. Must I?
LULU. He's staring straight at me.
SCHWARZ. And me – he's staring straight at me.
LULU. You're not a man. You're scared to do it.
SCHWARZ (*closing GOLL's eyes*). The first time in my life I've
   done it.
LULU. Didn't you do it to your parents?
SCHWARZ. No.
LULU. You were scared?
SCHWARZ (*violently*). No!
LULU (*cringing away*). I didn't want to offend you.
SCHWARZ. They're still alive.
LULU. At least you've still got someone.
SCHWARZ. Dear God – they're as poor as beggars!
LULU. So was I.
SCHWARZ. You?
LULU. Now I'm rich.
SCHWARZ (*looks at her, shakes his head*). You horrify me! (*Goes up
   and down in excitement, talks to himself.*) She can't help it.

LULU (*to herself*). What'll become of me?

> LULU *is still, her gaze fastened on* GOLL. SCHWARZ *looks at her from the side. He grasps both her hands* . . .

SCHWARZ. Look at me . . .
LULU. What d'you want?
SCHWARZ. Look at me.
LULU. What d'you want to see?
SCHWARZ. Your eyes.

> *He leads her to the ottoman and makes her sit beside him.*

Look in my eyes.
LULU. I see myself in them as Pierrot.
SCHWARZ (*jumps up*). Hell! This is hell!
LULU. I must get changed.
SCHWARZ (*holds her back*). One question – just one question.
LULU. I'm not allowed to answer.
SCHWARZ (*pulls her back on the ottoman*). Can you – can you –
LULU. Yes –
SCHWARZ. Wait! – tell the truth?
LULU. I don't know.
SCHWARZ. You must be able to tell the truth!
LULU. I don't know.
SCHWARZ. Do you believe in God?
LULU. I don't know. Leave me alone. You're mad.
SCHWARZ (*keeping her back*). Is there anything sacred to you to swear on?
LULU. I don't know.
SCHWARZ. Then what d'you believe in?
LULU. I don't know.
SCHWARZ. Have you got a soul?
LULU. I don't know.
SCHWARZ. Are you a virgin?
LULU. I don't know.
SCHWARZ. God above! (*Gets up and goes left, wringing his hands.*)
LULU (*without moving*). I don't know.
SCHWARZ (*with a glance at* GOLL). He knows.
LULU (*coming to him*). If there's something you want to know –

SCHWARZ. Everything! I want to know everything!

LULU. Since I've been married I had to dance every night God sent
   – half naked –

SCHWARZ. Not that! That tells me nothing!

LULU. Why don't I –

SCHWARZ. What?

LULU. You still can.

SCHWARZ. Have you no shame!

LULU. It was you who asked me to.

SCHWARZ. Get out! Get out! Cover yourself!

   LULU *goes.* SCHWARZ *is alone.*

SCHWARZ (*looking at* GOLL). She can't help it – I could save her
   – bring her soul to life – she'd come like a flash – she is utterly
   depraved – my parents, my poor parents – all this happiness –
   makes me so wretched! Do I love her? Does she love me? – She
   loves me – she says so – I love her – she loves me – loves me –
   it's the first time – I'll be married. I'm in such misery – I want
   to change – change places with you – get up – old man – I'll give
   her back to you – your puppet – and my youth, take my youth
   too – I don't have the sort of courage you need to live – to love –
   you can begin again – with my strength – in its prime – take it –
   you can catch me up – you can. His mouth's already open. Mouth
   open, eyes shut – like children. If I was gone – like that – so far
   – like children . . . I'm not a child. I never was. (*Groans.*) I (*He
   kneels and binds* GOLL's *jaw with his handkerchief.*) . . . am an
   old maid. I cry to heaven – to let me have the talent to be happy
   – the courage to be – and the power and the glory – just to be a
   little happy – for her sake – only for her sake.

   LULU *opens the bedroom door. Indicates the buttons on the back
   of her dress.*

LULU. If you'd be so kind and . . .

Act Two

Berlin.

A small, very elegant salon. Back left, the main entrance door. Side doors left and right. On the backwall, over the fireplace, in a sumptuous brocade frame, LULU's portrait as Pierrot. Right front, a few armchairs round a small Chinese table. Many pictures, some unfinished, in pretty gold frames. Right, a carved ebony writing desk.

SCHWARZ in an armchair, right front. Holds LULU on his knee. Brush and palette beside him on the carpet.

LULU (*in eau-de-Nil dressing-gown with a very low-cut neck – evading his advances.*) In the middle of the morning.
SCHWARZ. But you're mine.
LULU. You're horrible.
SCHWARZ. Can I help it?
LULU. You're murdering me.
SCHWARZ. Your own fault.
LULU (*hiding her face in his chest.*) Wait.
SCHWARZ. Till it's winter?
LULU. Till this evening.
SCHWARZ. Evening's started.
LULU. And then can I have all of you?
SCHWARZ. What more do you want?
LULU. You . . . you.
SCHWARZ. But I'm yours.
LULU. Till we're free.
SCHWARZ. Isn't it all the same?
LULU. No.
SCHWARZ. Please.
LULU. Like children.

SCHWARZ. Like children.

LULU. It's a sin.

SCHWARZ. Then let's sin.

LULU. You can do that on your own.

SCHWARZ. I've never done that. (*Tries to hitch up her dress.*)

LULU (*holds her dress firmly below her knees – so that her dark green slippers fall from her feet*). I'll tell you –

SCHWARZ. You're not nice.

LULU (*kisses him*). You get sweeter.

SCHWARZ. I'm too sweet.

LULU. Not by a long way.

SCHWARZ. So you say.

LULU. You know.

SCHWARZ. I just have to hear your feet –

LULU (*kisses him*). Darling.

SCHWARZ. – to say to hell with it!

LULU. I'll go barefoot.

SCHWARZ. Ah that's all I need.

LULU. I don't want to wear you out.

SCHWARZ. I'll die happy.

LULU (*kisses him*). Then what would be left for me?

SCHWARZ (*shakes himself*). Oh . . . Eve . . .

LULU. Wait . . . I'll tell you something.

SCHWARZ. A newspaper headline?

LULU. A surprise.

SCHWARZ. Surprises give me the jitters . . . every day I'm afraid the world will end . . . I wake up afraid that before the day's out you'll be bitten by a mad dog . . . I'll shake all day because there might be a revolution – and tomorrow I'll shake because an insect bite or something could end our happiness for ever – I can't even pick up a newspaper – I can hardly bring myself to go down in the street.

> LULU *resting on his chest, whispers in his ear.*

SCHWARZ. It's not possible!

LULU (*sits up smiling*). Ugh . . .

SCHWARZ. You're a mother?

LULU. Not yet.

SCHWARZ (*embracing her fiercely*). Eve – Eve – my Eve –

LULU. I wanted so much to go on drifting in the clear blue sky just a little longer.

SCHWARZ. No – you make me so happy!

LULU (*covering her face*). You're heartless!

SCHWARZ. I'm the opposite!

LULU. I wanted so much just to wait quietly.

SCHWARZ. Thanks thanks my darling – all my thanks.

LULU (*pulling herself up*). It's all your doing.

SCHWARZ. It's yours ten times more.

LULU. We won't fight over it.

SCHWARZ. And after all you did.

LULU. It's too late to change it.

SCHWARZ. Is it sure?

LULU. Since two weeks.

SCHWARZ. And you could keep quiet so long?

LULU. I spent half the nights crying myself to sleep.

SCHWARZ. The one happiness we still didn't have!

LULU. I tried everything.

SCHWARZ. You should be ashamed. I can face your confinement in cold blood – I'm not afraid. I've been able to feed two mouths for a long time now. Just go through with it bravely. These days I'm rated higher than almost all the others. The dealers break their necks when I turn up with a painting. Who have I done all this for? Who else should I work for? – if not my family!

LULU. I'm nothing to you.

SCHWARZ. I owe everything to you. Since I've had you, the whole world can see I'm marked out. This proves it again. Since I've had you, I know what I am. And the whole world knows it. My confidence, my creative joy, my pride as an artist – all – all – I owe it to you. And you ask if you're anything to me? You're my happiness. You don't know how you do it, but you can't help it. You flowered for me, and you'll wither for me. For me! For me! Your body lives for me. Take your happiness – it's all you've got. I dragged you out of the mud – I fought myself tooth and nail to make myself do it. I was man enough. Now happiness pours over me. Everyday I'm more famous and – whether you like it or not – every year you'll add another little blessing to my happiness.

LULU. I want some fresh air.

SCHWARZ. I must get to work. The model's waiting (*Takes the palette and brush from the floor, kisses* LULU.) Till – this evening.

LULU (*looking at him*). I dread it.

SCHWARZ. My Iphigenia's still missing everything that would make it my work – what a work of mine should be. It has to be finished by the end of March. Not to mention the five commissions from the United States.

LULU (*rocking on his knee*). Are you cross with me?

SCHWARZ (*lays the palette and brush down again*). I'm an artist – which excuses me for a lot of things. And you – you're a terrifying disruption.

    LULU *shudders*.

SCHWARZ. It's true – it's true.

LULU. I'm losing my shape.

SCHWARZ. That's not surprising.

LULU. It's easy for you to laugh.

SCHWARZ. God knows it's not my fault.

LULU. Who else's?

SCHWARZ. It's your beauty.

LULU. I'm going to be ripped open.

SCHWARZ. You are so sweet!

LULU. You're inhuman.

SCHWARZ. I can't help it.

LULU. And I can't help being what I am – I can only be a woman – when you're here.

SCHWARZ. Yes – you're a woman!

LULU. I want to be ugly!

SCHWARZ. Oh God help us!

LULU. Just once, for three weeks.

SCHWARZ. It'd be a disaster.

LULU. I could think I was young again – a little child – who knew nothing. I'd have something to look forward to – to growing up. I could laugh again, when I think of it – how beautiful it would be. I'd be a tiny little virgin for a while.

SCHWARZ (*stroking her hair*). Dear God.

LULU. . . . I want to play in the street again . . .

SCHWARZ. The world's brutal – brutal. Now fate's sacrificing you. Submit – to your death sentence – and die in bliss.

LULU. Often I want to scream.

SCHWARZ. I've often noticed it. I don't know what makes me so frightening.

LULU. I wouldn't wish it on anyone.

SCHWARZ. It's not just your skin.

LULU. My poor skin.

SCHWARZ. I've often tried to think what it is.

LULU. It's getting wrinkled.

SCHWARZ. You get used to everything.

LULU. Now I can hardly tell if I've got a silk sheet under me or the mattress webbing.

SCHWARZ. And it's not the way you twist and turn – though you do that beautifully.

LULU. I was so sensitive – when I ran my fingertips over my knees it left rosy marks.

SCHWARZ. I used to think it was the way you kissed me.

LULU. Or my underwear?

SCHWARZ. God no.

LULU. I won't wear any.

SCHWARZ. And it's not the way you kiss.

LULU (*kisses him*). No?

SCHWARZ. You're very mean with it.

LULU (*kissing him*). With kisses?

SCHWARZ. So where did you learn it?

LULU. Before I came into the world.

SCHWARZ. Idiot.

LULU. From my little mother.

SCHWARZ. So, so . . .

LULU. Some can –

SCHWARZ. I got it from you.

LULU. – the others never learn.

SCHWARZ. I'd never have got it without you.

LULU. You can.

SCHWARZ. So what is it? What is it – tell me – please.

LULU. It's all nothing.

SCHWARZ. I stand before a riddle. I only have to picture you in
   my mind.
LULU (*kissing him*). Poor boy.
SCHWARZ. Is it your beauty? Your limbs? The shape of your
   body . . .

   *He lifts her dress so that her bright green stockings are visible above
   the knee.*

These lines don't suggest voluptuousness.

   LULU *wards him off.*

SCHWARZ (*lost in gazing at her*). They're too cool, too chaste.
LULU (*covering her knees*). Why d'you have to rack your brains?
SCHWARZ. It can only be one thing.
LULU (*kissing him*). Still . . .
SCHWARZ. It is.
LULU (*closing his mouth*). No! – No!
SCHWARZ. It is.
LULU (*swamping him with kisses*). Bye – bye – bye – bye – bye –
   bye . . .
SCHWARZ. You know it.
LULU (*straightening herself, crossing her feet*). Then in that case it's
   not in my power and I can't change it.
SCHWARZ (*pressing her to him*). You mustn't change it – child – you
   mustn't change it – it's all you are – your life – everything.
LULU (*sinking back*). You make me wild. (*Closes her eyes, offers him
   her mouth*). I'm hot – oh – I'm –
SCHWARZ (*lifting her gently as he lays her back in the armchair*).
   Henriette's doing the shopping . . .
LULU (*hands between her knees*). Turn the key.

   SCHWARZ *goes to the back and locks the door. A ring from the
   corridor.*

SCHWARZ. Blast!
LULU. No one's in!
SCHWARZ. Perhaps the art dealer.
LULU. I don't care if it's the Kaiser!

SCHWARZ. One moment. (*He goes out*).

LULU (*alone, stares motionless into space*). You . . . You . . . You . . . you – here? Ah . . . Ah – that's good . . .

SCHWARZ (*coming back*). A beggar. Fought in the war. Give me some change. I haven't got any.

LULU. Just go.

SCHWARZ (*picking up the brush and palette*). Yes it's high time I got back to my Iphigenia. The model's sitting there, we're flirting here. (*Going*). Give him a few coppers.

> LULU *gets up, slowly straightens her clothes, strokes back her hair and goes to the door.*

SCHIGOLCH (*being let in by* LULU). I'd've thought he'd've been someone a bit more solid – bit more round the chest. He's rather jittery. Gave at the knees when he saw me.

LULU (*pushes a chair into place for him*). How could you bring yourself to beg from him?

SCHIGOLCH (*sits with a sigh*). That's what I dragged my cadaver here for. It's hard enough in this weather. You told me mornings he's busy with his brush.

LULU. He couldn't get started. How much d'you want?

SCHIGOLCH. Only two hundred – if it's not inconvenient – or say three hundred. My two best clients have gone travelling – without leaving me a word.

LULU (*goes to her writing desk and rummages in the drawers*). Am I tired!

SCHIGOLCH (*looking round*). This got me on my pins too. I've wanted to see how things are for a long time.

LULU. And?

SCHIGOLCH. Overwhelming. (*Looks round.*) Just like mine fifty years ago. Instead of the Chinese nicknacks we had rusty old sabres in those days. Damn it you've done well for yourself. (*Rucking up the carpet with his shoe*). Carpets too.

LULU (*gives him three banknotes*). I go barefoot when no one's here.

SCHIGOLCH (*noticing* LULU's *portrait*). That you?

LULU. Nice?

SCHIGOLCH. If it's the real goods.

LULU. – Drink?

SCHIGOLCH. Such as?

LULU (*getting up*). Elixir de Spaa.

SCHIGOLCH. It's all camomile tea to me – whether you get it from Spaa or Outer Mongolia. He drink?

LULU. That's all I need. (*Coming down*). Liqueurs affect people differently.

SCHIGOLCH. He lashes out?

LULU (*filling two glasses*). He goes to sleep.

SCHIGOLCH. When he's drunk you can know him down to his bowels.

LULU. Rather not. (*Sits opposite* SCHIGOLCH.) Tell me.

SCHIGOLCH. The streets get longer and my legs get shorter.

LULU. And your accordion?

SCHIGOLCH. It's got breathing problems – like me and my asthma. I keep telling myself it's not worth the trouble of doing it up. (*Clinks glasses with her*).

LULU (*empties her glass*). I thought your time'd run out by now.

SCHIGOLCH. That's what I thought. But just because the sun's gone down it doesn't mean you fall asleep. I'm hoping to make winter. And then my jolly old asthma will hitch me a one-way ride.

LULU (*filling the glasses*). You mean, they missed your turn?

SCHIGOLCH. Very likely – the driver doesn't always stop at the head of the queue. (*Stroking her knee.*) Now you tell me. Long time no see – my little Lulu.

LULU (*pulling back, smiling*). Life's incomprehensible!

SCHIGOLCH. You're still so young.

LULU. Fancy calling me Lulu!

SCHIGOLCH. Lulu, yes! Did I ever call you anything else?

LULU. I haven't been called that since before the flood.

SCHIGOLCH. You've got another handle?

LULU. Lulu sounds out of the ark.

SCHIGOLCH. Children, children.

LULU. Now I'm called –

SCHIGOLCH. What's in the honey pot still stays the same.

LULU. Meaning?

SCHIGOLCH. What's it called now?

LULU. Eve.

SCHIGOLCH. Tit spelt backwards.

LULU. I'm listening.

SCHIGOLCH (*looks round*). This is what I dreamt for you. It's what you set out to get. – And what's that supposed to be?

LULU (*spraying herself from a scent bottle*). Heliotrope.

SCHIGOLCH. Does it smell better than you?

LULU (*spraying him*). Sour grapes!

SCHIGOLCH. Who'd've guessed all this palatial luxury?

LULU. When I think back.

SCHIGOLCH (*stroking her knee*). And how are you? Still working at the French?

LULU. I loll about and sleep.

SCHIGOLCH. Very elegant. That always makes a good impression. And after?

LULU. I stretch – till my joints crack.

SCHIGOLCH. And when they've cracked?

LULU. Why're you interested?

SCHIGOLCH. Why am I interested? Why am I interested? I'd rather live to Judgement Day and see myself lose eternity in paradise, than know I'd left my little Lulu behind still struggling. My better self's already passed through the pearly gates – but I still have compassion for this world.

LULU. I don't.

SCHIGOLCH. You've got it too good.

LULU. It's making me stupid.

SCHIGOLCH. Better than the old dancing bear?

LULU. I don't dance any more.

SCHIGOLCH. It was time to cash him in.

LULU. Now I'm –

SCHIGOLCH. Tell me, tell me, how you really are – at heart, my child! I believed in you when all there was to see were two big eyes and a gaping mouth underneath.

LULU. An animal.

SCHIGOLCH. Devil take it! – and what an animal!

LULU. I know. I'm elegant.

SCHIGOLCH. A svelte animal! A mythical animal!

LULU. You trained me.

SCHIGOLCH. Yes well – and now they can bury me. I've got rid of all my prejudices now.

LULU. You did that when you started.

SCHIGOLCH. Even the one against washing the dead.

LULU. Why be afraid of being washed one last time?

SCHIGOLCH. You only get dirty again.

LULU (*spraying him*). This will bring you back to life.

SCHIGOLCH. We are corruption.

LULU. I beg your pardon! Every evening I rub my whole body in oil and then powder it. I look like a marble statue from top to bottom. My skin's like satin.

SCHIGOLCH. And it must be worth the trouble – for the louts with gold tiepins.

LULU. When the sheets are thrown back at night I look like a peeled apple.

SCHIGOLCH. As if that stopped you being muck!

LULU. Not me! I don't feel good unless I'm fit to eat all over.

SCHIGOLCH. Like me! I'm fit to eat all over. I'm throwing a dinner party. Open house – all comers welcome!

LULU. The worms won't live it up much on you!

SCHIGOLCH. Patience little girl! Your admirers won't preserve you in a bottle. It's the beautiful Helen when the skin stretches like elastic. Afterwards? – a pair of old boots. Even the zoo wouldn't take it in. It'd make the nice little animals belch! (*Getting up*). Perhaps they'll use you as artificial manure.

LULU (*Getting up*). Was it enough?

SCHIGOLCH. There'll be enough left to plant a bush on my grave.

LULU. I'll see it's done.

SCHIGOLCH. I can imagine how. D'you still remember how I yanked you out of the gutter?

LULU. How you strung me up by the wrists and made my bottom bleed with your belt. I remember that as if it were yesterday.

SCHIGOLCH. And it was necessary. And it was necessary. (*Giving her his cheek*). Bye-bye.

LULU (*kissing his cheek*). Bye-bye. (*She goes out with him and comes back with* SCHÖNING.)

SCHÖNING. What's your father doing here Mrs Schwarz?

LULU. My father? Why are you suddenly so formal?

SCHÖNING (*hesitantly*). I have to – for a moment – I have to talk to you.

LULU. With me? Then why didn't you do it yesterday?

SCHÖNING (*sitting*). If I was called Eduard Schwarz that relic would never cross my doorstep.

LULU (*dropping into a chair*). What's the matter with you – for God's sake –

SCHÖNING. Please listen to me Mrs Schwarz.

LULU. Why are you being so formal? He's in the studio.

SCHÖNING. I wanted to tell you yesterday – I've wanted to tell you for sometime.

LULU. Believe me – he's in the studio!

SCHÖNING. For God's sake don't start getting into a state.

LULU. It's because you're so – weird.

SCHÖNING. Yes – well – I must ask that your visits to me –

LULU. My visits?

SCHÖNING. Your visits, yes – are discontinued.

LULU. You're mad!

SCHÖNING. I must ask that your visits to me are discontinued.

LULU. What are you thinking of?

SCHÖNING. You understand me?

LULU. No.

SCHÖNING. I've been considering it for months. Above all I'm thinking of you and your happiness.

LULU. Let me get you an Elixir de Spaa?

SCHÖNING. Not now. I beg you – promise me.

LULU. What's happened to you – since yesterday?

SCHÖNING. Nothing.

LULU. You want to make a fool of me.

SCHÖNING. I've already asked you twice.

LULU. You've caught a cold – yesterday . . .

SCHÖNING. I feel excellent.

LULU. And me . . .

SCHÖNING. If you don't want to listen to me now.

LULU. I am listening.

SCHÖNING. If you don't want to listen to me, the – the door simply won't be opened to you. You force me . . .

LULU *stands up and goes up and down.*

SCHÖNING. For my part, I'll omit nothing to respect your position in society. You can be as proud of that as of my – intimacy. I won't be paraded about any more!

LULU. Don't play with me like this! What crime have I committed?

SCHÖNING. It costs me more than it costs you.

Pause.

LULU (*gracefully lowers herself into a chair, her hand on the back*).
   You intend to – marry?

SCHÖNING. That too.

LULU. A meeting of souls.

SCHÖNING. Will you shut up!

LULU. As you wish.

SCHÖNING. I don't want to fall between two stools.

LULU. May one ask . . .

SCHÖNING. The von Bergens' daughter.

LULU *nods.*

SCHÖNING. It's too late to change now.

LULU. So you know her well?

SCHÖNING. She sat on my knee when she was a child.

LULU. Pretty?

SCHÖNING. In that direction.

LULU. She doesn't know about it yet?

SCHÖNING. They're preparing her for it.

LULU. She's still at boarding school?

SCHÖNING. Her first step into freedom will take her into my arms.

LULU. Poor kid . . .

SCHÖNING. We visited her last week – I and her father. No one can see very far what lies ahead –

LULU. Is she sixteen yet?

SCHÖNING. – but she has the potential to become anything.

LULU. And – the Baroness?

SCHÖNING. A painful, motherly nod of the head.

LULU. How clever you are!

SCHÖNING. A gesture of gratitude.

LULU. I know. You saved daddy from prison.

SCHÖNING. He had his hand in the church till.

LULU. So you get the mother first.

SCHÖNING. Out of politeness.

LULU. Yes, you.

SCHÖNING. That's the truth as sure as there's a God in heaven.

LULU. I'll be happy if I look like that when I'm thirty-seven.

SCHÖNING. She brought six children into the world.

LULU. No one would believe it.

SCHÖNING. It doesn't show.

LULU. She wanted to repay you.

SCHÖNING. Her husband can't possibly have been blinded by the same infatuation. We saw each other only once by the way. I immediately asked her to confess everything to her husband.

LULU. You already had the child in mind.

SCHÖNING. That too.

LULU. I don't want to make the poor little creature even more unhappy. I won't put a foot in your house again.

SCHÖNING. I have your word?

LULU. We can meet wherever you like.

SCHÖNING. We won't ever meet again – except in your husband's presence.

LULU. You can't ask that of me!

SCHÖNING. When you married your husband you made him my friend.

LULU. And mine.

SCHÖNING. That you're going behind his back, I find – distasteful.

LULU. God in heaven!

SCHÖNING. I've grown used to him. Tomorrow if he found out I couldn't just say 'Go back from whence ye came!' I can't go on with it. At my age you don't make new friends easily. He's the one person in the world I'm close to.

LULU. You'll get enough friends – when you marry again.

SCHÖNING. Thank you.

LULU. Wait a little –

SCHÖNING. I don't want to quarrel with Schwarz.

LULU. There's no need.

SCHÖNING. Yes – he's too much of a child.

LULU. Too much of a sheep!

SCHÖNING. Too much of a child – otherwise he'd've found you out long ago.

LULU. It wouldn't hurt him if he did find me out. Perhaps he wouldn't be so ridiculous. He'd pull himself together.

SCHÖNING. Then why did you marry him?

LULU. Because I didn't know anyone could be such a fool.

SCHÖNING. Poor man.

LULU. He thinks he's in bliss.

SCHÖNING. If his eyes were opened.

LULU. He's banal. He's simple-minded. He's uneducated. He has no idea how he looks compared to others. He sees nothing. He doesn't see himself or me. He's blind – blind – blind as a bat.

SCHÖNING. Take him in hand a little.

LULU. I'm not a governess.

SCHÖNING. He bores you.

LULU. I'm his wife.

SCHÖNING. It's what ninety wives out of a hundred have to do.

LULU. It's not why I married.

SCHÖNING. Oh dear! – the illusions you still have about good society.

LULU. I have no illusions. None. Now – sometimes – I even dream of Goll.

SCHÖNING. The old magician. He spoiled you.

LULU. He wasn't banal.

SCHÖNING. God knows he wasn't – with his dancing lessons.

LULU. Sometimes I still see his big red head hanging over me.

SCHÖNING. You hanker for the whip.

LULU. Every three or four nights I dream his funeral was all a misunderstanding. He's there, as though he'd never gone away. Only he floats about as if he's in his socks. He's not cross with me for marrying Schwarz – just a bit sad – and awkward, almost shy – as if he's there without permission. Otherwise he feels quite at home with us – only he can't get over the fact that since he died I've thrown so much money out of the window.

SCHÖNING. That's real desecration of the dead.

LULU. He chooses to come.

SCHÖNING. So even now you still don't have enough?

LULU. What d'you call enough?

SCHÖNING. Huh – me? – you can't measure love by the yard. If he's untrained – initiate him into the sacred rites.

LULU. He loves me.

SCHÖNING. Fatal!

LULU. He wants to breed from me.

SCHÖNING. Love never rises above the animal.

LULU. I don't want to see myself in the mirror any more. I'm being made ridiculous. He doesn't know anything about me. He calls me his little love-bird and baa-lamb – he has no idea what I am. He'd say that to any piano teacher. He doesn't know the difference – because his whole life he's never had a girl. He says it himself.

SCHÖNING. Someone who's been ogling the juiciest little models since he was fifteen.

LULU. He even brags about it.

SCHÖNING. Hm –

LULU. He's afraid. He trembles for his life. Every time there's a full moon he thinks he's caught some unmentionable disease.

SCHÖNING. He's a hypochondriac.

LULU. I'm just his contraceptive.

SCHÖNING. Oho . . .

LULU. Why shouldn't I say it. I simply don't count. When I'm nauseated he thinks it's just childish bashfulness. That doesn't stop him cutting up rough. When everyone else is happy he's howling like a drainpipe.

SCHÖNING. God knows how many innocent little wives would count themselves lucky in your place.

LULU. Let him go and look for one. He'll find enough. When I scent my hair and get myself up in my dark silk chemise with the big lace flounces and bangles on the knees –

SCHÖNING. I remember.

LULU. And only my arms bare – he falls on me like an ape – rip, rip – everything to pieces and all I get is his grunts.

SCHÖNING. Unbelievable.

LULU. And then when I dance 'Daddy's Little Baby' in my baby costume – he goes to sleep.

SCHÖNING. Even though he's an artist.

LULU. He thinks he is anyway.

SCHÖNING. That's all that counts.

LULU. And he insists he's famous.

SCHÖNING. Another thing he owes to me.

LULU. He'll believe anything – anything. He's as mistrustful as a thief but lets himself be lied to so openly you lose all respect for him! When he married me I made him believe I was a virgin.

SCHÖNING. God almighty.

LULU. Otherwise he'd've thought I had no morals.

SCHÖNING. Can it be done?

> LULU *is silent.*

SCHÖNING (*half to himself*). That could be unpleasant . . .

LULU. I yelled.

SCHÖNING. For . . .

LULU. He misunderstood it.

SCHÖNING. And wasn't disappointed.

LULU. He flatters himself about it till today.

SCHÖNING (*getting up*). He's to be envied. I always said so.

LULU. He learnt to respect himself at one stroke! Since then he's full of admiration when he speaks about himself.

SCHÖNING. None of this changes anything. (*Pacing up and down*). I have to think of myself. This is the one moment I cannot afford to have a scandal.

LULU. I'll do everything – everything – to keep him happy.

SCHÖNING. That's not good enough for me! I want to take my wife home to a respectable house.

LULU. What d'you want with that child?

SCHÖNING. That's none of your business.

LULU. She's too young for you.

SCHÖNING. That 'child' is three years younger than you.

LULU. She'll bore you to death with her chatter and bore you to death with her silence.

SCHÖNING. I'll soon teach her the right style.

LULU. Merciful God – she'll fall to pieces in your hands.

SCHÖNING. Don't stand in my way! Since your marriage to Schwarz I've given you no cause to take our relationship seriously.

LULU. Oh God.

SCHÖNING. I gave you everything you had a right to expect of
me. You have a healthy young husband. I take an interest in his
career. You have a great deal of money at your disposal. You
move in society. Now please let me have my bit of freedom.
What's still left to me to live, I intend to live. When you come
to me, when you throw your clothes in the corner before I know
what's happening – then no one can expect me to treat you as a
married woman.

LULU. You've had enough of me – you've had enough of me.

SCHÖNING *bites his lips.*

LULU. That's it.

SCHÖNING. Yes – that's it.

LULU (*getting up*). But I won't let myself be pushed down.

SCHÖNING. Now it's starting.

LULU. I'm staying on top – as long as I've got the strength.

SCHÖNING. Be quiet!

LULU. I'm staying on top – even if everything else is destroyed.

SCHÖNING. Mignon . . .

LULU. From yesterday to today – all of a sudden you behave as if
you've never seen me –

SCHÖNING. It had to come to this in the end.

LULU. I can't let you throw me out – I'll go to pieces. The whole
world can tread on me – only not you – not you. It would be
wrong of you. You're taking my life!

SCHÖNING. Is it money?

LULU. If I belong to anyone in this world I belong to you! You
did everything for me! I've had everything from you! It all comes
from you! Take it! Take me as your slave if that's what you want!

SCHÖNING. I educated you; I gave you two marriages; now all I
want is to see you become a respectable woman.

LULU. What use is that to me – a respectable woman!

SCHÖNING. If you think you owe me gratitude, then show it –

LULU. Do anything you want with me! What else am I here for?
But not that! But not that! Don't throw me away!

SCHWARZ *comes from the right with the brush in his hand.*

SCHWARZ. What's happening here.

LULU. He's getting rid of me! He's told me a thousand times –
SCHÖNING. Be silent! Be silent! Be silent!
LULU. A thousand times – stammered – no one makes love like me.

SCHWARZ *takes* LULU's *arm and takes her out right.*

SCHÖNING (*alone*). A pretty kettle of fish.

SCHWARZ *returns with the brush in his hand.*

SCHWARZ. Is this some sort of joke?
SCHÖNING. No.
SCHWARZ. Please explain to me –
SCHÖNING. Yes.
SCHWARZ. Yes . . .? Yes . . .?
SCHÖNING. Let's sit – I'm tired (*Sits.*)
SCHWARZ (*hesitating*). What does it mean?
SCHÖNING. Sit – please.
SCHWARZ. What does it mean? Tell me. Tell me!
SCHÖNING. You've already heard.
SCHWARZ. I heard nothing.
SCHÖNING. You want to hear nothing.
SCHWARZ. I don't understand.
SCHÖNING. Just be clear – what you owe to her – and that –
SCHWARZ. Yes – I know that –
SCHÖNING. – you married half a million.
SCHWARZ. So – and –
SCHÖNING. You're swimming in luck.
SCHWARZ. Yes.
SCHÖNING. You owe that to her.
SCHWARZ. Yes.
SCHÖNING. You were a beggar.
SCHWARZ. Yes. – Yes. Has she accused me?
SCHÖNING. That's not the point.
SCHWARZ. She has accused me!
SCHÖNING. Pull yourself together. Take life a bit more seriously.
  We're not children!
SCHWARZ. What more does she want?
SCHÖNING. She wants the whip!
SCHWARZ. She already has everything she wants.

SCHÖNING. You are . . .

SCHWARZ. Tell me what all that was about just now!

SCHÖNING. She said it herself – here in front of you!

SCHWARZ (*going pale*). She didn't want –

SCHÖNING. You married half a million.

SCHWARZ. Did she want to deceive me?

SCHÖNING. Take what's happened as happened.

SCHWARZ. Happened?

SCHÖNING. It's your fault if you're deceived.

SCHWARZ. What has happened?

SCHÖNING. For half a year you've been living in seventh heaven –
  that can't be taken away. You owe that to her.

SCHWARZ. What has she done?

SCHÖNING. But she's already told you.

SCHWARZ. Just now?

SCHÖNING. Just now? No. – I've known her for thirteen years.

SCHWARZ. You.

SCHÖNING. You've made your name. You can work. That can't be
  done without money. You needn't deny yourself anything. You
  have your freedom.

SCHWARZ. You betrayed me.

SCHÖNING. D'you want us to use pistols?

SCHWARZ. Pistols? Pistols?

SCHÖNING. I won't harm you.

SCHWARZ. Oh God – oh God.

SCHÖNING. D'you feel unwell?

SCHWARZ. Oh God.

SCHÖNING. You haven't been betrayed.

SCHWARZ. Then I don't understand.

SCHÖNING. You don't want to understand. I came here to finish it.

SCHWARZ. Yes – I know.

SCHÖNING. I came to forbid her to visit me again. I came for
  your sake.

SCHWARZ. So it's true.

SCHÖNING. Help me to bring her to her sense of duty. She doesn't
  know what she does. She doesn't know anything else.

SCHWARZ. You – knew her.

SCHÖNING. Yes I knew her. When she was seven she

was selling flowers in the street. Barefoot without a
petticoat.

SCHWARZ. She said she grew up with a wicked aunt.

SCHÖNING. The woman I lodged her with.

SCHWARZ. Flower girl – without a petticoat.

SCHÖNING. She didn't tell you.

SCHWARZ. No. No.

SCHÖNING. Who could blame her?

SCHWARZ. Flower girl.

SCHÖNING. Why am I telling you? So you won't believe she's
depraved by nature. As long as I've known her she's tried to
improve herself. She was outstanding in school.

SCHWARZ. How long was she at it?

SCHÖNING. That's exactly the wrong question. When she was in
school the mothers held her up as an example to their daughters. I
still have her certificates.

SCHWARZ. When I got to know her she told me she was still –
untouched.

SCHÖNING. Must have been a joke.

SCHWARZ. She told me – she was still – untouched.

SCHÖNING. She was a widow!

SCHWARZ. She swore –

SCHÖNING *gets up and goes left.*

SCHWARZ. – by her mother's grave.

SCHÖNING. She never knew her mother – let alone her grave. Her
mother hasn't got a grave.

SCHWARZ. Oh God.

SCHÖNING (*coming back*). I'm not here to discuss your illusions.

SCHWARZ. No no. How long was she at school?

SCHÖNING. Five years. She was a little goddess to the other girls.
It was touching – the way she crossed the street with them at four
o'clock in the winter afternoons: they came to do their homework
with her. Later she spent half a year in Lausanne.

SCHWARZ. A boarding school?

SCHÖNING. Yes. They were just as impressed with her there.
She should have stayed longer. I took her away because the
headmistress was smitten with her.

SCHWARZ. Why didn't you tell me before?

SCHÖNING. Why? Why? Why didn't I tell you before? (*Sits facing him*). When old Goll died she had more claim on me than you.

SCHWARZ. Goll – she said he made her dance.

SCHÖNING. You married half a million.

SCHWARZ. Where did he get her?

SCHÖNING. Straight from me.

SCHWARZ. He never touched her.

SCHÖNING. He was married to her. How she managed to make you think all that, I don't know.

SCHWARZ. I saw her as my salvation.

SCHÖNING. You know by now.

SCHWARZ. Do I? – Yes.

SCHÖNING. Perhaps she told him I hadn't touched her.

SCHWARZ. My salvation. I told myself that – that – that heaven had made her for me – and me for her.

SCHÖNING. Yes – that's what Dr Goll told himself too.

SCHWARZ. Because I was so miserable.

SCHÖNING. It's to her credit. If she isn't what you imagined, then turn her into it. Take responsibility for your own mistake.

SCHWARZ. Oh God.

SCHÖNING. When she married you, that only added to her credit.

SCHWARZ. Really?

SCHÖNING. You've made your life with her.

SCHWARZ. She told me she was still –

SCHÖNING. You get nowhere if you can't make allowances. – You are funny.

SCHWARZ. – she was still untouched.

SCHÖNING. Untouched – untouched or not – what in the world –

SCHWARZ. Barefoot – without a petticoat.

SCHÖNING. – would you have done with a virgin?

SCHWARZ. She was – or I don't want to –

SCHÖNING (*gets up and goes to the back. Returns*). Let me stand by you. I can't watch you living like this – or her. That's no life. You can't look anyone straight in the face. Teach her to respect you. It's a pity she's what she is. She deserves a husband she can look up to. The chance to become a respectable woman. Afterwards you can quietly hide behind your curtains.

SCHWARZ. Afterwards?

SCHÖNING. With the start Mignon had, who could come up to your standards?

SCHWARZ. What are you talking about?

SCHÖNING. Her early days.

SCHWARZ. I don't understand a word.

SCHÖNING. I mean the squalor I found her in.

SCHWARZ. Who?

SCHÖNING. Your wife.

SCHÖNING. Eve?

SCHÖNING. I call her Mignon.

SCHWARZ. I thought – she was – Nelly.

SCHÖNING. Nelly's what Goll called her.

SCHWARZ. I call her Eve.

SCHÖNING. I don't know what she was really called.

SCHWARZ. Dr Goll called her Nelly.

SCHÖNING. Considering the sort her father is, it was up to you to keep things in order.

SCHWARZ. He had her . . .?

SCHÖNING. He creeps after me even now.

SCHWARZ. He's still alive.

SCHÖNING. Who?

SCHWARZ. Her father?

SCHÖNING. He was just here.

SCHWARZ. Where?

SCHÖNING. Here.

SCHWARZ. Here?

SCHÖNING. Here – in this room.

SCHWARZ. Here.

SCHÖNING. He left as I came. The two glasses are still there.

SCHWARZ. She said – she said – he went down in a typhoon in the Philippines –

SCHÖNING. What's the matter with you?

SCHWARZ (grasping his chest). A terrible pain.

SCHÖNING. Have you – have you any sodium bromide?

SCHWARZ. No.

SCHÖNING. Drink a glass of water.

SCHWARZ. You – you deflowered her!

SCHÖNING. Deflowered? – there wasn't much left to deflower.

SCHWARZ (*reels from the chair and staggers round the room*). It's crushing my chest – choking me – if I could cry – oh – if I could shout –

SCHÖNING (*supporting him*). Be your age. You married half a million. Everyone prostitutes themself! You've got her – the most beautiful woman in the world –

SCHWARZ (*straightening*). Leave me alone!

SCHÖNING (*stepping back*). It's stupid to make a pathetic song and dance out of the situation. Don't lose her! Keep her! She's your life.

SCHWARZ. You're right – you're – right –

SCHÖNING. Don't let the situation go off the rails. It depends on you. If you can be happy, you've lost nothing. She's your property – let her feel it. What d'you want – a spotless reputation without a rag on its back? You're a famous artist.

SCHWARZ. You're – right. (*Sways to the left.*)

SCHÖNING. Where are you going?

SCHWARZ. To – to – let her know her place . . .

SCHWARZ *goes out left.*

SCHÖNING (*alone*). He must set his mind at rest . . . Now for the trio. (*Pause. Looks right, then left and right again.*) I thought – he took her out there.

Terrible groan from the left. SCHÖNING *hurries to the door. Finds it locked from the inside.*

SCHÖNING. Open! Open!

LULU (*coming from right*). What's – (*The groaning goes on*).

SCHÖNING. Open!

LULU (*coming nearer*). It sounds – grisly.

SCHÖNING (*ramming his foot against the door*). Open . . . (*To* LULU.) Fetch an axe – if there's one there.

LULU. Shall I send for a doctor?

SCHÖNING. You're out of your mind! Heaven knows what's . . .

LULU. It serves you right.

A ring in the corridor. LULU *and* SCHÖNING *stare at each other.*

SCHÖNING. Let me – let me go and see to it. (*He goes to the back – stops in the doorway*). I mustn't be found here!

LULU. He groans – as if he had a knife in him.

SCHÖNING. Keep quiet. (*Softly*). No one need be in.

LULU. Perhaps – the picture dealer.

It rings.

SCHÖNING. Damn and blast! – if we don't answer –

LULU *creeps towards the door.*

SCHÖNING (*stopping her*). Wait! Wait! After all, it's not always convenient to go to the door when . . . (*Goes out on tiptoe.*)

LULU *creeps to the locked door and listens.*

SCHÖNING (*leading* ALWA *in*). I beg you – be quiet.

ALWA. There's been a riot in the Reichstag.

SCHÖNING (*hiss*). I told you – be quiet!

ALWA (*to* LULU). You're as white as a corpse.

SCHÖNING (*rattling the door*). Eduard! Eduard!

From inside a hoarse croaking.

LULU. God help us!

SCHÖNING. Haven't you brought the axe?

LULU. I don't know if there is one in the kitchen. (*Goes out uncertainly, left*).

ALWA. He caught you *in flagrante*?

SCHÖNING. An over-excitable fool.

ALWA. A poor soul in torment.

SCHÖNING. There's been a riot in the Reichstag?

ALWA. The editor's office – they're dashing their heads against the wall! No one knows what to write!

A ring in the corridor.

SCHÖNING (*stamping*). Damnation! Damnation! (*Pressing on the door handle*). Eduard . . .

They both listen.

ALWA. Not a sound! Shall I break it down?

SCHÖNING. Anyone can do that. So could I. Now who's here?
(*Straightening up.*) The brute! The fool! The idiot!

ALWA. Hm – he's making fools of us.

SCHÖNING. All day long – jubilation – doesn't bother about
anything – then leaves the others to face the music.

LULU (*an axe in her hand*). Henriette's back.

ALWA (*taking the axe*). Give it to me, give it. (*He pushes it between
the door and the frame.*)

LULU (*her hand at her breast*). This could be – a surprise!

ALWA (*working*). I'll base a tragedy on it.

SCHÖNING. You have to grip it further back! Further! It won't
work like that!

ALWA. It's already giving.

   The door springs open.

(*Lifting both hands to his head, staggering back into the room.*) Oh! Oh!

   Pause.

LULU (*her whole body shaking, pointing to the door, to* SCHÖNING).
Look what you've done!

SCHÖNING. Will you shut up! (*Wipes his brow and goes in*).

ALWA (*in an armchair*). Revolting! Revolting! – Revolting!

LULU (*steadying herself with her left hand on the doorpost, excitedly
putting her right hand to her mouth*). I – I've – never seen –
anything like it.

ALWA. My breakfast's churning up in my stomach. I feel sick. I'll
never get over it.

LULU (*suddenly screaming*). Oh God oh no! Help! (*Hurries right.
Grabs* ALWA *by the shoulder.*) Let's go! He's pushed his head
back on – oh! Let's go –

ALWA (*struggling to get a grip on himself*). Horrible! Ghastly!

LULU. Let's go! I can't stay here! – I can't be alone!

ALWA. I can't – I'm paralysed.

LULU. I beg you!

   LULU *takes* ALWA's *hand and leads him out right.*
   SCHÖNING *comes back from the left, a key-ring in his hand.*

*Blood on his sleeve. He pulls the door to behind and goes
uncertainly to the writing desk, sits and writes two notes.*

ALWA (*coming back from right, flops into an armchair*). She's
changing. Wanted to change.

SCHÖNING (*looking up*). She's gone?

ALWA. To her room. She's in her room. She's changing . . .

SCHÖNING *rings. Goes left.* HENRIETTE *comes in.*

SCHÖNING. D'you know where Dr Bernstein lives?

HENRIETTE. Of course. Next door.

SCHÖNING. Take this note to him. But – hurry.

HENRIETTE. What if the doctor's not at home?

SCHÖNING. Then leave it. And this – this you take to the police
station. Go.

HENRIETTE *leaves.* SCHÖNING *goes to the broken door.*

ALWA (*gets up*). I must see him again.

SCHÖNING (*turning in the doorway*). I don't like the look of you.

ALWA. I –

SCHÖNING. I don't like the look of you. Let yourself go as much
as you like – but not at an unsuitable moment.

ALWA. I'm not used to these jokes. I'm not that hard-boiled.

LULU *comes in right – in mourning: a grey raincoat and black
gloves, with a black lace hat and a black sunshade in her hand.*

LULU. I see it on all the walls.

SCHÖNING. Where did he keep his papers, his valuables?

LULU. I don't know. (*To* ALWA.) Come with me.

ALWA. You look nice.

SCHÖNING *goes to the writing desk and opens drawers.*

LULU. My heart's beating like a drum.

ALWA. It's affected my legs.

LULU. Take me away.

SCHÖNING (*at the writing desk*). Damned country!

LULU. It's all your doing!

SCHÖNING. Shut up – or . . .

LULU. You're the murderer!

SCHÖNING. I'm a fool for being so kind to the lad.

> LULU *starts to sob.*

ALWA (*staring stiffly in front of him*). Before the poor wretch is even properly cold!

LULU (*sobbing*). He'll never warm himself again.

ALWA. That's true. We're all alone. (*Sinks into a chair.*)

SCHÖNING. The only time in my life I've allowed myself to own up! –

LULU. What've you got to be afraid of?

SCHÖNING. – and a schoolboy brings the whole house down on my head!

ALWA. I'm wondering how this story could be staged.

LULU (*to* SCHÖNING). You can cover it up – like a lot of things.

SCHÖNING. How does that help me?

ALWA. Write his obituary tomorrow. You knew him best. Squeeze out a few tears and call him Raphael. Then no one'll believe you're guilty.

SCHÖNING (*pacing up and down*). I already see myself as a headline: 'Don Juan claims victim!'

ALWA. He's worried about his engagement.

LULU. He'll have to invent something.

SCHÖNING (*to* LULU). What will you tell the police?

ALWA. It's certainly not in my interest to see you married again.

SCHÖNING. I have no reason to consider your interest.

ALWA. Winter sowing! I'll have to get used to a whole nursery full of uproar.

SCHÖNING. You managed to endure getting half my fortune twice already.

ALWA. Marry your lover –

LULU. Everything's spinning before my eyes.

ALWA. Fortunately she's on the open market again.

SCHÖNING (*goes to the writing desk*). The lad lived on his own too long . . .

ALWA. If you must marry.

LULU. I can only see blood.

ALWA. She's my guarantee against a population explosion in the family.

LULU. Who said so?

ALWA. You promise me.

SCHÖNING (*half turns away*). A whore.

> LULU *throws herself on him with her raised sunshade.*

ALWA (*throwing himself between them*). Children, children! Behave yourselves . . .

> *Leading* LULU *to the left.*

> He has to let off steam. He's like a
> schoolboy in love . . .

SCHÖNING. You marry her. You couldn't do better. Put on your plays with her money. Use it to pay your women.

ALWA. Thank you father.

SCHÖNING. I've had enough of her!

ALWA. I've not yet reached that tragic necessity.

LULU. I don't want you either – I'd rather die!

ALWA. There's no danger, madam!

SCHÖNING. My hair stands on end.

ALWA. I love to watch the beginning of a break-up.

SCHÖNING. A blow that would strike a hangman's assistant dumb – at least temporarily speechless! – and this inhuman rabble –

LULU. It takes time to get used to.

ALWA. I still can't keep a grip on my objectivity.

SCHÖNING. And I'm not master of myself.

ALWA. And on top of it all there's a riot in the Reichstag.

SCHÖNING. After this? – that's just a detail.

ALWA. The chaos in the editor's office! – you'd think they were building the Tower of Babel.

SCHÖNING. I'll wait for the police. Get back there. I'll come in five minutes.

ALWA. I must see him once more. (*Goes to the broken door and opens it*).

LULU (*to* SCHÖNING). Blood on you.

SCHÖNING. Where?

LULU. Wait – I'll dab it off.

> *She sprinkles Heliotrope on her handkerchief and cleans the blood from* SCHÖNING's *sleeve.*

SCHÖNING. His.

LULU. I've seen it before.

ALWA. He bled easily?

LULU (*smiles*). It's the last we'll see of it.

SCHÖNING (*through his teeth*). Monster.

LULU. Even so, you'll marry me.

ALWA (*in the open doorway*). Blood – blood – blood – it's horrible.

LULU (*coming to the door*). There was always something frightening about him.

SCHÖNING (*coming closer to the door*). For heaven's sake don't touch him.

LULU *and* ALWA (*together*). God save us from that.

ALWA. A mad lad.

LULU. How could he do it!

ALWA. With an open razor.

LULU. It's still in his hand.

SCHÖNING. At least that's one good thing.

ALWA. It must be a horrible feeling.

LULU. To cut your throat with an open razor.

ALWA. Look at the sheets – the floor.

LULU. A piggery!

ALWA. It's dripping everywhere.

LULU. And his hands.

ALWA. He was too highly strung.

SCHÖNING. He goes before us on the path.

LULU. He had no education.

ALWA. He was behind his times.

SCHÖNING. He was living on tick.

HENRIETTE *comes in with* DR BERNSTEIN.

HENRIETTE. Dr Bernstein.

BERNSTEIN (*goes breathlessly to* SCHÖNING). How is it possible Mr Schöning?

SCHÖNING. Depression . . .

Act Three

Berlin.

A magnificent hall in German Renaissance style with a heavy ceiling of carved oak. The lower half of the walls panelled in dark wood. Above this, on both sides, faded Gobelins. The back of the hall is closed off by a gallery hung with drapes, and from the right of this a monumental staircase runs to halfway down the stage. Under the gallery, an entrance door with a pediment supported by twisted pillars. In the middle, opening to the left and right, a closed Portière (door-curtain) in heavy Geneva velvet.

In front of the bottom pillar of the outer bannister, LULU's Pierrot portrait on a decorated easel. Its frame is mock antique – gold with the red undercoat showing through. Right front, a deep ottoman. In the middle of the hall a square oak table with two upholstered high-back chairs. Old padded armchairs, antiques, oriental objets d'art, weapons, animal hides, etc. On the table, in a porcelain vase painted with flamingoes, a bouquet of white hyacinths.

GESCHWITZ sits on the ottoman, her black-gloved hands clutched convulsively in her muff. LULU, at her left in an armchair, wears a low-cut morning dress patterned with big, bright flowers; her hair in a simple knot with a gold clasp; white satin shoes and flesh-toned stockings. SCHÖNING stands down right. RODRIGO is unseen left, behind the Portière.

GESCHWITZ (*to* LULU). You won't believe how much I'm looking forward to seeing you at the Ladies' Arts Ball.

SCHÖNING. I hope to goodness my wife's costume doesn't go beyond the bounds of good taste.

GESCHWITZ. We're quite confident about that. My friend's taste is far too delicate.

SCHÖNING. As men are so firmly excluded we'll never know what your fantasies run to. (*To* GESCHWITZ.) Is there really no chance of smuggling us in?

GESCHWITZ. None Mr Schöning. The slightest suspicion that there was a male animal in the hall would ruin the evening.

SCHÖNING. Ruin? – Ruin?

GESCHWITZ. We must feel completely free. The Ladies' Arts Ball is known for its exclusivity. It would be high treason if one of us were involved in an intrigue. Our ladies have other opportunities – as many as they wish – to dance with men. On this evening they belong to us.

SCHÖNING. I should think if I came as – say – a lamp-post – that would avoid any suggestion of rivalry?

GESCHWITZ. We are adamant.

SCHÖNING. You've nothing to fear from me. (*Taking his cigarette case from his pocket, to himself.*) I deserve a medal for self-composure. (*Aloud.*) Will the ladies smoke?

GESCHWITZ. If I may.

SCHÖNING (*to* LULU). And you Mignon . . .?

LULU. No thanks.

GESCHWITZ (*to* LULU). You don't smoke?

LULU. I don't like to.

SCHÖNING (*giving* GESCHWITZ *a light*). My wife regards smoking from an exclusively artistic point of view.

LULU. But if I may offer you a liqueur.

SCHÖNING. Thank you.

LULU. You Countess?

GESCHWITZ. Please don't go to any trouble for me.

LULU. Please, please – it's just to hand. (*She goes to a little cupboard under the staircase.*)

SCHÖNING (*going to the table*). Hyacinths – how magnificent. (*Sniffs.*) Ah.

LULU. Aren't they! The Countess brought them for me.

SCHÖNING (*to* GESCHWITZ). You'll bankrupt yourself. (*To* LULU.) Surely it's not your birthday?

LULU (*brings a little Japanese table forward, puts the liqueur on it and sets it before the ottoman. Pours*). My birthday? – that's what I asked myself.

GESCHWITZ (*to* LULU). You want to hurt my feelings.

LULU (*touching glasses with* GESCHWITZ). Don't worry . . . (*She gulps down her glass in one go.*)

GESCHWITZ (*after a sip, looks round the room. Her eyes stop at* LULU's *portrait*). You are fascinating. No – ravishing. If only I could see you once like that. Is it by anyone we know?

LULU. Someone called Schwarz.

GESCHWITZ. Schwarz – I seem to recall the name.

LULU. You'd hardly have heard of him.

GESCHWITZ. Isn't he still alive?

LULU. No.

SCHÖNING. He cut his throat.

LULU. You're in a huff.

GESCHWITZ. If he was in love with you – I understand.

LULU. He was a bit weird.

GESCHWITZ. Who isn't? (*Getting up.*) I must go Mrs Schöning. This evening we have a life class – and I still have so much to do for our Ball.

LULU (*accompanying her to the door*). Thank you Countess – for calling on us.

SCHÖNING. Have a really good time – at the Ladies' Arts Ball.

> RODRIGO *left, sticks his head out of the Portière – when he sees the others he disappears with a start.*

SCHÖNING. Is there really no chance – you could let us into the boxes?

GESCHWITZ (*taking leave of him*). Dear Mr Sch-ön-ing.

> LULU *accompanies* GESCHWITZ *out.*

SCHÖNING (*coming forward*). My own son! (*Goes to the table, glares at the flowers and goes right.*) He's here now . . . (*Pulling himself together.*) It's gone beyond suspicion. So be it. (*He goes to the Portière left, for a moment stands before it.*) He'll show up in a minute. (*Coming back.*) I'm not afraid of the scandal. He's not taking my place. They'll say I wanted the publicity. But my respectable name – the honour of my house! Only – proof first. And there's a feeling I've never had before. I must fight for my life. I know enough. Now it depends on the remains of my strength – what's left of it. (*Looking at the liqueur bottle.*) If only the drink helped her. It would be paradise. But quick – or else –. Oh she can swallow unbelievable amounts.

LULU (*coming back*). She kissed my hand.

SCHÖNING. Aren't I going to be allowed to see you in your costume?

LULU. No no.

SCHÖNING. I'd just like to see you before you go.

LULU. You'd be cross.

SCHÖNING. You're not very obliging.

LULU. It's only for the ladies.

SCHÖNING. That's exactly why.

LULU. Please.

SCHÖNING. Very well (*Goes right, to himself.*) It would've been more friendly.

LULU. Where are you going?

SCHÖNING. The paper needs a review of the matinée.

LULU. You spend half your life away from home.

SCHÖNING. Of course.

LULU. You could stay in a little today.

SCHÖNING. I – I write for your splendour, my child. When someone wears as little as you – the upkeep of your naked shoulders costs me more than five racing stallions cost a duke.

LULU. Then why d'you do it?

SCHÖNING. Because I admire you. You're quite right – one tells an artist by what he leaves out.

LULU. It's better to die than make your life miserable.

SCHÖNING. That sounds fine.

LULU. Dying's easy. I always used to be terrified of it.

SCHÖNING. Those who live easy . . .

LULU. Yes – and I will! The last thing I'll worry about are my naked shoulders.

SCHÖNING. Those who live hard . . . Oh well! . . . That's why I married you.

LULU. You didn't marry me.

SCHÖNING. Then what did I do?

LULU. I married you.

SCHÖNING (*Kissing her brow*). A risky undertaking.

LULU. You're going?

SCHÖNING. I must laugh

LULU. Why don't you then?

SCHÖNING. Later, later. (*He goes out right.*)

RODRIGO (*sticks his head out of the Portière*). May I – madam . . .?

LULU (*finger on her lips*). Wait – one moment.

RODRIGO. It's not exactly entertaining. It's almost an hour – according to my watch. At least give me a drink.

LULU. For God's sake.

> RODRIGO *comes out. He wears a bright chequered suit, tight-fitting and tightly buttoned up; the sleeves are a bit too short; bell-bottom trousers. A fiery red tie, golden ear-rings.*

LULU (*giving him a little glass*). Are you bored?

RODRIGO (*upending the glass*). I'm used to hardship. Thank you. If Madam hasn't got the time –

LULU. Yes, yes. In a minute.

RODRIGO (*looking round*). This place is a – a real show-stopper. Only it doesn't exactly make you feel at home. If Madam's busy –

LULU. If you just wait a moment.

RODRIGO. Then may I at least ask for the fifty marks?

LULU. What muscles you've got.

RODRIGO. The fifty marks actually – for my poor bed-ridden wife.

LULU. Ah yes – you're married.

RODRIGO. I can't stand before her bed of pain with empty hands.

LULU. Wait. Please do. I have to wait too.

RODRIGO. Madam isn't well?

LULU. Oh yes. I'm very lively. I have so much to think of.

RODRIGO (*shyly putting his arm round her waist*). Just think of my poor bed-ridden wife.

LULU (*pushing him off*). One more minute. I promise you.

RODRIGO. Hm – as you like. At least give me another drink.

LULU (*pouring his drink*). He could still come back. It would be fatal – after we've waited so long.

RODRIGO. In that case I'd like to offer the suggestion that in future Madam gives me an appointment in a hotel. In a hotel you don't get all this keep-your-eyes-peeled malarkins. Here there's all the trimmings – and the drinks are well up to standard: but a guarantee of survival is the essential basis of any fulfilling relationship.

LULU. It makes me anxious.

RODRIGO. Just give me fifty marks and write.

LULU. One more second . . . It's nicer here. It's so cool.

RODRIGO. Then give me another drink.

LULU (*suddenly starting up*). God help me!

RODRIGO. God stone me – another one?

LULU (*dragging him left*). Behind the curtain – I knew it!

RODRIGO. Give me the fifty marks – and open the door!

LULU (*pushing him behind the Portière*). Quick! Quick!

RODRIGO (*stopping her*). At least give me twenty –

LULU. Quick for God's sake!

RODRIGO. Then just give me my marching orders.

LULU. D'you want to be shot dead?

> RODRIGO *vanishes behind the Portière.*

You're out of your mind . . .!

> SCHÖNING *comes in from the right.*

SCHÖNING (*very white*). I forgot.

LULU (*motionless behind the table*). Your opera glasses?

SCHÖNING (*to himself, with a glance at* LULU). He's here now . . .

> *Opens an encrusted casket, takes out two étuis, puts the larger in his breast pocket and comes forward with the smaller.*

What did the Countess really want?

LULU. I don't know. She wants to paint me.

SCHÖNING (*to himself*). I'm shaking like a leaf.

LULU. I think she's weird.

SCHÖNING (*down left, has opened the smaller étui and turns away to give himself an injection in the arm*). I think she's – weird too.

LULU. You shouldn't do that.

SCHÖNING. She comes like misfortune personified – paying a social call.

LULU. You promised me you wouldn't do it again.

SCHÖNING. That's why I locked it away . . .

LULU. You're nothing to me any more.

SCHÖNING. I've tried to.

LULU. It'll kill you.

SCHÖNING (*to himself*). Thanks to you.

LULU. It's better to drink.

SCHÖNING (*closes the étui and buttons his cuff, recovering his breath*). I'll probably dine at Peter's. (*Puts on his hat.*)

> LULU *falls on his neck and kisses him.*

SCHÖNING (*gently freeing himself*). Ah well you're a well-behaved girl. Doesn't everyone know that? (*Squeezes her hand.*) Till this evening.

> LULU *accompanies him out, stands in the open doorway listening.* RODRIGO *sticks his head out from the Portière.* LULU *waves him back. Suddenly* ALWA *steps into the open doorway – in superb evening dress, his top hat in his hand. He encloses* LULU *in his arms.*

ALWA. At last – at last!

> RODRIGO *ducks back behind the Portière.*

LULU (*her whole body shaking*). Oh God . . .

ALWA (*leading her forward*). I was hiding behind the door. The old buffer can never get to the end.

LULU. If I was a hundred miles away.

ALWA. While I'm here –?

LULU. Oh – if you knew – I don't know any more – I'm unspeakably unhappy – if you knew –

ALWA. You asked me to come! You promised me everything. You set every fibre of me on fire!

LULU. For God's sake – stay! – you're the only one – I can talk to – you're so sweet to me – . When he went out he growled as if he had a stone between his teeth.

ALWA. Haemorrhoids! Haemorrhoids! Please don't tell me about it. His self-regard – it's almost monstrous. I can't be jealous – I

assure you, I simply can't – however much I try. He's nothing to
me! I know who you belong to. I feel you when I'm out riding –
when I sit in a café – when I lie on the couch – I feel you! You –
your body!

LULU. It's yours. Or will be yours. But calm me – make me numb
– make me numb, I beg you – or I can't go on . . . (*With a glance
left.*) Didn't you hear it . . .?

ALWA. Dead quiet.

LULU. Sh. – I think – we're being overheard . . .

ALWA. You're not well.

LULU. Yes, yes – I'm really lively. I've been a virgin for a fortnight
– I don't know what it is . . .

ALWA. Then why did you ask me to come here? You said we'd have
a little orgy. I went to extra trouble with my clothes.

LULU (*lost in gazing at him*). You're beautiful.

ALWA. White tie!

LULU. To love you – and die!

ALWA. Ah!

LULU. I've had everything prepared. I ordered a little supper. If –
if only there wasn't so much agitation –

ALWA. Don't push me over the edge my darling. You don't seem
to realise it's me! Me! You can't imagine the state my nerves are
in! The cab jolted really badly – I'm panting! Since you raised the
prospect of this little orgy – night after night it's as if I already
had you. And now I'm here and you're here – I see your knees
under those flowers – your movements – your burning eyes – I
must let my ravings out or you'll turn me into a sex killer!

LULU. I've got something important to ask you.

ALWA. Oh God oh God what else is important! You're dicing with
death. Gloating over the last twitches of a starving man!

LULU. It's lovely to hear you talk like that.

ALWA. I know – but where does it get me? (*Takes her to the
ottoman.*) Perhaps I was a bit quick off the mark. I came in a
horsecab.

LULU. I'd love to fall into the hands of a sex killer.

ALWA. Just tell me what you wanted to chatter about.

LULU. The Ladies' Arts Ball – if only it was the Men's Arts Ball!
They invited me three times. The Geschwitz woman was just

here. She wants to paint me. In the end – you're not listening! –
in the end, I said to myself, it's best to go in something as simple
as possible.

> SCHÖNING *appears on the gallery between the pillars, right, at
> the top of the stairs, pulling the curtain a little apart.*

ALWA. As simple as possible.

LULU. I tried something out this morning when I came out of the
bath. My hair in a simple knot with a clasp –

ALWA. As it is now.

LULU. Yes – exactly like this!

ALWA. It suits you wonderfully.

LULU. I left it as it was. This morning I would have got between
my legs if I could. I understood Geschwitz when I saw myself in
the mirror. If I could be a man – just for me – just once! If I had
myself on the cushions like this –

ALWA. Oh!

LULU. Otherwise I wouldn't like it. Not at all. No, it's much nicer
– when you're being kissed all over, all over!

ALWA (*nestling his head on her lap*). You're fantasizing – it's driving
the blood to my head! Katja! And your warm firm body under
this soft silk – I can't feel a slip – no thick underclothes – only
you – everywhere I feel. Now you're a woman. You were always
too thin like a girl. Now you're perfect. And you've still got the
feel of a girl. You dressed yourself up so tantalizingly for me
Katja! I need that! You know your people. I'm spoiled! This
slippery silk – that lies on every swelling –

LULU (*digging her fingers into his hair*). This is just my house dress.

ALWA. God no – I want to make love to you in it – this silk under
my fingers.

LULU. I put it on to please my lord and master.

ALWA. The dirty swine!

LULU. That's why it's cut so low.

ALWA. It's not too low.

LULU. They all want to see a little bit of heaven.

ALWA. It's not cut too low Katja!

LULU. For their astronomical studies.

ALWA. I swear to you it's not cut too low –. It – is – not – (*He begins to unbutton her from the top.)*

LULU *stretches her arms behind her head and smiles into space.*

ALWA (*under the morning dress – he discovers an elf costume*). What's this! I'm mad! What's this! I'm having hallucinations!

LULU (*jumps up. Her dress stays on the ottoman*). This is for you!

She wears light silk tights, a pale red silk blouse – split to the waist back and front, armless, finishing high over the hips in front and at the back drawn down in a narrow band and fastened between her legs. White satin shoes. Dark roses at the breast. SCHÖNING – on the gallery – lets the curtain fall and vanishes. ALWA has slid to the ground – he presses his lips to LULU's feet.

ALWA. I'm afraid – it'll vanish – before my open eyes! I'm afraid – it'll slip from my hands! It's too much! How can you go so deep inside me Katja – in my spine! I'm having a nervous breakdown! Oh Katja – Katja!

LULU (*trying to free herself*). Ow. Ow – you're biting.

ALWA. No – I won't leave these feet! These little ankles! – This – this gentle crescendo – every inch a – a –! These knees – oh merciful God – this girlish voluptuous capriccio – between the andante of lust – and the – and the unspeakably tender cantabile of these calfs! – These calfs! – I hear it – like children's voices! On all my finger tips – Katja – I feel your caress! I don't think – I don't think – I can rise . . .

LULU (*touching his shoulders*). It's not necessary – yet. (*She goes back and rings.*) Come here.

ALWA (*dragging himself to the table*). My head's empty – as if I'd downed sixty bottles of champagne –

LULU. You're my ray of light – you make me happy again.

ALWA sits at the table left and LULU right. Behind ALWA's back, RODRIGO sticks his head out from the Portière. LULU throws him a withering look. He draws back again. FERDINAND enters through the middle with a serving tray. He lays the table, sets two places and serves partridge pâté and a bottle of Pommery on ice.

LULU (*rubbing her hands*). I've arranged everything as you like.

ALWA (*taking the bottle*). I don't think I can find the proper appetite.

> FERDINAND *snaps the napkin under his arm, throws a look over the table and goes out through the middle door.*

ALWA. But I'm dying of thirst

LULU. He's discreet.

ALWA (*filling the glasses*). I feel like an angel in heaven rubbing the sleep out of its eyes.

LULU (*rubbing her hands between her legs*). I feel like a bird using its wings for the first time.

ALWA (*clinking glasses with her*). Your eyes are flickering . . . black water in the bottom of a well when a stone's thrown in.

LULU (*glass at her lips*). You're letting your moustache turn up?

> ALWA *nods, fills the two glasses. They both eat and become lost in their own silence.*

LULU (*giving ALWA a truffle from her plate*). I couldn't love a man who didn't dress well.

ALWA. Not when he comes in a healthy string vest?

LULU. I'd rather be strangled by him than make love.

ALWA. Doesn't he still wear them?

LULU. How can you ask me that?

ALWA. Well you should know!

LULU. How?

ALWA. My sweet little whore.

LULU. You're all I want to be happy.

ALWA. Oh Katja!

> ALWA *rings. Pause.* FERDINAND *comes in with a dish of asparagus. He changes the plates.*

ALWA. Are you sweating?

FERDINAND. Not at all Sir.

LULU. Leave him alone.

FERDINAND. I'm only human.

ALWA. Bring us another bottle.

FERDINAND. Certainly Sir.

FERDINAND *goes out with the pâté.* SCHÖNING *appears in the gallery between the two pillars, carefully parting the curtains. He takes up a place behind the bannister and cleans his opera glasses.*

ALWA. I'm beginning to get over my fuddle. Your plate –

LULU *reaches him her plate and fills the glasses.*

ALWA (*serving her*). You'll drown my strength.
LULU. I have your word for it.
ALWA. Now I see you clearly for the first time. Now I see the details. Your little fingers – how they handle the asparagus. I've never seen such thick asparagus.
LULU. I'm almost afraid to take them in my hand.
ALWA. And your little cupid-head – between your naked shoulders.
LULU. I want to feel like this for the rest of my life. My legs feel so free, my head's clear . . .
ALWA. And your tongue – how you enjoy licking with it.
LULU (*taking the asparagus from her mouth*). And how it dangles . . .
ALWA (*sinking back*). You're driving me mad.
LULU. Eat – to please me.
ALWA (*rising*). Kiss me.
LULU (*pushing him back*). Aren't you ashamed?
ALWA. Kiss me! – Kiss me!
LULU. He can't even take supper with a lady.
ALWA. This is the condemned man's last meal not supper.
LULU (*giving him her hand across the table*). You still need bringing on.

ALWA *covers her hand with kisses, pulls her middle and ring finger apart and kisses between.*

LULU. There's still some butter in there.

ALWA *sinks to his knees, lays her bare arms above her head and kisses her armpit.*

LULU. Oh you're exciting me.
ALWA. Caviar! – Caviar!
LULU (*pushing him back to his place*). Behave yourself (*Hands him her*

full glass.) Pour that down. (*Wiping her finger on a napkin.*) There's more to come . . . (*She rings*).

ALWA. What are three dozen oysters to this?

> FERDINAND *enters, changes the plates, serves roast quail on mushrooms with salad, and two new bottles of Pommery, one of them uncorked.*

LULU. See the coffee's nice and hot.
FERDINAND. Madam can rely on me.
LULU. Shall we take it in the conservatory?
ALWA. No.
LULU (*to FERDINAND*). In the bedroom.
FERDINAND. With rum, arrack, whisky, curaçao?
LULU (*to ALWA*). Rum or whisky?
ALWA. Both please.
FERDINAND. Madam may rely on me completely.
ALWA. You're trembling.
LULU. Let him alone.
FERDINAND. I'm still not used to serving.
ALWA. The world's full of surprises.
LULU. I said let him alone.
FERDINAND. Usually I'm the stable boy. (*Goes out with the asparagus.*)
SCHÖNING (*on the gallery, to himself*). He's another one!
ALWA (*dismembering a quail*). You're stoking my greed for your body with these superb titbits. These aromas – I should be marching at the head of a column of demolition workers! And this meat – this Byzantine flesh – so expert – but yours . . .
LULU (*putting her arms behind her head*). But mine . . .?

> RODRIGO *sticks his head out of the Portière. When he sees SCHÖNING sitting in the gallery he pulls back in alarm.*

SCHÖNING (*to himself*). And there's another one!
LULU (*helping ALWA to salad*). If only you could come to the ball with me. The women chase me like bloodhounds.
ALWA. What's that?
LULU. Celery.

ALWA (*collapsing helplessly*). You can't work me up any higher! If
you've got one spark of feeling in your body. God help me you're
damaging my health. I'll be a wreck for the rest of my life. (*He
slips from the chair and embraces her knees.*) Let me die here! Let
me die here! I can't go on staring into your terrible eyes! I'm
hardly human anymore. I warn you Katja! – I warn you.

LULU (*makes his head slide between her knees*). Your face is burning –

ALWA (*murmuring*). Let me enjoy the torments – to the limits of
human power! Save me now! – before I go too far. Your body,
its breath – so pure – my lust's tearing itself – shaking me – no
woman – a cool – ring of silk . . . let me get up . . .

LULU (*holding him down by the hair*). No.

ALWA. Now.

LULU. Finished?

ALWA. Oh God!

LULU. Get up.

ALWA. I can't get up.

LULU. Let's finish the food off.

ALWA. I can't eat.

LULU. Let's go to –

ALWA. Shut your face.

LULU. – my room.

ALWA. You sewer! You meat grinder! You latrine! You cess pit!
You snotrag! You liquid shit! You steam hammer! You puss hole!
You dirty drain!

LULU (*backs away trembling. Sees* SCHÖNING *sitting in the gallery*).
His father! He'll box his ears.

> SCHÖNING *has got up rapidly and closed the curtains.* ALWA
> *remains lying motionless, his hands folded over his head.* LULU
> *takes a rose from her breast and puts it in her hair. She goes
> up the stairs – half-way up stops, leans backwards against the
> bannister, her feet crossed, her bare arms stretched along the
> velvet-covered rail.*

LULU (*to herself*). This is the most beautiful moment of my life.

> SCHÖNING *enters through the middle with a revolver in his
> hand, sees* ALWA *lying on the carpet, lands a kick on his behind.*

SCHÖNING. Get out.

ALWA (*looking up*). You!

SCHÖNING. Get out!

ALWA. That's rich!

SCHÖNING. Shall I shoot you!

ALWA (*grins at him*). The Idealists! The Moral Guardians! Impotent old men! Decrepit editors!

SCHÖNING. D'you know I could shoot you down like a dog!

LULU (*on the stair, to herself*). He won't do it.

ALWA (*has got up*). Yes that's the way to get revenge!

SCHÖNING. Get out!

ALWA. I congratulate you!

SCHÖNING. Have I accused you?

ALWA. Your books would be more readable then! No – first try writing something with blood in its veins!

SCHÖNING. Show me one reason why you should be here!

ALWA. Sentimental hack!

SCHÖNING. All I'm doing is chucking you out!

ALWA (*retreating*). Your old German melodramas –

SCHÖNING. Your feeble plagiarisms! (*Seizes him by the collar.*) Let's be original!

> SCHÖNING leads ALWA out. The door closes behind them.
> RODRIGO bursts from the Portière, hurries over the room and
> stumbles up the stairs. LULU bars his way.

LULU. Where are you going?

RODRIGO. Out.

LULU. Where?

RODRIGO. Let me out!

LULU. You can't leave me alone now!

RODRIGO. I'll toss you over the bannister.

LULU. You can't get out this way. You'll run into his arms.

RODRIGO (*falls to his knees*). I implore you Madam, get me out of here! You invite me to a bottle of champagne, stick me behind moth-eaten curtains, while that maniac fiddles with a pistol and you stuff your belly with partridge! I'm not even allowed to see which way he's pointing!

LULU. He's coming!

RODRIGO (*staggering down into the room*). Oh God I'll kiss Jesus' arse! (*Looks round.*) How do I get out of this madhouse? He'll put a bullet through my head! What harm have I done!

> SCHÖNING *is heard coming.*

LULU. He'll kill you.

> RODRIGO *vanishes under the tablecloth.* SCHÖNING *comes back with the cocked gun, goes to the Portière, throws open the curtains.*

SCHÖNING (*to* LULU, *who still stands on the stairs*). Where's he gone?
LULU. Away.
SCHÖNING. How?
LULU. Through the window.
SCHÖNING. Over the balcony?
LULU. He's an acrobat.
SCHÖNING. I didn't know that.

> SCHÖNING *goes to the back and bolts the door.* RODRIGO *reaches for the plate of quails and vanishes with it under the table again.*

SCHÖNING. You look beautiful.
LULU (*coming down the stairs*). Don't I.
SCHÖNING. From another world – beyond the sunset.
LULU. I put it together myself.
SCHÖNING. A tightrope artist.
LULU. I had in mind an elf.
SCHÖNING. If it weren't for your big round child eyes, people would be scandalised at the way you flaunt your hips.
LULU. I think this is more dignified – than if I'd pulled a pair of plush knickers over them.
SCHÖNING. Beauty triumphs over shamelessness. Your flesh mortifies your body.
LULU. My flesh is Lulu.
SCHÖNING. Perhaps it's because of your corset.
LULU. I'm not wearing one.
SCHÖNING. I beg your pardon.

LULU. I feel so free like this. D'you like my hair?

SCHÖNING. You intend to go to the Arts Ball like that?

LULU. Don't you like it?

SCHÖNING. And you're not ashamed?

LULU. They'll pull me apart to get a bit.

SCHÖNING. Then you have no shame at all.

LULU. No.

SCHÖNING. I'm an old fool.

LULU. You are . . . (SCHÖNING *takes her to the ottoman.*) What d'you want?

SCHÖNING. I want to curl up against you one last time.

LULU. But put the revolver down.

SCHÖNING. It's not in the way.

LULU (*on his knee*). Give it to me.

SCHÖNING. That's what I brought it here for. (*Puts the revolver in her hand.*)

> LULU *stretches her arm high and fires a shot into the ceiling.*

SCHÖNING. Don't play the fool.

LULU. Didn't it bang!

SCHÖNING. The bullets are live.

LULU (*looking at it*). It's pretty.

SCHÖNING. Not pretty enough for a charming devil like you.

LULU. What am I supposed to do with it?

SCHÖNING. Kill yourself.

> LULU *stands and pulls her blouse straight over her tights.*

LULU. If only you'd brought your horsewhip with you.

SCHÖNING. That's just play.

LULU. It might put other ideas in your head.

SCHÖNING (*holding her waist*). Kiss me.

LULU (*sinks down on his knees, throws her arms round his neck and kisses him*). But put the revolver away.

SCHÖNING. Kiss me – kiss me.

> LULU *kisses him.*

SCHÖNING. You get more desirable all the time.

LULU (*kisses him*). Put it away.

SCHÖNING. You need it.

LULU (*kisses him*). Please.

SCHÖNING. It's been like this since I've known you.

LULU. Then why don't you do it?

SCHÖNING. Because I'd go to prison.

LULU. You love me too much to do it.

SCHÖNING. Quiet, sweetheart.

LULU. It's going black before my eyes.

SCHÖNING (*stroking her*). Do as you're told.

> LULU *yawns*.

SCHÖNING. Put it to your breast.

LULU. It's still warm.

SCHÖNING. Fire!

> LULU *tries it a few times*.

SCHÖNING. Use the trigger finger (*He tries to guide her hand.*)

LULU (*lets the weapon sink*). Ah.

SCHÖNING. I'm bungling this.

> LULU *lays her head back and rubs her knees together*.

SCHÖNING. Little goose – it would be over by now.

LULU (*breathing out*). Then I'd be in the soup.

SCHÖNING (*he has taken back the revolver without her noticing*). Your legs, your legs.

LULU. They've gone to sleep

SCHÖNING. They cuddle up so nicely together because each one of them's sure it's the most beautiful.

LULU. Oh God (*Stretching her feet.*) Tie them together.

SCHÖNING. Then as soon as their wicked mistress is touched –

LULU. – they spring wide open –

SCHÖNING. – like jealous lovers.

LULU. – Why don't you – one last time.

SCHÖNING. What?

LULU. What else? Tie me up and whip me.

SCHÖNING. Pointless.

LULU. Till the blood flows. I won't scream. I'll bite my hanky.

SCHÖNING. The stuffing's gone out of me.

LULU (*lets her hand glide over his grey hair*). Then why don't you forgive me.

SCHÖNING. It's the morphine. It destroys me. I forgave you long ago. I was always like a father to you. Now I'm really one.

LULU. I'll get dressed. We'll go to the opera.

SCHÖNING. They're playing Pagliacci. You're breaking your little head trying to find some way out.

LULU (*pressing against his chest*). Let me go – let me go.

SCHÖNING. If you were stronger.

LULU. Let me – I must go to the toilet!

SCHÖNING. It's not worth it now.

LULU *stares at the ground.*

SCHÖNING. You know very well where you must go.

LULU. I can't – can't think of it.

SCHÖNING. Just think you're already lying . . . (*While he kisses her with deep emotion.*) . . . in the arms of . . .

LULU (*restraining his arm*). Not yet! Not yet! I'm still so young.

SCHÖNING. Give me your hand. This fuss. It doesn't hurt.

LULU (*holding the revolver*). It'll kill me!

SCHÖNING. Quiet! Quiet!

LULU. Why should I leave the world so soon?

SCHÖNING. Don't be a fool.

LULU. Oh God.

SCHÖNING. Ugh – pitiful!

LULU (*breaks out in sobs*). The animals can still – afterwards I'll be nothing –

SCHÖNING. It's like getting drunk.

LULU (*crying*). Why should I leave the world so soon?

SCHÖNING. Quiet, quiet . . .

LULU (*breaking into sobs*). I'm so happy – so happy – why must I – I'm alive – why must I – the animals – they can live – the animals – can – can – I – I've done what they all do – I'm a woman – I'm a woman – I'm twenty years old.

SCHÖNING. Don't be silly.

LULU. Oh God.

SCHÖNING. You don't feel it.

LULU (*putting the revolver to her breast*). God help me.

SCHÖNING (*giving her a jerk with his knee*). You're boring.

LULU. It's going black before my eyes

SCHÖNING (*guiding her hand with the revolver under her left breast*).
There – there – why waste time thinking about it?

LULU (*wide-eyed*). Soon.

SCHÖNING. I've never seen you like this.

LULU. Don't – don't –

SCHÖNING. Ugh.

LULU. Soon.

SCHÖNING. Now.

LULU. Afterwards I'll be nothing – a dead woman.

SCHÖNING. Dammit!

> *He pulls her from his knees and throws her on the ottoman. Goes
> left – agitated.*

LULU (*lying in front of the ottoman, pressing the revolver against
her breast, crying and sobbing*). I can't – not yet – I can't – oh –
my life –

> SCHÖNING *comes back.*

LULU (*half sitting up, the revolver still at her breast, her face distorted*).
Be patient – I beg you – be patient – one minute – of life – soon
– (*Crawling to him on her knees.*) I beg you – I beg you –

SCHÖNING (*stamping nervously*). Now!

LULU (*beats her brow on the floor*). I can't – I can't – I can't –
(*Doubling up.*) – can't think – night – night – night – God –
(*Threshing about.*) – Oh – Oh . . . Oh!

SCHÖNING (*suddenly white, unsure*). Haven't you any – any –

LULU. Everywhere's night – when it breaks – when it breaks – I'll
shoot myself – in the heart!

SCHÖNING (*in the left proscenium, stammering*). Sh – shall – 'll I . . .

LULU. No – no – no –

> SCHÖNING *takes the étui from his pocket and injects himself
> with morphine.*

LULU. I will . . . (*Lifts her head.*)

> ALWA *comes out of the curtain and down the gallery steps, silently*

wringing his hands. RODRIGO *dashes from the table, seizing*
SCHÖNING's *arm.*

RODRIGO. Look out!

Two shots.

SCHÖNING (*tumbling forwards*). I . . .
RODRIGO (*catching him*). I warned you.
SCHÖNING (*spewing blood*). I've copped my number.

LULU *has jumped up, rushes up the stairs and clings to* ALWA.

RODRIGO (*leading* SCHÖNING *to the ottoman*). How could you
  – walk right into it – (*Showing his right hand, from which blood
  streams down.*) I copped mine too – . (*He lays* SCHÖNING *on the
  ottoman.*) Wait – I'll just – nip out to the doctor's –
SCHÖNING. You stay – here . . . (*Pause.*)
LULU (*coming closer on tiptoe*). Did I hurt you?
SCHÖNING (*catches sight of* LULU). My – murderess – it – it burns
  – get – to safety – to safety – the keys – the keys – from my
  pocket.
LULU. It doesn't hurt.
SCHÖNING. In the safe – sixty thousand – don't – lose time –
  water – give me – a glass – water – please –
LULU. I can't go out like this.
SCHÖNING. Elf . . . my elf . . .
RODRIGO. Would the gentleman take champagne?
SCHÖNING. If you happen – to have – any.

  RODRIGO *has quickly filled a goblet from the open bottle and
  takes it to the ottoman.*

SCHÖNING. Thirst – the thirst –
LULU (*taking the goblet from* RODRIGO). Let me. (*Kneels and puts
  it to* SCHÖNING's *lips.*)
SCHÖNING. My – little murderess – (*Drinks.*) you always – stay –
  the same.
LULU. It's like getting drunk.
SCHÖNING (*after he has emptied the goblet*). Oh – Oh – it burns –
  I'm shrivelling up – my tongue – my tongue –

RODRIGO (*uncorking the other bottle*). Drink. That's just the first
glass. Keep drinking – as much as you can –

   ALWA *has come close to the ottoman.*

SCHÖNING. You too – my son.
ALWA. Et tu Brute.
SCHÖNING. I see – you – you plotted – the next – next – you're –
the next – you –
RODRIGO (*has filled the goblet and gives it to* SCHÖNING *to drink*).
Down at the old Bull and Bush – Bush-Bush!
SCHÖNING. Swimming – in it – blood.
RODRIGO. It's only mine.
SCHÖNING. I'm – dreaming –
RODRIGO. It's not poisoned . . . (*To* LULU.) If Madam would be
so kind . . .
LULU (*takes the bottle and goblet from him*). God knows I didn't
see you.
RODRIGO (*binding his hand with his handkerchief*). It's not worth
talking about.
SCHÖNING. You are – an acrobat –
RODRIGO. Wrestling – free-style – mostly. (*To* LULU.) Keep
topping him up.
LULU (*giving him champagne to drink*). You can't be cross with
me . . .
SCHÖNING. My elf-murderess.
RODRIGO (*to himself*). A little scratch.
LULU. It was me who got the . . .
SCHÖNING. Better – it's getting – better.
ALWA. Shall I send for a doctor?
SCHÖNING. Take – take – the keys – from my – pocket – I can't –
can't move – you know – the papers – my mother – she hid – hid
– hid – the – how could she know – a beautiful summer – month
– summer – sum – oh . . .
LULU (*kissing him*). Look at us! Look at us! You can't see us!
SCHÖNING. Are you still – still – afraid – heart-burn – morphine –
morphine – mor –
RODRIGO. Give him more champagne.
LULU (*pouring*). It was almost me who got the –

SCHÖNING. Go – get – to safety – you're – you're lost – doctor
   – no doctor – I give you money – money – with – bridges – you
   build a – bridge – over – over – over – over – the isthmus –
   already I – (*Groaning.*) Oh . . .
LULU. It goes right through you.
SCHÖNING. Yes, yes – kiss me – once – more.

> LULU *bends over him and kisses him, putting her right hand over
> his heart.*

RODRIGO (*to* ALWA). As white as chalk already. Clown's make-
   up. That colour makes you think. I wouldn't like to look like that
   – oh dear no. Still at least he's drawn the lucky number – being
   kissed like that. Not long before he's down the hole. All the same,
   she's giving him the farewell treatment. That's what I call the last
   rites. People like us don't even get a fag stuck in their snout.
ALWA. Where d'you come from actually?
RODRIGO. The billiard hall. (*Pause.*)
LULU (*straightening up*). He's dead.
ALWA. My father –
RODRIGO. If Madam and the gentleman will allow, I'll pay my
   respects and run – or I'll end up Muggins.
ALWA. We must put the revolver in his hand – while there's time.
RODRIGO. Not very convincing Sir – I don't know what your
   speciality act is, but he couldn't've made a good job of shooting
   himself in the back.
LULU. I'm going to Paris. (*To* ALWA.) Get the keys – quick!
ALWA (*emptying* SCHÖNING's *pockets*). Why Paris?
SCHÖNING (*toneless*). A bridge –
ALWA (*stepping back*). Ah – ah –
LULU. Quiet.
RODRIGO. That sounds like a voice from the crypt. He's well on
   the way.
ALWA (*keys in his hand*). Take me with you.
LULU. I must change.
ALWA. I won't give you the money if you don't.
LULU. I can't stop you going to Paris.
ALWA. You can't leave me behind in poverty!
LULU. Give me my dress.

ALWA. You're my evil destiny.

LULU. Give me my dress.

ALWA. Yes.

LULU. He's lying on it.

ALWA *(pulling the morning dress from under SCHÖNING and throwing it over LULU)*. I can't live without you.

RODRIGO. Madam's dirtying her tights.

ALWA. It's full of blood.

LULU. It doesn't matter any more. I'll soon be taking them off.

ALWA. I'll empty the safe. Then we'll lock up.

LULU *(in the doorway, right)*. The train leaves at eight.

RODRIGO. I hear something.

SCHIGOLCH *(lifting the curtain in the middle of the gallery)*. It smells of gunpowder.

ALWA *(giving at the knees)*. Who's that?

LULU. My father.

Act Four

Paris.

A spacious salon in white stucco. In the back wall, wide double swing doors. On either side of them a large mirror. On both side walls, two doors. Between them – to the right – a rococo console with a white marble top on which stands a large mirror – and to the left – a white marble fireplace and over it in a narrow gold frame set into the wall LULU's Pierrot portrait. In the middle of the salon an elegant, brightly upholstered Louis XV sofa. Broad, brightly upholstered armchairs with thin legs and slender armrests. Down left a small table.

GESCHWITZ sits alone downstage. She wears a pale-blue Hussar jacket edged with white fur, with silver-braid facings, white bow-tie, close fitting stand-up collar and stiff cuffs with enormous ivory cuff-links.

Off, in the gaming room beyond the open double doors, the sounds of a social gathering. ALWA is heard speaking. RODRIGO comes through the doors. Like all the men in the scene he wears evening dress. He surreptitiously goes to the console and scribbles a note. He is so intent that at first he does not see GESCHWITZ. She ignores him.

ALWA (*off*). Mesdames et Messieurs – excusez. Mesdames et Messieurs – vous me permettez – soyez tranquilles – c'est L'anniversaire – the birthday of our – de notre bien aimable hôtesse – comtesse, qui nous a reunis ici ce soir. Permettez Mesdames et Messieurs – c'est à la santé de la comtesse Adelaide d'Oubra que je bois, à la santé de la comtesse – donc c'est L'anniversaire . . .

Applause. Calls of congratulations. RODRIGO has finished writing the note. He folds it, puts it in an envelope and props it on the console. He sees GESCHWITZ.

RODRIGO. A la bonne heure! – Hm – . Your grace –

> GESCHWITZ *gives a little start.*

RODRIGO. Do I look as dangerous as that?

> GESCHWITZ *stares vacantly at the floor.*

RODRIGO. Your Grace is searching for a subject of mutual interest . . .

> GESCHWITZ *throws a despairing look at the middle doors.*

RODRIGO (*to himself*). You must go at it a bit more lively, lad. Try a joke. (*To* GESCHWITZ.) May I be so bold as to –

> GESCHWITZ *gives a little shriek.*

> CASTI-PIANI *leads* LULU *from the gaming room. She wears a white directoire gown with enormous puff sleeves and white lace falling from the high waist to the feet. Her arms are in white kid gloves. Her hair is piled high with a small plume of feathers.*

CASTI-PIANI. May I have a few words?
LULU. Please do.

> RODRIGO *leaves through the double doors.*

CASTI-PIANI. Sit down. (*To* GESCHWITZ.) Leave us alone.

> GESCHWITZ *does not move.*

LULU (*sitting on the sofa*). Have I upset you?
CASTI-PIANI (*to* GESCHWITZ). Are you deaf?

> GESCHWITZ *throws him a furious look and goes into the gaming room.*

LULU. Have I offended you?
CASTI-PIANI (*sitting opposite her*). How are your nerves today?
LULU. Ask me for anything you want.
CASTI-PIANI. What have you got left?
LULU. You're disgraceful.
CASTI-PIANI. I've even got your heart.

LULU. It's true – it's stronger than me. I'd be grateful if you didn't abuse it.

CASTI-PIANI. I envy you.

LULU. Now what more d'you want?

CASTI-PIANI. You should count yourself lucky.

LULU. That I came across you? What shall I say? You're right.

CASTI-PIANI. Oh I don't count.

LULU. I'd never have dreamt this!

CASTI-PIANI. Emotions – they're something people like us should never allow ourselves.

LULU. You should thank God!

CASTI-PIANI. It's bitter – especially when you're born with a heart made for them.

LULU. I'd give half my life never to have seen you!

CASTI-PIANI. When you have to fight for your life the heart becomes hard.

LULU. You haven't got one.

CASTI-PIANI. It's my weak point.

LULU. Hypocrite!

CASTI-PIANI. My Achilles heel – especially as I have no power over women.

LULU. God above.

CASTI-PIANI. If you hadn't – following your own pig-headed whim – thrown yourself at my feet – how could I have ever hoped to share the joys of paradise with you?

LULU. You can mock now.

CASTI-PIANI. And then the terrible boredom of avoiding getting hooked. The world lost an ideal husband in me.

LULU. Why're you telling me this?

CASTI-PIANI. Because – at this moment – I'm being crucified again. May this cup pass from me.

LULU. Crucified? – What cup?

CASTI-PIANI. It's pure murder . . .

LULU. You're a –

CASTI-PIANI. Whatever you like.

LULU. – police spy.

CASTI-PIANI. Whatever you like. I started out as a Guards Officer.

LULU. Oh God!

CASTI-PIANI. There was nothing in it for me – I don't fancy being shot to pieces for other people's amusement.

LULU. You're a police spy?

CASTI-PIANI. After I'd handed back my sword I founded an employment agency.

LULU. What's that got to do with me?

CASTI-PIANI. I arranged situations in Hungary – in Siberia, India, Persia, America.

LULU. What sort of situations?

CASTI-PIANI. Lucrative ones. At least for me. Until a vicar's wife got between my legs.

LULU. Oh God, oh God.

CASTI-PIANI. Little Gerta or Berta – or whatever she was christened – had the time of her life. What use was that to me? I was given a situation by the state.

LULU. In prison.

CASTI-PIANI. To be frank, yes. After six months – thanks to my exemplary conduct and wide knowledge of languages – my cell door opened. I was given the opportunity – which I allowed myself to be talked into taking – of putting down roots here to keep an eye on my fellow countrymen.

LULU. Police spy.

CASTI-PIANI. I couldn't deny myself the satisfaction of reopening my employment agency. I have the best possible connections, and the territory here is much more profitable. Parisian women love Paris, especially if they're poor – but the constant flow of foreigners supplies me with an enormous stock-in-trade.

LULU. You're making fun of me.

CASTI-PIANI (*taking an open letter from his pocket*). I have an offer from Epaminondas Oikonomopoulos – an establishment in Cairo. I sent them your photographs.

LULU. The ones I gave you?

CASTI-PIANI. You in your elf costume; as Pierrot; in the flouncy chemise; as Eve in front of the mirror.

LULU. Why didn't I realise!

CASTI-PIANI. What use were they to me? (*Indicates letter.*) Six hundred pounds – that makes fifteen thousand francs or twelve

thousand marks. I can read it – so you don't take me for a
swindler.

LULU. You're a monster.

CASTI-PIANI. Not enough to please me. I advise you to take it. I've
written to the people to say you're very versatile and experienced.
You'd be completely safe there.

LULU. I don't know – if I understand.

CASTI-PIANI. Let me help you to understand. If I grabbed you
by the throat and held on till the police came – I'd earn three
thousand.

LULU. You couldn't.

CASTI-PIANI. That's four thousand less than Epaminondas
Oikonomopoulos will pay for you.

LULU. Give me an assurance – that you won't hand me over – to
the axe – then take out of what I've still got more than your Oik –
Oik – Oik –

CASTI-PIANI. You haven't got anything left – you've given me
everything.

LULU. That's not true.

CASTI-PIANI. All you've got left are Jungfrau shares.

LULU. They're going up. You can sell them.

CASTI-PIANI. I never waste my time with shares. Epaminondas
Oikonomopoulos pays in sterling – and the relatives of your –
suddenly deceased husband – would pay in –

LULU. Give me time to sell them.

CASTI-PIANI. I need it fast.

LULU. Three days.

CASTI-PIANI. Not even one night. So far I'm the only one in
possession of your valuable secret. You won't blab it out –

LULU. How do you know – prove –

CASTI-PIANI. That's not my job. I led the Public Prosecutor's
Office to understand that I'd been on your traces – but you're
supposed to have emigrated to America.

LULU. America?

CASTI-PIANI. I advise you – pack yourself off to Cairo. The
Epaminondas Oikonomopoulos house will protect you from any
bother.

LULU. A brothel!

CASTI-PIANI. Have you heard of anyone taking a girl out of a brothel to cut off her head? They usually do that to the clients.

LULU. I won't go to a brothel!

CASTI-PIANI. Actually you don't belong anywhere else.

LULU. God help me!

CASTI-PIANI. It's a shame. If you don't do it now, you'll end up on the streets.

LULU. That's not true.

CASTI-PIANI. Only because they'd chopped off your head.

LULU. God – God –

CASTI-PIANI. You won't find such a marvellous house anywhere else. A more fashionable trade than you get in Paris – Scottish lords, Indian governors, high Russian officials, rich industrialists from the Ruhr.

LULU. Heaven help me.

CASTI-PIANI. You'll be dressed in the best taste. Stroll about on carpets as thick as your fist – your own fairytale room with a magical view of the El Azhar mosque. You're completely your own mistress. You won't get that anywhere in Europe – not here or in London – not to mention Germany.

LULU. Heaven help me – heaven help me.

CASTI-PIANI. Four weeks ago I sent a young Berlin beauty there – from the highest social circles, married for half a year. She did it purely out of the urge for self-fulfillment. Her husband put a bullet through his head.

LULU. I'll never go with anyone who pays for it at a till! I'd rather have my skin torn off.

CASTI-PIANI. It's your choice.

LULU. Those women are children – empty creatures – I'm not a wild animal any more.

CASTI-PIANI. That will come back.

LULU. When I was seventeen I'd've jumped at the chance.

CASTI-PIANI. Love is love – whether it's with a Chinese or a Japanese – that's why it's never soiled your soul.

LULU. I'd go mad. All I've got is myself – my body – and you want me to give that to every riff-raff – some hairy orang-outang – the next one with stinking breath – God help me –

CASTI-PIANI. You can still cheer yourself up – in the bad times –
with your brandy –

LULU. You're a devil – no feeling or heart –

CASTI-PIANI. Where would I be if I let myself be touched by my
client's righteous anger?

LULU. Why d'you want to sell me – why! Take me – as I am –
anywhere you wish – do anything with me – I'd do it for you –

CASTI-PIANI. I have a wife and child.

LULU. You're married?

CASTI-PIANI. Yesterday evening about ten I went into a tobacco
shop on the Boulevard. As I left a girl spoke to me. It was my
daughter – (*Pause.*)

> LULU *stares at him.*

CASTI-PIANI. Sacrifice yourself on silk sheets –

LULU. To rot in a hospital!

CASTI-PIANI. – or on the scaffold.

LULU. On the –

CASTI-PIANI. I'd prefer the sheets.

LULU. It's my head they cut off – my body they dissect – my flesh
they torment –

CASTI-PIANI. I lose four thousand francs by this.

LULU. You can't do it.

CASTI-PIANI. I can do anything.

LULU. You're not human – you're not human.

CASTI-PIANI. Thank God. (*Getting up.*) I can get you to safety
today. The police are outside. Think it over till the guests have
finished playing.

LULU. Send Mr Puntschuh to me. He's at the roulette.

> CASTI–PIANI *goes out through the double doors.* LULU
> *goes to the console and takes out a folder of Jungfrau
> shares. Each certificate has a startling colour print of an
> Alpine sunset in the heading. For a moment she stares
> lost in thought. She sees* RODRIGO's *note. She opens
> it, reads it and shrieks with laughter.* PUNTSCHUH
> *comes in.*

LULU. What are these shares worth?

PUNTSCHUH. Les actions du Funiculair de la Jungfrau. Their
value increases à la bourse –

LULU. Sell them.

PUNTSCHUH. They are Madame's dernier security. She must wait
a few more days. The price will be better. Madame must choose
the moment that benefits her the –

   LULU *laughs*.

PUNTSCHUH. I recommend Madame to wait –

LULU. Sell them – sell them – sell them. (*Puts the certificates in his
hands*.) Bring me the money today.

   PUNTSCHUH *bows and goes out through the side door. A
   moment later* GESCHWITZ *comes in through the double
   doors*. LULU *is looking at* RODRIGO's *note – she looks up*.

GESCHWITZ. What did that creature want with you? How can you
even speak to him?

LULU (*stares at* GESCHWITZ *for a moment. Puts the note away*).
You've made a conquest.

GESCHWITZ. Don't mock me. I've come to the point where I could
shoot myself.

LULU. Enjoy what's on offer.

GESCHWITZ. You're tireless in finding new torments.

LULU. He's leaving me for you.

GESCHWITZ. Have pity!

LULU. You have it – the poor man's in despair.

GESCHWITZ. So am I!

LULU. He begged me to sing his praises to you.

GESCHWITZ. Who are you talking about?

LULU. He never leaves your side.

GESCHWITZ. That circus creature?

LULU. He'll throw himself in the Seine.

GESCHWITZ. I'm in misery – God knows! – misery – misery –

LULU. He's an acrobat.

GESCHWITZ. But I wouldn't change places with someone as
heartless as you!

LULU. And I wouldn't with you! – even if I had to die!

GESCHWITZ. You're murdering yourself! You go with the vilest – most depraved –

LULU. *You* say that?

GESCHWITZ. What are you doing with Casti-Piani?

LULU. Shut up!

GESCHWITZ. A vulgar creature like that!

LULU. Shut up!

GESCHWITZ. It's written on his face.

LULU. Shut up! – Shut up!

GESCHWITZ. The most bestial expression I ever saw!

LULU (*going to her with blazing eyes*). Shut up! – or –

GESCHWITZ. Hit me! (*As LULU steps back.*) You won't even do that –

LULU. Not to you!

GESCHWITZ. Listen to me – please – please – if you don't utterly – I've given everything – everything for you – I beg you – please – tell that monster to go.

LULU. And hand myself over to you!

GESCHWITZ (*sinking to the ground*). My love – my angel –

LULU. God help me – haven't I got enough horrors –

GESCHWITZ. Then stamp on me.

LULU. Get up.

GESCHWITZ. Stamp on my life!

LULU. Get up – or I'll call –

GESCHWITZ. Stamp on my life!

LULU. Get up –

GESCHWITZ. Stamp on my life – and it's finished.

LULU. I wouldn't dirty my shoes on you.

GESCHWITZ. Stamp me to death – for pity's sake!

LULU. I'll open the doors.

GESCHWITZ. Stamp me to death – or strangle me –

LULU. Go to the Moulin Rouge! Go to a circus!

GESCHWITZ. My love! My life!

LULU. Spend your money –

GESCHWITZ. You! You!

LULU. Buy some other women!

GESCHWITZ. One night!

LULU. There are plenty of women who'll do anything for money.
GESCHWITZ. One night – then I'll die.
LULU. You make a spectacle of yourself for nothing!
GESCHWITZ. One – night.
LULU. Not for a million!
GESCHWITZ. Lulu!

> RODRIGO *comes in through the double doors.* GESCHWITZ
> *gets to her feet.*

RODRIGO (*offering* GESCHWITZ *his arm*). If your Grace permits.
GESCHWITZ. Go and take a running jump!

> GESCHWITZ *goes out through the double doors.*

RODRIGO. You'll pay me for that. (*To* LULU.) Have you read
  my note?
LULU. Where did you learn such outrageous spite?
RODRIGO. I can explain.
LULU. I don't have fifty thousand francs.
RODRIGO. I can explain.
LULU. I've nothing left.
RODRIGO. You've got three times more than that.
LULU. What if I –
RODRIGO. You're not brushing me off!
LULU. Shameless!
RODRIGO. If my name was Casti-Piani –
LULU. Not even if it was Vasco da Gama.
RODRIGO. Why d'you chuck it down these strangers' throats!
LULU. I don't have any left.
RODRIGO. You're swimming in it.
LULU. God almighty.
RODRIGO. I've just been speaking to the Count.
LULU. The Count?!
RODRIGO. Mr Alwa.
LULU. Then ask him!
RODRIGO. You know he wouldn't give me a button.
LULU. He lets anyone bamboozle him till it's a joke!
RODRIGO. Make him give you the fifty thousand francs.
LULU. Because you're shameless enough to threaten me?

RODRIGO. He can't refuse you anything.

LULU. You have no feelings!

RODRIGO. He wants you so much he's going loopy!

LULU. Betray me! Betray me!

RODRIGO. It costs you one night!

LULU. Just betray me!

RODRIGO. He loves you more than ever! – he opened up to me.

LULU. Just because he loves me –

RODRIGO. Give him one night.

LULU. – he can be robbed?

RODRIGO. He'd give the whole caboodle for it.

LULU. I can't.

RODRIGO. Even if it's me who's asking?

LULU. He makes me sick.

RODRIGO. Well he is your husband after all.

LULU. Hand me over – betray me! – it'll be you or someone else!

RODRIGO. Don't take it all so tragic – I only wrote that about
informing just to make it clear – if you'd just listen to the reason.

LULU. I don't have fifty thousand francs any more.

RODRIGO. But I need them! Not a penny less!

LULU. Then you'll have to betray me!

RODRIGO. The fact is – I want to – well –

LULU. What?

RODRIGO. Get a grip on yourself.

LULU. Shoot yourself?

RODRIGO. Get married. – Please – get a grip on yourself –

LULU. With Geschwitz?

RODRIGO. Are you mad?

LULU. I don't care who it is.

RODRIGO. It's the toilet lady at the Folies-Bergère – get a grip on
yourself.

LULU. For all I care you can marry the Queen of Spain!

RODRIGO. You know I appeared as 'guest-artiste' at the Folies-
Bergère. They wanted to engage me at three thousand francs. But
the Parisians don't know my real worth. I wasn't a success. If I'd
been a kangaroo I'd've been in all the papers. That's how I made
the acquaintance of Coelestine Rabeux – a real all-round angel.
She's been in charge of the loos for thirty years. She's put away

fifty thousand francs. She'd take me tomorrow if I could match her fifty thousand. I said I wasn't sure – but I'd probably get them. She wants to retire from the public gaze. We're like two children. If she told me to kill my father I would.

LULU. Then why did you frighten the poor Countess with your billing and cooing?

RODRIGO. To show the Parisians I have savoir-vivre –

LULU. You are –

RODRIGO. You have to do that here when you move in society.

LULU. You never do anything you promise.

RODRIGO. I regret –

LULU. Someone only has to meet you to get a knife in the back.

RODRIGO. That's why I have such difficulties in my artistic career. My appearances as the Strong Man bring me one disappointment after another – with the weaker sex. First they tear the clothes off your body – then they're rolling about with the chamber maid. I'm left to sort out the dirty washing. God help me! My Coelestine loves me for myself.

LULU. I don't want to stand between you and your shy little bride.

RODRIGO. Sacrifice one night for us.

LULU. I wish I was as cold-blooded as she is.

RODRIGO. She lost all her girlhood illusions.

LULU. You can thank God for that!

RODRIGO. She knows when it comes to marriage you don't judge a desert by the oasis.

LULU. As long as you love each other – yes?

RODRIGO. And have the money.

LULU. I honestly don't know if I can get fifty thousand francs for you.

RODRIGO. If you're really nice to him – and don't always think of your own pleasure.

LULU. To please you?

RODRIGO. You wouldn't believe how grateful I'd be.

LULU. Please, please.

RODRIGO. Four people made happy at one blow.

LULU. With the exception of me.

RODRIGO. Two men and two women – including a happy young couple. You still love me a little bit in spite of yourself . . .

LULU. Come to lunch tomorrow?

RODRIGO. Vous êtes charmante, Madame la Comtesse!

LULU. Because you play your little games with me so charmingly.

> RODRIGO *goes out through the side door. Immediately* CASTI-PIANI *comes in through the double doors.*

CASTI-PIANI. What've you been saying to him?

LULU. Who?

CASTI-PIANI. Your old lover! Your jumping Jonny! He was here!

LULU. Lovers' secrets.

CASTI-PIANI. You'll lose your head.

LULU. You simply couldn't do it.

> SCHIGOLCH *comes in through the double doors.* CASTI-PIANI *glares at him and goes out through the side door.*

SCHIGOLCH. I need five hundred francs – my mistress – I must furnish an apartment – elle veut se mettre dans ses meubles.

LULU. Good God – you've got a mistress!

SCHIGOLCH. With God's help!

LULU. At eighty?

SCHIGOLCH. Why else come to Paris?

LULU. Good Lor'!

SCHIGOLCH (*lowering himself into an armchair*). She wasn't born yesterday either.

LULU. God almighty.

SCHIGOLCH. I've spent too long in Germany sending chocolates and flowers.

LULU. I – oh God –

SCHIGOLCH. You haven't seen me for six weeks.

LULU. I – I – I can't go on – I can't go on – it's too – it's too –

SCHIGOLCH. What's too?

LULU. Too horrible! (*Breaks down, buries her head on his knees and is convulsed by sobs.*) – too – horrible –

SCHIGOLCH. I was inside the whole time – . (*Stroking her hair.*) You go at it too hard. You must give it up for three days.

LULU. Oh! – Oh! – What have I done to – deserve this! What have I – done! Oh – dear God – oh God, oh God – what'll become of me! – What – oh, what I suffer! – Oh merciful

God! I can't go on – I can't go through with it – oh – it's too – horrible!

SCHIGOLCH. They let me out yesterday. (*Stroking her.*) Wash yourself in snow. Cry – if it does you good – cry it out.

LULU (*groaning*). Oh! – Oh! – Oh God – oh God –

SCHIGOLCH. I learnt some French inside. Take salt baths. Cry it out. Once a week spend a day in bed with a novel.

LULU. What'll become of me! – Oh – what'll become of me!

SCHIGOLCH. It'll soon be over. Cry yourself better. I had you like this on my knee – must be – good lor' – almost twenty years ago. How time passes! How you've grown! You cried then just like this. I had you here, I stroked your hair and rubbed your knees warm – but there was no white satin dress then – no feathers in the hair – no stockings you could see through – hardly a shirt for your back. But cry, that you could already do . . .

LULU. Please – take me with you – take me with – with you. Please have pity on me – take me back again – now – take me with you – to your attic.

SCHIGOLCH. Me – take you with me?

LULU. To your attic! To your attic!

SCHIGOLCH. And my five hundred francs?

LULU. Oh God!

SCHIGOLCH. You indulge yourself – more than you can take. You must give your body the time it needs – to be at peace again.

LULU. They want my life.

SCHIGOLCH. Who wants your life? Who? Who?

LULU. They'll betray me.

SCHIGOLCH. Who'll betray you? Tell me.

LULU. They'll – oh –

SCHIGOLCH. What?

LULU. Cut off my head! Cut off my head!

SCHIGOLCH. Who'll cut off your head? I've lived eighty years – but –

LULU. I can see myself in their ropes!

SCHIGOLCH. Who'll cut off your head?

LULU. Rodrigo! – Rodrigo Quast!

SCHIGOLCH. Him?

LULU. He just said so.

SCHIGOLCH. Don't lose your sleep over that. I'll take him out for a drink . . .

LULU. Kill him! Please! – Kill him! – Kill him! You can – if you want to!

SCHIGOLCH. He's a fancy man. He says all sorts of things he doesn't believe.

LULU. Kill him! – Kill him!

SCHIGOLCH. He likes to pretend he counts.

LULU. For your child's sake – kill him!

SCHIGOLCH. I've never known – whose child you are –

LULU. I won't get up till you promise me.

SCHIGOLCH. The poor devil.

LULU. Kill him.

SCHIGOLCH. When he's gone – you won't be able to bring him back. I could throw him out of my window into the Seine.

LULU. Please . . .!

SCHIGOLCH. And what's in it for me?

LULU. Do it! – Do it!

SCHIGOLCH. What's in it for me?

LULU. Five hundred francs.

SCHIGOLCH. Five hundred francs – five hundred francs.

LULU. A thousand.

SCHIGOLCH. If I liked to put my hand to this – in Paris – I'd soon be rich again.

LULU. How much do you want?

SCHIGOLCH. Then even at my age – I could drive round like a lord again.

LULU. How much – how much?

SCHIGOLCH. If you could . . .

LULU. Me?

SCHIGOLCH . . . lower yourself to . . .

LULU. Have pity on me.

SCHIGOLCH . . . as you used to . . .

LULU. With – you?

SCHIGOLCH. You have such beautiful clothes now.

LULU. What d'you want – to do with me?

SCHIGOLCH. You'll see.

LULU. I'm not like – like I was.

SCHIGOLCH. You think I'm ancient?

LULU. You've already got someone.

SCHIGOLCH. A girl of sixty-five.

LULU. What d'you do then?

SCHIGOLCH. Play patience.

LULU. And with me?

SCHIGOLCH. You'll see.

LULU. You're a brute.

SCHIGOLCH. We haven't known each other for so long.

LULU. In – God's – name.

SCHIGOLCH. We'll refresh old memories.

LULU (*getting up*). But you give me your solemn word –

SCHIGOLCH. When will you come along?

LULU. Dear God.

SCHIGOLCH. So I'll be alone.

LULU. When you like.

SCHIGOLCH. Day after tomorrow?

LULU. If it has to be.

SCHIGOLCH. In white satin.

LULU. But you'll throw him in?

SCHIGOLCH. With diamonds and pearls.

LULU. As I am now.

SCHIGOLCH. Just one more time – I want to make the walls shake.

LULU. You swear to me.

SCHIGOLCH. Just send him to me.

LULU. You swear, you swear.

SCHIGOLCH. By all that's holy –

LULU. To throw him in.

SCHIGOLCH. I swear.

LULU. By all that's holy.

SCHIGOLCH (*groping under her dress*). What more d'you want . . .

LULU (*trembling*). By all that's – holy.

SCHIGOLCH. By all that's holy.

LULU. Now I'm cool.

SCHIGOLCH (*letting her dress fall*). You're burning with hate . . .

Pause.

LULU (*goes left. Smooths her dress straight. Tidies her hair in the mirror and dries her eyes*). Go – *now* – go.
SCHIGOLCH. Today then?
LULU. So you're in when he comes with her.
SCHIGOLCH. With who?
LULU (*feels her cheeks then powders them*). He'll come with the Countess.
SCHIGOLCH. With a Countess?
LULU. Make them drink. Say it's the Countess' room – you live next door. The Countess will get drunk. Put something in his glass – anything you've got.
SCHIGOLCH. He'll get enough to last.
LULU. If only you can lift him – oh God – oh God.
SCHIGOLCH. Three steps to the window.
LULU. The Countess will creep away in the morning.
SCHIGOLCH. And if I have to roll him.
LULU. She certainly won't know the house again.
SCHIGOLCH. My window reaches down to the floor.
LULU. Don't forget – bring me his ear-rings.
SCHIGOLCH. When he's gone – I'll be up and away.
LULU. You hear – his gold ear-rings.
SCHIGOLCH. What is it?
LULU. I think –
SCHIGOLCH. What on earth is it?
LULU. I think – my garter –
SCHIGOLCH. Why're you gaping at me?
LULU. My garter's – broken.
SCHIGOLCH. Then I'll look for a room behind the Bastille.

LULU *has pulled up her dress and fastens her garter.*

SCHIGOLCH. Or behind the Buttes-Chaumont – Yellow stockings.
LULU. Orange.
SCHIGOLCH. Ah – the smell.
LULU. All orange – to white satin. (*Straightens up.*) Go – go now –
SCHIGOLCH. Orange –. Hm! – who's this Countess?
LULU. The mad woman – you know her. You must take a cab.

SCHIGOLCH. Of course I must – of course! (*Getting up*.) What mad woman?

LULU. The one who kisses my feet –. Please go.

SCHIGOLCH (*going*). His golden ear-rings . . .

> LULU takes SCHIGOLCH *back left*. CASTI-PIANI *pushes* RODRIGO *into the saloon through the middle door*.

RODRIGO. At least treat me with respect

CASTI-PIANI (*shaking him*). What has she told you?

RODRIGO. Nothing – nothing –

CASTI-PIANI (*knees him*). You mongrel.

RODRIGO. Oh God.

CASTI-PIANI. You've arranged a meeting.

RODRIGO. I can only tell you – what's true.

CASTI-PIANI. Admit it! (*Hits him*.)

RODRIGO. I'm getting married – please – spare me – I'm getting married – oh God – I'm getting married honestly –

CASTI-PIANI. A meeting! A meeting!

RODRIGO. A local girl – on my life – spare me – it's all to do – with money – she's got to – give me money . . .

CASTI-PIANI (*taking out a revolver*). Liar!

RODRIGO. Don't – don't – ask her – it all hangs – on the money – only money – she – she shot someone.

CASTI-PIANI (*lets him go and goes right*). Then forgive me. You see, I'm in love, and when I'm in love I'm a . . .

RODRIGO. Nasty brute!

CASTI-PIANI. Good evening. (*Goes into the gaming room*.)

RODRIGO (*alone*). Mad dog! God help me! A brute! A brute I could throw up on the ceiling with one hand – (*Looks round with a start*.) What –? You – thank God!

LULU. Yes, me. I've come.

RODRIGO. Phew! – Thank God.

LULU. I've come from Countess Geschwitz.

RODRIGO. Oh, so – yes. Yes, yes – I just told her.

LULU. She's just told me.

RODRIGO. What I said was – I sort of said –

LULU. That she was the first girl –

RODRIGO. Sort of. Yes.

LULU. – that you wanted to make love to.

RODRIGO. That I'd like to take a few liberties. Naturally she immediately – ha-ha!

LULU. You've driven her half wild.

RODRIGO. A lot I care!

LULU. It's the first time she's been told anything like that –

RODRIGO. If only it was as easy with Coelestine.

LULU. Haven't you got any further with her?

RODRIGO. I still haven't got your fifty thousand francs.

LULU. But I've promised them.

RODRIGO. Oh – woman!

LULU. On one condition.

RODRIGO. What time d'you want me?

LULU. That you make the Countess happy today.

RODRIGO. I honestly couldn't do it.

LULU. As you wish.

RODRIGO. I couldn't.

LULU. As you wish.

RODRIGO. I don't believe it'd work.

LULU. As you wish.

RODRIGO. As you wish? It's got nothing to do with wishing. All she's got going for her – as far as I'm concerned – is that she's strictly top-drawer.

LULU. That's always something – have you ever had an aristocrat?

RODRIGO. Dozens! They drop on me like flies. Duchesses – princesses – but they had legs – bums – God almighty!

LULU. You haven't seen her legs.

RODRIGO. I don't want to.

LULU. As you wish.

RODRIGO. It wouldn't work. You could bet your life on it.

LULU. You – the Strong Man.

RODRIGO. My strength's in my arms. Look at the biceps.

LULU. Spare me your biceps. If you don't want to, then – you see, she's my friend.

RODRIGO. But I didn't mean that! – I meant a platonic relationship. That happens among the educated classes. We don't all take our clothes off the moment we're introduced – like you.

LULU. Me?

RODRIGO. Who else? When were you any different? Have you ever
  loved anyone for their own sake?
LULU. I'm not a toilet acquaintance.
RODRIGO. Toilet yourself!
LULU (biting her lip). What may I tell the Countess?
RODRIGO. Tell her I've been castrated.
LULU. As you wish. (Goes back.)
RODRIGO (turning to her). What – what is it she wants?
LULU. You.
RODRIGO. I just can't believe it.
LULU. Blame it on your tummy muscles.
RODRIGO. If I'd ever imagined –
LULU. Then why did you make her drool?
RODRIGO. That hat rack!
LULU. She's still a virgin.
RODRIGO. You're a –! If a man was hanging on the gallows you'd
  wiggle your tongue at him.
LULU. I'm not like that any more.
RODRIGO. I know!
LULU. And you found me – ungrateful . . .
RODRIGO. I'll do it. I'll show her. What can't you do, when you're
  in love! (Goes back right.)
LULU. Where are you going?
RODRIGO. I need a caviar sandwich.

  RODRIGO goes out back right. LULU opens the middle door and
  calls into the gaming room.

LULU. Marthe . . .
GESCHWITZ (entering with downcast eyes). Lulu . . .
LULU (leading her down). Do what I ask – tonight – you hear?
GESCHWITZ. Yes.
LULU. Listen to me – then tomorrow night you can –
GESCHWITZ. What? – What?
LULU. Sleep with me.
GESCHWITZ (seizing LULU's hand and covering it with kisses).
  Oh . . .!
LULU. Undress me.
GESCHWITZ. Oh! – Oh!

LULU. And arrange my hair.

GESCHWITZ. Oh – Lulu!

LULU (*freeing her hand*). But now –

GESCHWITZ. Tell me.

LULU. Now – you must go with Rodrigo.

GESCHWITZ. Why?

LULU. Why? Why?

GESCHWITZ. Why – of all things!

LULU. At least you know that much . . .!

GESCHWITZ. With a man?

LULU. Yes! Yes! Enjoy yourself!

GESCHWITZ. For God's sake!

LULU. With a man! That's why you're a girl!

GESCHWITZ. Demand – demand everything of me – everything – demand every abomination – everything –

LULU. I had to do it before I could count to three. That wasn't fun either.

GESCHWITZ. My life – anything you want – demand it – I implore you.

LULU. It might even cure you.

GESCHWITZ. I can't – I can't – not a man.

LULU. And I can't – not a woman!

> GESCHWITZ *turns away, reeling, straightens herself, clenches her fists, breaks out in hysterical sobs and – supporting herself on the mantelpiece – cries quietly into her handkerchief.*

LULU. D'you think – d'you think – I'd let you – you! – come to me – if this man didn't want – to send me to the scaffold – didn't threaten – to sell me – if I didn't have to – save my head!

GESCHWITZ (*straightening herself*). What is it you want – me to do?

LULU. He'll be here in a moment –

GESCHWITZ. And – then –

LULU. You must overwhelm him – implore him –

GESCHWITZ. To what?

LULU. To what? Don't pretend to be so stupid.

GESCHWITZ. No no – but – I don't know – it's – the first – the first time –

LULU. Behave as if you're panting for him –

GESCHWITZ. Dear God!

LULU. He needs that. Otherwise he'll get in a rage.

GESCHWITZ. I'll do – what I can.

LULU. He's an athlete – and you've hurt his feelings.

GESCHWITZ. If only he believes me.

LULU. Call a cab and tell the driver soixante-quinze Quai de la Gare.

GESCHWITZ. Yes.

LULU. Soixante-quinze Quai de la Gare.

GESCHWITZ. Yes.

LULU. Shall I write it down?

GESCHWITZ. Yes.

LULU (*writes on the mantelpiece and gives the card to* GESCHWITZ). Soixante-quinze Quai de la Gare – you must pay the driver.

GESCHWITZ (*taking the card*). Yes.

LULU. It's a hotel. Tell him you live there.

GESCHWITZ. Yes.

LULU. And that's all you have to worry about.

GESCHWITZ *shudders.*

LULU. He can't take you back to his room because – he hasn't got one. He hasn't got a penny to his name. (*Opens the door back right and calls.*) Monsieur – s'il vous plait . . .

RODRIGO *comes on from back right, his mouth full.*

LULU (*whispers to* GESCHWITZ *as she passes her*). Throw yourself round his neck.

RODRIGO (*chewing*). Pardon me?

With downcast eyes GESCHWITZ *goes to* RODRIGO *and hangs round his neck.*

RODRIGO. We'd better get started.

LULU. D'you want a cab? There's a rank down in the street.

RODRIGO (*groaning*). Will you let go of me!

GESCHWITZ (*avoiding his eyes*). I love you.

RODRIGO. Well I never!

GESCHWITZ (*trying to drag him with her*). Please.

RODRIGO. Who'd've thought the old bag had it in her!

GESCHWITZ (*her hands covering her face*). I can't go on!

RODRIGO (*wringing his hands*). Couldn't you have another go at it?

LULU (*icy, close to* GESCHWITZ). You know what hangs on it.

GESCHWITZ (*her hands at her temples*). Oh God, oh God, oh God, oh God!

RODRIGO. Have I ever tried to tell you a smutty joke? Have I ever overstepped the line in your presence? Have I ever – as much as once – pinched your bum? If you don't want the other – tomorrow I'll lend you a gadget and every night God sends you can wind it up ten times – which you can't do with me!

LULU (*close to him*). And your fifty thousand francs?

GESCHWITZ (*with haggard face, violently tugging at his jacket*). Please – force me – throw yourself on me – I'm going to faint.

RODRIGO (*getting a grip on himself*). For God's sake, my lad! Look at the facts! When did you get such an upper-class return for services rendered? (*Offers her his arm.*) Let's mount the scaffold! (*He leads her back left.*)

LULU (*close to* GESCHWITZ). You've got the card?

GESCHWITZ. It'll kill me! – kill me!

LULU (*opening the door*). Bonne nuit, chers enfants.

> LULU *closes the double doors. Immediately the side door opens.* PUNTSCHUH *comes in.*

PUNTSCHUH. Madame – tragedy! Disaster! A monstrosity! The second flood!

LULU. The shares!

PUNTSCHUH (*holding out the certificates*). Fallen! The Jungfrau is a mountain no more! An abyss!

LULU. Oh God!

PUNTSCHUH. The city's in uproar!

LULU (*takes the shares*). But can't you try? Your friends? Your colleagues? (*Sits in an armchair.*) Why didn't you warn me! If I'd sold yesterday my life would be . . . (*Stops.*) Oh I am tired . . . (*To herself, low.*) To Cairo – quick – to Cairo! (*To* PUNTSCHUH.) Send the Marquis to me.

PUNTSCHUH. The Marquis de Casti-Piani left.

LULU (*stands*). When?

PUNTSCHUH. When he heard the shares are fallen. Perhaps he had an interest?

LULU (*runs to the double doors and shouts through them*). Alwa! Alwa! Alwa!

> *She throws the share certificates in the air – they scatter about the room – and goes out through the side door. ALWA comes in through the double doors. He stares at the share certificates.*

ALWA. My God! She's drunk! Our capital! Our capital!

> ALWA *runs round collecting the shares – pushing the furniture aside as he searches – picking others from* PUNTSCHUH's *feet.* PUNTSCHUH *watches impassively.*

ALWA. Help me! Help me! How many were there? (*Counting.*) Fifteen – twenty –. Our capital!

> ALWA *stops – realising that* PUNTSCHUH *is watching him.* ALWA *gets to his feet – clutching share certificates to his chest.*

PUNTSCHUH. Worthless. They fell faster than Satan fell after his famous quarrel with the Lord.

ALWA. You had shares in Jungfrau. That's why we invested!

PUNTSCHUH. I sold mine yesterday. My son I give you advice – if you should live long enough to use it. Put on armour when you deal with women – Jews – and Christians.

ALWA. Dirty yid!

PUNTSCHUH (*with the side of his shoe edges a share certificate towards* ALWA). Survival is not as easy as fixing a roulette wheel – Monsieur le Comte.

> PUNTSCHUH *goes out.* ALWA *sits on the floor grizzling in anger.*

ALWA. The bastards – bastards – bastards.

> LULU *opens the door down right, without coming in. She wears a red jacket and a cycling cape round her shoulders. She holds a jockey cap. Her hair is cut short.*

LULU (*low*). Alwa! Alwa!

ALWA (*looks up*). Mais voilà – are you mad?

LULU. Not a moment to lose.

ALWA. Why not? We can get back to the top. I'll run *two* gaming houses. We'll be –

LULU (*stepping into the room*). We're betrayed!

ALWA (*throws the share certificates in the air – they scatter about the room*). Wa – wa – wa . . .

LULU. They'll put you in prison and cut off my head –

ALWA (*knees giving*). Lulu –

LULU. Take the money box – wrap it in your coat –

ALWA. I've got – the key.

LULU. Quick! – another minute and –

ALWA (*stunned*). But who –

LULU. What's the use of that! Quick!

ALWA. You've let yourself be panicked.

LULU. Casti-Piani!

ALWA. Your darling!

LULU. Quick!

> They both go out through the side door. The double doors are thrown open by a gendarme – the archetypal kepi, cloak and moustache.

GENDARME. Au nom de la loi! – vous êtes arrette! Tous! (*Looks round.*) C'est vide! Pas de peuple! Mon Dieu! (*Looks round. Sees the scattered share certificates.*) Oh. (*Starts to collect the share certificates. He stuffs them into his jacket.*) Oh – oh – oh –

Act Five

London.

An attic without a mansard. Two large panes set in the sloping roof, opening outwards. Down left and right, a badly fitting door of bare wood with a primitive lock. Right, a torn grey mattress. Front left, a red-painted flower-stand. On it a bottle of whisky. Next to the bottle a little, smoky paraffin lamp. In the back left corner an old green chaise-longue. Right, next to the middle door, a wicker chair with the seat poking through. The walls white-washed with a reddish tinge.

The sound of rain beating on the roof. Front left it drips through the skylight. The floorboards are awash with water.

SCHIGOLCH lies on the mattress, right, in a paletot (a long grey coat) with tight waist and tails down to the feet. At the back, left, ALWA SCHÖNING lies on the chaise-longue, his hands clasped behind his head, wrapped in a red rug. The strap used to bind the rug hangs above him on the wall. LULU, with half-length hair that hangs loosely on her shoulders, in a torn black dress, comes in from the left carrying a wash-basin.

SCHIGOLCH. Where were you?
ALWA. She has to wash herself first.
SCHIGOLCH. They don't bother with that here.
ALWA. She has grand ideas!
LULU (*putting the wash-basin under the rain drip*). If only you'd die.
ALWA. That's what she's waiting for!
LULU (*straightening up and throwing back her hair*). God knows that is true!
SCHIGOLCH. Go child.
ALWA (*writhing on his back*). My wife! My wife! My wife!

LULU. It's not worth dirtying my hands on you.

SCHIGOLCH. Getting started always means tears and complications. The same with any business.

ALWA. The basin's running over already.

LULU. What am I supposed to do about it?

ALWA. The rain's beating like a roll of drums. It's setting the mood for your debut.

LULU (*shaking*). I wish I was lying where I could never be kicked awake.

SCHIGOLCH. When she's been at it three days wild horses won't keep her off it. First they have to learn to enjoy it. I've seen it twenty times in my life. At first they think it's hell. Then they wouldn't give it up for a million.

ALWA. Are you going on a pilgrimage in bare feet?

LULU. My shoes are wet.

SCHIGOLCH. That won't put Old England off.

LULU. If the old man would go!

SCHIGOLCH. In this filthy weather – you wouldn't put a dog out.

LULU. Only me!

SCHIGOLCH. She'd rather let us starve than go and have some fun.

ALWA. I don't blame her. No one enjoys prostituting their sacred being.

SCHIGOLCH. Bloody ass!

LULU (*sits on the floor with her back to the wall and clasps her arms round her knees*). Wuh – it's cold!

ALWA. I dreamt we were dining chez Sylvain.

SCHIGOLCH. With her gift for languages she'll have a great future here.

ALWA. I'd ordered fers de cheval.

LULU. I want to warm myself on one of you.

ALWA. I was so happy I could've cried. The plates clattered. My shirt was sopping with champagne. I was so drunk. It ran out of my mouth.

SCHIGOLCH. Yes yes.

LULU. I can't feel my hands and feet any more.

SCHIGOLCH. She's wasting the time when they come out of the restaurants.

LULU. I'd rather freeze to death.

ALWA. That's what I say. Why drag out this dog's life? This is the last station of the cross.

LULU. I'm supposed to feed other people's faces with the little bit of life I've got left.

SCHIGOLCH. Get up! Get your shoes on!

ALWA. I won't touch a penny of it.

SCHIGOLCH. She was at it before she could even feel it.

LULU. You drank it!

SCHIGOLCH. When she was ten she could've kept her father and mother.

ALWA (squirming). A beefsteak, Katja! A beefsteak! My kingdom for a – a – a –

SCHIGOLCH. Give her a kick so she lands downstairs. I can't any more. I'm too old and weak.

LULU. You want me to go on the streets so I can never go anywhere else. I could've found something here. I only needed to ride in Hyde Park once. Now I've got nothing but rags to put on. You held me back as your gold mine – till I've ended up in hell!

SCHIGOLCH. You shall be punished according to your sins. She'll weep before her maker, when the truth stands written on her face. Wonder-children like you come into the world to be bound in chains – so that they die and turn into angels.

> SCHIGOLCH *coughs in his hollow chest, slowly gets up, hacks and spits on the floor.* LULU *is emptying the wash-basin through the window into the guttering.*

LULU. They spit on my face! – They kick me in the stomach!

ALWA. If only there was something to smoke. I dream of a cigarette – that beats everything that's ever been smoked. The Ideal Cigarette.

LULU. Men you don't even see. Their hats over their faces, collars up to their ears, hands in their pockets. They'd go without their jackets and coats rather than go without what they came for. And that's what I'm supposed to –

SCHIGOLCH. Yes . . .

LULU. Why should I go down? I've never cost either of you a penny. There's a writer lying there! Let him get busy and sell his talent.

ALWA. Harpy! Who dragged me in the mud? Stole my ideals!
   Stifled the last spark of humanity in me!

LULU. Trash!

ALWA. Who turned me into my father's murderer!

LULU. You? You? Did you shoot him?

ALWA. She's still trying to take the credit for it!

LULU. Lazy oaf! When I look at you, I wish I'd cut off the hands
   that did it. Not to save him – he lost nothing – he had nothing
   left. But to spite you – dear God!

ALWA (*laughs*). Look what she's turned me into!

LULU. Did I run after you?

ALWA (*laughs*). Look what she's turned me into!

LULU. Have you forgotten how you begged me on your bended
   knees?

ALWA. How happy I was then! What success lay before me –
   the most brilliant future a man could strive for – on the way
   to becoming one of the Great Men of the times – all wasted –
   squandered – blown away! Oh God what have I done!

SCHIGOLCH. He's getting convulsions.

ALWA. I'll bear it to the end. I searched the highways for all things
   human! Now why not starve! Why not starve!

SCHIGOLCH. He should try searching for a sympathetic nurse.

ALWA. For what you left of me? – my rotting bones – my hideous
   lust!

LULU. Cry-baby!

ALWA. She-wolf! Hyena!

SCHIGOLCH (*to* LULU). Don't stand on ceremony – you've got
   everything you need.

LULU. If I go, it's for my pocket. I'll do it to get myself out of this
   hole. I can get back to the top when I'm on my own.

SCHIGOLCH. All I want is a slice of Christmas pudding. I don't
   need more for myself.

LULU. I'm not letting myself be turned into money for your sakes.

SCHIGOLCH. Yes yes.

ALWA. I made charts – spent nights poring over them – the perfect
   gambling system based on eternal laws! All I did was lose money
   faster than if I'd thrown it out of the window with both hands!

SCHIGOLCH. Oh yes.

LULU. He let himself be fleeced by every man and woman he met!

SCHIGOLCH. I don't understand women.

ALWA. I never have.

LULU. I do.

ALWA. I offered myself up to them.

SCHIGOLCH. If I only had some pudding – a slice of pudding, child.

ALWA. The first one threw me into the arms of the next. And these English women's feet! The men have their women, then compensate themselves with the orgies they have with ours.

LULU. He's too stupid to tame a dog.

ALWA. I tried everything! In Paris it goes to their hearts! I saw their desires in their eyes! God protect me! Here one woman – afterwards she still wanted money for it – broke my umbrella in two! I shouted police – she grabbed a handful of steaming horse-droppings from the street and threw them in my face! That's what they call their daughters of joy! I didn't spare myself one disappointment! I'd rather starve – freeze – to death than go to their ministering angels for a little human warmth!

SCHIGOLCH. When you're young it's easy to talk of death.

ALWA. Since we've been stuck here I haven't sniffed at a woman! And the less you get to eat the more lust gnaws at your vitals! Katja! – you're a monster – but when it's a choice between you and madness –

> ALWA *gets up and sways in torn trousers towards* LULU. *She grips his outstretched arms, wrestles him to the floor and throws him on his back.*

LULU. Go to a hospital first!

ALWA. Who made me ill?

LULU. Am I ill?

ALWA (*on all fours, neck craned forwards*). No – no – you're not ill – you're healthy – you'll make lots of men happy!

SCHIGOLCH. Don't let your dependants cry out for bread any longer.

ALWA. You're not ill! You're not ill!

LULU. I kept myself clean all my life – to drown in filth.

LULU *sits at the end of* SCHIGOLCH's *mattress and props her elbows on her knees.*

SCHIGOLCH. She wants to see our tongues hanging out.

LULU. Make me warm.

SCHIGOLCH. Child, child – this is what I get for the sleepless nights of worry!

LULU. I'll get the blanket.

ALWA (*picking himself up from the floor*). You'll drive me so far I'll kill you! I'll kill you, you bloodhound! I'll slake my thirst on your blood! (*He drags himself back to his couch.*)

LULU (*to* SCHIGOLCH). Undo your coat. Let me put my feet inside.

SCHIGOLCH. If you still had silk knickers and garters . . .

LULU. Please.

SCHIGOLCH. Make them pay up. I'd prefer a slice of Christmas pudding.

LULU. It's still me.

SCHIGOLCH. Yes yes.

LULU. Undo it. Please, please. I'm dying of cold.

SCHIGOLCH. I could pop off any moment. I've felt nothing in my finger-tips since Paris. They're bluer every day. I'd like Christmas pudding one last time. At midnight I'll go back down to the bar. Perhaps they'll be gambling. I shan't like that. But there's a beautiful blonde miss floating behind the bar.

LULU. For God's sake – (*Goes to the flower stand and puts the whisky bottle to her mouth.*)

SCHIGOLCH. So they can smell her from thirty feet – before she opens her mouth.

LULU (*with a poisonous look at* SCHIGOLCH, *puts down the bottle*). I won't drink it all.

LULU *goes out left.* ALWA *wraps himself in his rug.*

ALWA. She could've been Empress of Russia. The second Catherine the Great . . .

Pause. LULU *comes back with a pair of worn lace-up boots and sits in the chair by the door.*

LULU (*babbling*). I already feel – the – the – the – the – . If only

I didn't have to go – down the stairs – I must laugh – je jouirai
– ah – je jouirai – . (*Stamping her feet firmly into the boots.*) It's
cold! I must just –

LULU *goes to the flower stand and puts the bottle to her lips.*

SCHIGOLCH. A dog wouldn't piss on her.
LULU (*gulping*). Ca m'excite!

LULU *takes another gulp and sways out through the middle.*

ALWA. It's a real shame about her – when I think back. (*Pause.*)
SCHIGOLCH. When we hear her coming we must creep away in my
hole till it's done.
ALWA. I grew up with her more or less . . . (*Long pause.*)
SCHIGOLCH. She'll last as long as I live.
ALWA. The first time – I met her – she – she was dressing. At once
we were like brother and sister. She lay in her vest in the rocking
chair – pompon slippers on her little feet – having her hair done.
Mama was still alive. We talked about my first poem. It was
printed in *Vienna Mode*. The hairdresser had read it too. 'Chase
your hounds far over the mountains – they will return covered in
sweat and dust.'
SCHIGOLCH. Yes yes – (*Pause.*)
ALWA. And then the Museum Ball. She was in pink tulle – a white
bodice under it. Father had arranged for her to go with Dr Goll.
They weren't yet married. Mother went too at the last moment.
She'd had a headache all day. Papa didn't want to speak to her.
So I had to dance. Papa didn't take his eyes off me the whole
night. Later on she shot him. It's hideous.
SCHIGOLCH. I'm not sure anyone'll bite.
ALWA. I was there. I wouldn't recommend it.
SCHIGOLCH. That ox!
ALWA. In those days she was still three years younger than me. But
she already treated me like a mother. She was my step-mother –
then my little sister.
SCHIGOLCH. So long as she doesn't clear off.
ALWA. I made love to her for the first time in her swirling wedding
dress – at Papa's wedding. She'd mixed us up.
SCHIGOLCH. They're coming . . .

Heavy footsteps are heard outside on the stairs.

ALWA (*jumping up*). She shan't –

SCHIGOLCH (*laboriously getting up from his place*). Forwards!

ALWA (*standing by his chaise-longue, throwing his rug round his waist*). I'll beat the dog to the ground!

SCHIGOLCH (*drags himself over the room and takes* ALWA's *arm*).

Forwards! – he can't unload his troubles to her with us falling about all over the place.

ALWA. Let me go – I'd rather be beaten to death!

SCHIGOLCH. Little coward – little oaf – little fool! Will you feed your family? (*Pushes him down right.*)

ALWA (*menacingly*). What if he demands something dirty from her?

SCHIGOLCH. So what?

ALWA. God help him!

SCHIGOLCH. Forwards! (*Pushes him into his hiding hole.*)

ALWA. Leave the door open.

SCHIGOLCH (*following* ALWA *into the hiding hole*). You'll hear nothing.

ALWA. I will hear it!

SCHIGOLCH. Shut your face!

> LULU *opens the door and lets in* MR HOPKINS. *He is a big, bulky man, with a rosy, clean-shaved face, blue eyes and a welcoming smile on his mouth. He wears a top-hat and a long Havelock and holds a dripping umbrella in his hand. He lays a finger to his lips and looks meaningfully at* LULU.

LULU. This is my little room. It's not very comfortable.

> HOPKINS *puts his hand over her mouth.*

LULU. What d'you mean?

> HOPKINS *puts his hand over her mouth and holds his index finger to his lips.*

LULU. I don't understand.

> HOPKINS *holds her mouth shut.*

LULU (*freeing herself*). We're alone. There's nobody.

HOPKINS *lays his index finger to his lips, waves his hand in a negative sign, points to* LULU, *opens his mouth as if he's speaking, points at himself and then at the door.*

LULU. Mon Dieu, mon Dieu . . .

HOPKINS *holds her mouth shut. Then goes to the back, folds up his Havelock, lays it across the chair by the door, opens his umbrella and stands it to dry on the floor.*

SCHIGOLCH (*behind the half-open door, front right, to* ALWA). This one's cracked.
ALWA. He'd better watch out.
SCHIGOLCH. Couldn't she find any worse rubbish?

HOPKINS *comes down with a grinning smile, takes* LULU's *head in his hands and kisses her forehead.*

LULU (*stepping back*). I hope you'll give me some money.

HOPKINS *holds her mouth shut and presses a ten-shilling piece into her hand.*
LULU *examines it and throws it from one hand to the other.*
HOPKINS *looks at her uncertain and questioning.*

LULU (*putting the ten-shilling piece into her pocket*). All right.

HOPKINS *quickly holds her mouth shut, gives her a five-shilling coin and throws her an intimidating glance.*

LULU. You're generous.

HOPKINS *jumps round the room like a madman, brandishing his arms in the air and stares despairingly up to heaven.* LULU *comes closer to him, throws her arm round his waist, puts her index finger to his lips and shakes her head negatively. He takes her head in his hands and kisses her mouth.* LULU *throws her arms round his neck, presses against him and kisses him for a long time on the mouth. He frees himself from her, laughing soundlessly, and looks questioningly at the mattress, front right, and the chaise-longue, back left.* LULU *takes the lamp from the flower stand, throws*

HOPKINS *an inviting look and opens the door down left. He nods and enters smilingly, taking off his hat as he passes under the door. LULU follows him. The stage is dark except for a ray of light that comes left from under the door gap.*

ALWA (*in the half-open door, down on all fours*). They're in.
SCHIGOLCH (*behind him*). Wait.
ALWA. Can't hear from here.
SCHIGOLCH. Stupid brat.
ALWA. I'm going to the door.

LULU *comes from left carrying the lamp. She smiles and shakes her head. She takes the rug from the chaise-longue and goes to pick up the wash-basin on the floor. When she sees SCHIGOLCH and ALWA she jumps and motions them to stay inside.*

SCHIGOLCH (*sharp*). Did he pay you in dud?

LULU *lays her index finger to her lips and anxiously creases her forehead in pleading. She takes the wash-basin from under the rain drip, goes out left and closes the door behind her.*

ALWA. Now.
SCHIGOLCH. Stupid sod.

SCHIGOLCH *turns the Havelock inside out and goes through the inside pockets. Pulls out a book, holds it in the ray of light and with difficulty deciphers the title page.*

SCHIGOLCH (*reads*). Lessons for Those Who Are and Those Who Want to Be Christian Workers – with a preface – by Rev W. Hay M.H – Very Helpful – price three-shillings and sixpence. (*Putting the book back into the pocket.*) God's certainly abandoned that one.
ALWA. Now . . .
SCHIGOLCH (*feels his way back*). There's nothing left in London. The nation's greatness is behind it. (*In the doorway right front, whispering across to ALWA.*) What's the situation?
ALWA (*after a pause*). Il fait sa toilette.
SCHIGOLCH. The world's never as bad as we think.
ALWA. My wife! My wife!

Creeps back right and pulls SCHIGOLCH with him into the hiding hole.

SCHIGOLCH. The oaf didn't even bring a silk scarf.

ALWA. Quiet now!

SCHIGOLCH. And this is the nation the Germans crawl to on their stomachs.

ALWA. He's got a repeating rifle.

SCHIGOLCH. For his miserable handful of coppers!

ALWA. I envy him his romp!

SCHIGOLCH. Me too – me too.

> HOPKINS *comes back from the left.* LULU *follows him with the lamp. They look at each other.*

LULU. D'you think you'll come again?

> HOPKINS *holds her mouth shut.* LULU – *a little dazed – looks in bewilderment at heaven and nervously shakes her head.* HOPKINS *has thrown on his Havelock and comes close to her, grinning. She throws herself on his neck. He frees himself gently, kisses her hand and turns to the door. She starts to go with him but he waves her back. He goes out through the middle.*

LULU (*coming down*). Did he exhaust me! Did he exhaust me!

SCHIGOLCH. How much did you get?

LULU. Did he exhaust me! (*She puts the lamp on the flower-stand*). I – I must go back –

ALWA (*barring her way*). Not again!

LULU. Shut your –! Oh God, oh God.

SCHIGOLCH. She's possessed! The spirit's come upon her. As I prophesied!

LULU (*throwing her arms up*). I can't stand it.

SCHIGOLCH. All the better. Business is beginning to tick. How much?

LULU (*pushing ALWA aside*). I must! It's no use – (*Stops – stands as if rooted.*)

ALWA. What is it?

LULU. He's coming back . . .!

SCHIGOLCH (*taking ALWA's arm*). Quick.

LULU. It's someone else.

ALWA. Who – can it – be?

SCHIGOLCH. Quick.

LULU. Heaven knows.
ALWA. It's here.

> *A knock. The three stare at each other in silence. The door is opened from the outside. GESCHWITZ comes in with a pale, haggard face, in poor clothes, a rolled canvas in her hand.*

LULU. You!
GESCHWITZ. If I've come at the wrong time . . .
LULU. You're late.
GESCHWITZ. I haven't spoken to a soul for nine days.
LULU. Did you manage to –?
GESCHWITZ (*eyes cast down*). No – nothing.
LULU (*goes left front, her chin stuck out*). I can't stand it.
SCHIGOLCH. Her Grace might like to enquire after our health.
GESCHWITZ. I wrote to my brother. He sent nothing.
LULU. In a barracks . . .
GESCHWITZ. Today I had nothing left to buy food.
SCHIGOLCH. She'd be delighted to get her feet under our table.
(*He goes to GESCHWITZ and feels the canvas roll.*)
GESCHWITZ. Lulu.
LULU. I must go down quickly.
GESCHWITZ. Lulu.
LULU. I'll be back soon.
SCHIGOLCH. What've you got there?
GESCHWITZ (*to LULU*). I've got it.
LULU. It's driving me off my head.
GESCHWITZ. The picture.
ALWA. What? – You've got her portrait?
LULU (*at the door*). I'll jump into the Thames if no one takes pity on me.
ALWA (*he has taken the picture from GESCHWITZ and unrolled it*).
There! We've got her back again!
LULU (*Turning back*). What's that?
GESCHWITZ. Your picture.
ALWA. It seems to have darkened.
LULU (*cries*). Oh – oh God in heaven.
SCHIGOLCH. It must be nailed up.
ALWA (*to GESCHWITZ*). How did you get it?

SCHIGOLCH. It'll impress our customers.

GESCHWITZ. I cut it from the frame. I crept back the next day.

ALWA. There's a nail (*Goes right and hangs the picture on a nail in the wall.*)

GESCHWITZ. It's cracked. I couldn't carry it any better.

SCHIGOLCH. It needs hammering at the bottom.

ALWA. I know what to do!

> ALWA *takes a nail from the wall, takes off his shoe and hammers the nail with the heel through the bottom of the canvas.*

SCHIGOLCH. It'll straighten itself out. It was rolled up too long.

GESCHWITZ. A dealer in Drury Lane offered me half-a-crown for it. I didn't want to let it go.

ALWA (*putting on his shoe*). It just needs to hang a bit.

SCHIGOLCH. Gives the room a touch of society.

ALWA (*stepping back, to LULU*) The lamp, my dear

> LULU *comes with the lamp.*

SCHIGOLCH. They'll flatter themselves when they see it.

ALWA. She had everything to make a man happy.

> LULU *laughs.*

SCHIGOLCH. What's not there any longer, they'll have to imagine.

> LULU *laughs.*

ALWA. She's thinner.

SCHIGOLCH. That's nothing – I'm thinner.

ALWA. The eyes are exactly the same.

SCHIGOLCH. Those days she pigged herself on pâté de foie gras. Look at those arms!

ALWA. That beautiful bust. It was just before she was at her best.

SCHIGOLCH. At least she can say 'that was me'.

> LULU *laughs.*

ALWA. The likeness was hypnotic. The pose – the line – the young flush on the skin.

GESCHWITZ. He must have been a gifted artist.

> LULU *laughs*.

SCHIGOLCH. What legs! You don't find legs like that now.

> LULU *laughs*.

ALWA. The subtle way her whole face smiles. Enough to shake the earth to its foundations.

SCHIGOLCH. Anyone whose hands she fell into today, they'd have no idea.

ALWA. The rosy white. Dazzling light – drops of air on the skin.

SCHIGOLCH. Her whole body shines.

> LULU *laughs*.

ALWA. A girl who feels happiness in every limb. Below desire, above the dawn.

SCHIGOLCH. Yes. It was a gift from God. All flesh is grass.

ALWA. You feel the old excitement.

> LULU *laughs*.

ALWA. That picture shows me all my downfall.

SCHIGOLCH. I saw the milk-teeth drop out of that mouth.

ALWA. You don't see the ravages when you live close to someone for years.

SCHIGOLCH. In those days I could still let myself be seen in broad daylight. I had a fancy bit in every other street.

ALWA. My self-respect's coming back.

SCHIGOLCH. It all went off in the dustcart. It's the times.

ALWA. It's the trick nature plays on us to trap us. Woman blossoms for the few seconds in which mankind must betray itself for ever.

SCHIGOLCH. She doesn't need tricks here. Under the street lamps she's still a match for ten of these English rattling bone-bags.

ALWA. Providence hangs the noose but you put your head in it. You can't complain.

SCHIGOLCH. Anyone who feels the urge this time of night isn't looking for much.

ALWA. And in what woman has nature fought with more powerful weapons?

SCHIGOLCH. He just chooses the eyes with the least glint of thievery in them. He asks for the soul. He doesn't look at the body.

ALWA. Other men are spared my suffering but they'll never know my joy.

SCHIGOLCH. We don't count any more. If someone's handing out money he's usually got a good reason for it. Survivors like us are too cunning to pay. She's not as dumb as she wants us to think. Right, girl?

LULU (*setting the lamp on the flower-stand*). I'll soon be back.

ALWA. Don't go!

GESCHWITZ. Where are you going?

LULU. Out – out –

ALWA. To prostitute herself.

GESCHWITZ (*cry*). Lulu!

LULU (*with tears in her eyes*). Don't make my sufferings worse.

GESCHWITZ. Lulu, Lulu, I'll go with you – wherever you go.

SCHIGOLCH. That's all we needed!

GESCHWITZ (*falling at LULU's feet*). Come with me – I'll slave for you.

LULU. Get off – you monster!

GESCHWITZ. I – I'll go in your place.

SCHIGOLCH (*treading on GESCHWITZ's fingers*). If you want to exhibit your skeleton on the pavement with a cap for the pennies! God help you – slake your thirst, it's lasted a hundred years –

GESCHWITZ. Lulu! Lulu!

SCHIGOLCH. – but don't frighten off our customers! Find your own shop doorway. Don't fish with other people's worm.

LULU *has run downstairs.*

GESCHWITZ (*picking herself up*). I won't leave her side – I've got a weapon . . . (*She rushes after her.*)

SCHIGOLCH. Damn! – Damn! – Damn! – Damn! Why didn't you grab her by the throat!

ALWA (*writhing on his chaise-longue*). My suffering's burned me out – body and soul.

SCHIGOLCH. She'll drive everything away – like rat poison – with her bony face.

ALWA. She tied me to the whipping post and crowned me with thorns – inside and out.

SCHIGOLCH. Don't be ungrateful for what providence sends –

ALWA. She's eaten me like a plague of boils.

SCHIGOLCH. – she's the best fate we could have – (*Stretching out on his mattress.*) – she lured that oaf back to my hole.

ALWA. Who'd be more grateful for the *coup de grâce* than me?

SCHIGOLCH. The toilet-bridegroom.

ALWA. I envy him his fate!

SCHIGOLCH. She let him rob her of her fossilized virginity.

ALWA. She made me the receptacle of all the poisons and parasites that came to her Babylonian orgies.

Pause.

SCHIGOLCH. Turn up the lamp a little.

ALWA. All the same it's terrible to think about the end.

SCHIGOLCH. By the time I was twenty-three I knew how to help myself. Even when all I owned to cover my nakedness was a tie. Later I owned three houses in the new suburbs. You learn to do without.

ALWA. What have I made of my life?

SCHIGOLCH. Do we have to sit in outer darkness till she comes?

ALWA. The year's going – you can hardly remember one hour exactly.

SCHIGOLCH. What's this filthy weather done to my fool's cap?

ALWA. You can't hear the rain anymore. It wants to be fine by the morning.

SCHIGOLCH. It's no good in twos. Thank God she's got the sense to use her fists to keep that crow off her body.

ALWA. One wins the respect of his nation –

SCHIGOLCH. I think – I hear something.

ALWA. – the other lies in London on a trash heap – and can't die.

SCHIGOLCH. Can't you hear it?

ALWA. Where? – We spent such happy times together. Sharing our inspiration – doting on the future.

SCHIGOLCH. They're here! They're here!

ALWA. Who?

SCHIGOLCH (*getting up*). The Countess!

ALWA. I'm staying put.

SCHIGOLCH. Oaf!

ALWA. Staying put. I'll crawl under the rug. At least I'll be here for it.

SCHIGOLCH. Mother's boy! (*Creeps into his hole, front right, and closes the door behind him.*)

    ALWA *crawls under his rug.*

LULU (*opening the door*). Come in, come in.

    KUNGU POTI *in a light top hat, light overcoat and light trousers is stumbling up the stairs.*

KUNGU POTI. It's very dark here.

LULU. Come in darling. Here's more light.

KUNGU POTI. Is this your sitting-room?

LULU (*closing the door*). Yes sir. Why are you looking so serious?

KUNGU POTI. I feel cold.

LULU. Would you like a drink?

KUNGU POTI. Well. Have you any brandy?

LULU. Yes. Come on. (*Taking the bottle.*) I don't know where the glass is.

KUNGU POTI. That does not matter. (*Puts the bottle to his lips.*) Well – well –

LULU. He looks like a burned pancake.

KUNGU POTI. What's that?

LULU. I said you're a nice young man.

KUNGU POTI. Well. Do you think so?

LULU. Yes sir. – Down in the street he didn't look so black.

KUNGU POTI. My father is the Sultan of Ouaoubée.

LULU. Is he? How many women does he keep?

KUNGU POTI. Only four. I have six here in London. Three English and three French. Well, I don't like to see them.

LULU. Aren't you on good terms with them?

KUNGU POTI. Well. They are too stylish for me.

LULU. You prefer to come with me?

KUNGU POTI. Yes, I do.

LULU. He reeks like a menagerie.

KUNGU POTI. What do you say?

LULU. Will you stay long in London?

KUNGU POTI. Well. When my father is dead I must go to
Ouaoubée.

LULU. What d'you want to do there?

KUNGU POTI. I shall be king of my country. That kingdom
is twice the size of England. Well, I would rather stay in
London.

LULU. I believe that. How much will you give me?

KUNGU POTI. What's your name?

LULU. Daisy.

KUNGU POTI (*sings and wiggles his feet*).

> Daisy Daisy!
> Give me your answer do!

LULU. Tell me – what do you want to give me?

KUNGU POTI. Daisy – I give you a sovereign.

LULU. Well.

KUNGU POTI (*sings and wiggles his feet*).

> I'm half crazy
> All for the love of you!

    KUNGU POTI *tries to kiss her.*

LULU (*fending him off*). Let me see your money first.

KUNGU POTI. Yes. I will give you one pound. I give always a
sovereign.

LULU. You can give it to me afterwards but you must show it to
me first.

KUNGU POTI. Never I pay beforehand.

LULU. All right but show me your money.

KUNGU POTI. No Daisy. Come on –

LULU. Go away please!

KUNGU POTI (*seizing her round the body*). Come on, come
on.

LULU. Let me go! Let me!

KUNGU POTI (*grabs her by the hair*). Come on Daisy – where is
the bed?

LULU (*shrieking*). No! – No! – Don't do that! Oh!

KUNGU POTI. Well. (*Throws her to the ground.*)

> ALWA *has unwrapped himself from his rug – he strides down and flies at* KUNGU POTI'*s throat.*

LULU (*crying out*). Holy Jesus!

> KUNGU POTI. *reaches into his pocket for a cosh – gives* ALWA *a blow to the head.*

ALWA (*collapsing*). Mama . . .

KUNGU POTI. Well – that's a den. That's a murder hole! I am going!

> KUNGU POTI *goes out through the middle.*

LULU (*getting up*). He's lying there now. Alwa! – I can't stay here. Why did I go with the black? Crowds of men – go by every minute – you have to ask the time – what's the time, time, please? – Where've you been so late? Make them talk – why d'you look so sad? Show them you understand everything –

> LULU *goes out through the middle.* SCHIGOLCH, *groping in from the right, bends over* ALWA.

SCHIGOLCH. That's what you get! Don't mix with strangers' love affairs. (*Touching his head.*) Blood . . . Blood . . . (*Goes to the table and comes back with the lamp.*) Nothing to see. Alwa. Good lad! – He's got wax-paper in his ears. (*Puts the lamp on the floor and his ear to* ALWA'*s back.*) A murmur. (*Turns him over and feels his forehead.*) No fever. He's cool. (*Shouts in* ALWA'*s ear.*) Alwa! – Alwa! (*With his thumb he lifts his left eyelid.*) I know that, I know that, I know that. (*Takes his head in both hands and feels it.*) The cannibal! Deep – deep. (*Lets it fall. The head strikes the floor.*) Hay-oops! He should be in bed. (*Grips* ALWA *with one arm under the shoulders, the other under the knees, tries to lift him and lets him fall. Straightens up.*) The boy doesn't weigh much any more. If there was someone here . . . (*Bending over him.*) Say something then! You didn't land on your tongue. Sleepy head. You've got the whole world before you. (*Shakes him.*) Now now! Don't take it so much to heart. He didn't mean any harm. A hundred times you could –. Don't be a fool. It's not worth the bother. You're

still too young for this life. Look – see reason! (*Straightens up.*)
Those who won't be told, can't be helped. Let him think it over
a little while. You smile as if he'd put a lump of sugar in your
mouth. (*Grips him again under the arms and knees and drags him
a few paces to the left.*) These cases are either-or – but when they
can't make up their own mind . . . (*Shakes* ALWA.) You can still
dote on the future. Can't you hear now? (*Boxes* ALWA's *ears.*) I'll
knock the sulks out of you! (*Picks him up again.*) He wants to be
left in peace.

> SCHIGOLCH *drags* ALWA *into* LULU's *room. Pause.*
> SCHIGOLCH *comes back, takes the lamp from the floor and sets
> it on the flower-stand.*

SCHIGOLCH. You won't last long either. (*Turning it up, stares at*
LULU's *picture.*) Still doesn't hang quite right. There's something
there – the white legs – the arm in the air – of death. It comes to
you in a dream. By and by our time will come. God knows when
she'll be back from her expedition. When she's lived as long as
us – seen so much flare up, and sink down to nothing – there'll
be no more howling – no more jumping in the Thames. (*Goes to
his hole and comes back with a dented top hat.*) Now it's off to buy
a scotch whisky and eat a slice of Christmas pudding. (*Suddenly
starts.*) God alive! – someone there.

> GESCHWITZ *opens the door soundlessly.*

SCHIGOLCH. You.
GESCHWITZ. Me.
SCHIGOLCH. I thought – it might've been – the –
GESCHWITZ. He'll come soon.
SCHIGOLCH (*going to the door*). I won't disturb him.
GESCHWITZ. I won't keep you.
SCHIGOLCH. Goodbye.
GESCHWITZ. How dark it's getting.
SCHIGOLCH. It'll get darker.
GESCHWITZ. I'm maimed.
SCHIGOLCH. Everyone must go.
GESCHWITZ. I can't.
SCHIGOLCH. I can – thank God.

GESCHWITZ. I can't go and I can't stay.

SCHIGOLCH. I think because you're so flat-chested you want to play the heavy father.

GESCHWITZ. I've learnt to wait.

SCHIGOLCH. Wait quietly. At least it's more sensible than trying to be her rival. – Perhaps you'll still fill out . . .

GESCHWITZ. She sent me ahead.

SCHIGOLCH. Then I'm sure to meet her.

SCHIGOLCH *goes out through the middle.*

GESCHWITZ. I'm maimed. She said it. I'm maimed. (*Sitting in the wicker chair by the door.*) Perhaps she's right. She used me as a murder weapon. She deceived me – deceived and deceived me. I've waited three years for one minute. If she saw me in my death throes at her feet –. My life's all I have left – she's got the rest. The shares – the bank books – bonds – redemptions – rents – my part in the estate – my reputation – happiness – I still wait. What will I get when I'm dead? She won't even cry. Now I don't believe in a loving God. Who maimed me. For a long time – I believed in him. But as I'm maimed – as I'm maimed! – When he comes – I'll shoot him! Everyone else is fit – whole. Every gutter-lout. They can make her shout with joy! I can't! I'm the last one who could do that! The last one on earth! Why – why – why – why – am I the one who's damned . . .?

She takes a small black revolver from her bag and aims it at her head. A long pause.

GESCHWITZ (*letting the revolver sink*). Better to hang. Then I won't hear anything any more. What is the rest of my life? Pain, pain. I could throw myself from a bridge. The water's cold. My bed's cold. What's colder? The water? My bed. The railings in Paris aren't so high. You're not cold long. I could dream of her – till it's over. Better to hang. She's cold too. A knife? I couldn't – use – a knife. No courage. It can't be that way. I dreamt so often – she kissed me. One more minute. No, no, no – something always comes between. It's better to hang. I couldn't cut my wrists – it wouldn't work. I can't take poison. Better to hang. I'm so dirty, dirty, dirty, dirty. Hang! (*She hides the revolver.*) I can't shoot myself. Can't go in the Thames. The water's too clean! Hang yourself! (*Suddenly jumps up.*) God knows! –

> *She takes the rug strap from the wall, climbs on the chair, fastens the strap on a hook in the wall above the door, puts the strap round her neck, knocks the chair over with her feet and falls to the ground. She runs her hand along the strap – finds the hook, torn from the wall.*

GESCHWITZ. Damned life! Damned life! Damned life! (*For a while she stays leaning against the wall. Then she speaks in a tearful voice.*) Lulu – Lulu – if only – if only – I could still – if this was only a trial – Lulu – and I didn't have to go – if you'd let me – speak to your heart – once – you only have to open your heart to me once – then everything will be good! I'll wait. I'll wait. If only you promise me – once – at least once – then I don't have to go. Not till I've been happy – once. I know it. Now I know it. Or I'd suffer all eternity. God doesn't want that! He won't let me go! Not till I've been happy! Once. Once! Lulu – happiness! Listen to Him! He's speaking to you for me! Lulu! – listen to Him or He will punish you – the dear Lord will punish you!

> GESCHWITZ *drags herself right, sinks on her knees before the portrait and clasps her hands.*

GESCHWITZ. My angel! My love! I worship you! Adore you! Who suffered more? Gave you more? You laugh – so full of happiness! Who had more patience? Your skin's as soft as snow. Your heart's as cold. Have pity! – Have pity! – Have pity!

> LULU *leads* JACK *in.*

LULU (*to* GESCHWITZ, *with blazing eyes*). You're still here . . .

> JACK *is stockily built, with lithe movements, white face, inflamed eyes, scrofulous nose, heavy arched eyebrows, drooping moustache, thin beard, matted side-whiskers and raw hands with chewed fingernails. While he speaks he shifts from one posture to another and keeps his eyes on the ground. He wears a dark overcoat and a bowler hat.*

JACK. Who is it?

LULU. My sister sir.

JACK. Your sister.

LULU. She's mad. She's always under my feet.

GESCHWITZ (*cringing back like a dog*). I didn't hear you.

JACK. Does she disturb us?

LULU. No – stay, stay! Don't go please . . .

JACK. You have a beautiful mouth when you're speaking.

LULU (*opens the door, to* GESCHWITZ). Get out! Wait on
   the stairs!

JACK. Don't send her away!

LULU (*closing the door*). Will you stay with me sir?

JACK. How much do you want?

LULU. All night . . .?

JACK. You have a strong pretty chin. Your lips. Red – bursting.

LULU. As soon as you've seen me you'll leave me. You'll tell me
   you have to go home –

JACK. Liar!

LULU. Oh God, oh God.

JACK. You understand your business. Where did you get your
   beautiful mouth?

LULU. From my mother.

JACK. I do know that. – How much do you want?

LULU. Just what you like.

JACK. I can't waste money. I'm not Baron Rothschild.

LULU. Will you stay all night with me sir?

JACK. No. I haven't time.

LULU. Why won't you stay all night sir?

JACK. I'm a married man.

LULU. You say you missed the last bus and had to spend the night
   with one of your friends . . .

JACK. Time is money. – How much do you want?

LULU. A pound.

JACK. Good evening. (*Goes to the door.*)

LULU (*holding him back*). Stay! – Stay!

> JACK *goes past* GESCHWITZ *to the hiding hole, opens the door
> and taps round inside.*

LULU. I'm living with my sister.

JACK (*coming back*). You are insolent!

LULU. I am not insolent. – You can pay me tomorrow . . .

JACK. When I'm sleeping you'll file my pockets.

LULU. I don't do that.

JACK. Why d'you want me to stay all night?

> LULU *is silent.*

JACK. That is suspicious.

LULU. Just give me what you like . . .

JACK. Your mouth is the best part of you.

LULU. Half-a-sovereign . . .

> JACK *laughs and goes to the door.*

LULU (*holds him back*). Don't leave! – I beg you.

JACK. How much do you want?

LULU. I don't want anything at all.

JACK. You want nothing? What does it mean?

> LULU *throws* GESCHWITZ – *who has pulled herself up against* JACK – *to the floor.*

JACK. Let her go! That's not your sister. – She loves you.

LULU. We are sisters-in-law . . .

JACK (*comes closer to* GESCHWITZ *and strokes her head*). We don't hurt each other. We understand each other. Don't we? (*Fondling her cheek.*) Poor beast . . .

> GESCHWITZ *crawls away and throws him poisonous looks.*

LULU. Are you gay?

JACK (*holding* GESCHWITZ *on the strap round her neck*). What is that? – What is that?

LULU. She's insane – I told you. If you prefer to go with her . . .

JACK (*firmly holding* GESCHWITZ, *to* LULU). Tell me what you want.

LULU. Give me eight shillings.

JACK. Too much.

LULU. If that's too much . . .!

JACK. How long have you walked the streets?

LULU. For two years.

JACK. I don't believe that.

LULU. Since my birthday.

JACK. Why do you lie?

LULU. What can I say?

JACK. You are a beginner!

LULU. I'm starting today.

JACK. How many did you have already?

LULU. A gentleman came first. He was really mad. He didn't let me speak. He covered my mouth. I wasn't allowed to laugh or groan. – Did he excite me! – I could've bitten off his nose!

JACK. And then?

LULU. Won't you stay with me?

JACK. Then?

LULU. A nigger came. – We began fighting over money. He didn't want to pay. He promised to pay afterwards . . .

JACK. And then?

LULU. Oh I would like you – to stay with me all night.

JACK. I pay in advance.

LULU. I don't want any money.

JACK. Who followed the black man?

LULU. Nobody.

JACK. Have you been a mother?

LULU. I don't know what you mean.

JACK. Did you ever have a child?

LULU. No sir. Never. – Why?

JACK. Because your mouth is still so fresh.

LULU. What's the matter with my mouth?

JACK. Now what is it you want?

LULU. I was a nice looking woman.

JACK. How much is it when I stay all night?

LULU. Give me five shillings.

JACK. No miss. (*Going to the door*.) Sleep well . . .

LULU (*stopping him*). Give me four . . .

JACK. Have you a friend living with you?

LULU. I'm all alone – with my sister.

JACK (*pointing left*). What is in there?

LULU. There's my kitchen.

JACK. Your kitchen?

LULU. There's no window in it.

JACK (*stamping his foot*). Who is living down below?

LULU. Nobody. – The room is to let.

JACK. Would three shillings do?

LULU. Yes sir.

JACK. I don't have so much . . .

LULU. Two . . .

JACK. I judged you from your way of walking.

LULU. Did you see me before?

JACK. Never. – I saw your back. I followed you.

LULU. My skirt is torn behind.

JACK. I didn't make a mistake. I saw – your body is perfectly formed.

LULU. You saw that from behind?

JACK. I saw the way you put your feet down. I said to myself she must have a very expressive mouth.

LULU. It seems you took a fancy to my mouth.

JACK. Yes. Indeed. – You are intelligent. – You are generous. – You are ambitious. You are all right at heart.

LULU. What harm can that do . . .?

JACK. I saw that when I saw you walking on the pavement.

LULU. You are original.

JACK. I was coming behind you.

LULU. Why are you staring at me!

JACK. I only have a shilling.

LULU. You are excited too.

JACK. It's three years since I slept with a girl.

LULU. Come on – give me the shilling.

JACK. What did you live on till today?

LULU. I was a parlour-maid.

JACK. Parlour-maids have rougher hands than you.

LULU. I had a rich friend. Give me your shilling.

JACK. You've loved too much already.

LULU. Yes . . .

JACK (*taking out his purse*). I must get sixpence change.

LULU. I haven't any change.

JACK. You must. I have to take a bus tomorrow morning.

LULU. Why are you trembling?

JACK. Come on. Look in your pocket.

LULU (*searching her pockets*). Nothing – nothing –

JACK. Let me see.

LULU. That's all I have (*She holds a ten-shilling piece in the flat of her hand.*)

JACK. I want that half sovereign.

LULU. I'll change it tomorrow morning.

JACK. Give it to me.

LULU. You're richer than me.

JACK. If I stay all night with you.

> LULU *gives him the money and takes the lamp from the flower-stand.*

JACK (*noticing the portrait*). You are a society woman. You took care of yourself.

> LULU *opens the door to the hiding hole.*

LULU. Come on, come on.

JACK. We don't need light.

LULU. In the dark?

JACK. Why not? It's going out. It stinks.

LULU. That's true (*Puts the lamp on the flower-stand.*)

JACK. What's the use of that stink? (*Goes to turn down the lamp.*)

LULU. Let it burn.

JACK. The moon is shining.

LULU. Come on.

JACK. As you like.

LULU. Why don't you?

JACK. I am afraid.

LULU (*falls on his neck and kisses him*). I wouldn't do you any harm. I love you. You are like a baby. You're too bashful. You look puzzled. Why don't you look at me?

JACK. I ask myself whether I will succeed or not.

LULU. You too? Yes yes. (*Her hand under his overcoat.*) What more is it you want? Don't let me beg you any longer, you needn't be afraid of me. I was never ill.

JACK. Aren't you ashamed – to sell your love?

LULU. What could I do?

JACK. That's very mean!

LULU. You love me! You pity me!

JACK. I have never found a more beautiful girl in the street.

LULU (*holds him in an embrace*). Come on. I'm not as bad as I look . . .

JACK. All right.

> JACK *follows* LULU *into the hiding hole.* GESCHWITZ *writes with her fingers on the boards.*

GESCHWITZ. You put this love in me – in my heart – child – can I help it – my finger bleeds – I'm – I'm too hot – there's still something – I must think about . . . Lulu . . .

> *The lamp goes out. On the boards under the windows two glaring squares. Everything in the room is clearly discernible.*

GESCHWITZ (*speaks as if in a dream*). When it gets dark – when it gets dark – she's all I think of – especially when it gets dark. If only – she hadn't married – I must think about –. I'm so dirty, so dirty! – I must still think about – if my father had never married – I'd never have seen her – never seen – if my mother . . . they make the children – why am I maimed – I – I can't marry . . . I – I knew a . . . Lulu . . . (*Jumps up.*) Oh! – Oh.

> *Shrieking from right.* LULU, *barefoot in a slip, screaming, tears open the door and holds it shut from the outside.*

LULU. Help! Help! Martha!

> GESCHWITZ *rushes to the door, takes out her revolver and aims it at the door, pushing* LULU *behind her.*

GESCHWITZ (*to* LULU). Let go!

> JACK *bent double to the ground, tears the door open from inside and runs a knife into* GESCHWITZ's *body. She fires a shot into the ceiling and collapses howling.* JACK *has posted himself in front of the way out.*

LULU (*down left*). – Oh! – Oh! – Oh God . . .

> *Pause.* GESCHWITZ, *her head bent into her neck, stretches out the revolver to* LULU.

GESCHWITZ. Lulu . . .

> JACK *jerks* GESCHWITZ *towards him on the strap and takes the revolver from her hand.*

LULU. Police! – Police!
JACK (*aiming the revolver at her*). Be quiet!
GESCHWITZ (*death rattle*). It – doesn't – shoot.

> JACK *throws himself on* LULU *and tries to hold her. She flees to the way out.* JACK *throws himself against the door.*

JACK. I've got you safe!
LULU (*staggering back*). He'll slit my belly open!
JACK. Shut up!

> JACK *throws himself on the floor and tries to catch her feet.* LULU *escapes into her room and leans on the door from the inside. Her shouts are heard.*

LULU. Help! – Help! – Help! – Police! – Police!

> *With his knife in his hand* JACK *tries to force open the door.* GESCHWITZ *tries to get up and falls on her side.*

GESCHWITZ. – My angel! – My angel!
LULU (*from inside*). Murder! Murder! Get help!
JACK (*working at the door, to himself*). There is no finer mouth in the four seas.

> *The door gives way.* JACK *crashes in. For a moment only* GESCHWITZ's *rasping breath is heard.*

LULU (*from inside, suddenly screaming*). No! – No! – Have pity! Mercy!

> JACK *carrying* LULU *in his arms comes through the door and tries to cross the room.* LULU *presses against his forehead with both hands and screams.*

LULU. Murder! – Murder! – Murder! – they're ripping me up . . .
JACK. The bed is occupied.
LULU (*with all her voice*). Police!

JACK *puts her down, holds her head fast and bores his thumbs between her teeth.*

JACK. I will make you quiet!

LULU escapes. JACK throws himself against the door to the stairs.

JACK. Goddam . . .

Sweat drips from his hair, his hands are bloody. He pants from the pit of his chest and stares at the floor with bulging eyes.

JACK. That is a hard piece of work . . .

LULU looks round wildly, every limb shaking, suddenly seizes the whisky bottle, smashes it on the table and throws herself on JACK, pointing the jagged edge with her right hand. JACK has lifted his right foot – he catapults her onto her back. He stays motionless in his place. LULU has her hands over her belly, her knees pressed to her breast, writhing on the floor.

LULU. – Oh – Oh – Oh . . .
GESCHWITZ. Lulu – I can't –

JACK shakes himself together, lifts LULU from the floor and carries her right, her legs flailing.

LULU. Martha! He's slitting me up! He's slitting me up!

JACK carries her into the hiding hole.

GESCHWITZ. Help! Help! – Murder! – Help! –
LULU (*from inside*). – Oh! – Oh! – Oh! – Oh! – Oh! – Oh don't! – Don't! – No! – No!
GESCHWITZ (*dragging herself to the door with her last strength*). – Lulu! – Murder! – Police! – Police!

After a pause JACK comes back from the right, unbuttons his overcoat and hides a small, newspaper-wrapped packet in his inside breast pocket. He gropes his way across the room and goes through the door of LULU's room.

LULU (*in the hiding hole, whimpering*). Oh – oh – oh . . .

GESCHWITZ. Lulu – my love!

> JACK *comes from the room with the full wash-basin, puts it on the flower-stand and washes his hands.*

JACK. I would never have thought of a thing like that. That is a phenomenon that wouldn't happen in two hundred years. I am a lucky dog to find this curiosity.

GESCHWITZ. Lulu – alive – my angel?

JACK. When I'm dead and my collection is put up for auction, the London Medical Society will pay three hundred pounds for the prodigy I have conquered tonight. The professors and students will say 'That is astonishing!' – Not so much as a towel in this place. It looks awfully poor here . . .

GESCHWITZ. Speak – Lulu . . .

JACK. Well . . .

> JACK *jerks back* GESCHWITZ's *dress and dries his hands on her white petticoat.*

JACK. This monster is quite safe from me. (*To* GESCHWITZ.) It will be all over with you in a second.

> JACK *goes out through the middle.* GESCHWITZ *is alone by the hiding hole – she struggles to go towards the half-open door, propped on her arms and leaving a thin trail of blood behind her.*

GESCHWITZ. Once more – once more – my angel – see you – once more – see you – once more – I love – I love – love – I am in misery –

> GESCHWITZ's *elbows give way.*

GESCHWITZ. – s-s . . . submit . . .

> *Dies.*

Select Bibliography of Books in English

Translations of Wedekind's plays:

Tragedies of Sex, translated and introduced by S.A Elliot, Jnr, London: Henderson, n.d.; New York: Boni & Liveright, 1923. Includes *Spring Awakening, Earth-Spirit, Pandora's Box, Damnation!*.

Five Tragedies of Sex, trans. F. Fawcett & S. Spender, intro. L. Feuchtwanger, New York: Theatre Arts, n.d.; London: Vision, 1952. Includes *Spring Awakening, Earth-Spirit, Pandora's Box, Death and Devil, Castle Wetterstein*.

The Lulu Plays and other Sex Tragedies, trans. Stephen Spender, London: Calder, 1972. Includes *Earth-Spirit, Pandora's Box, Death and Devil, Castle Wetterstein*.

King Nicolo in *The Genius of the German Theatre*, ed. Martin Esslin, London & New York: Mentor, 1968.

Lulu, translated and abridged by Peter Barnes, London: Heinemann Educational, 1971.

The Singer in *Frontiers of Farce*, trans. Peter Barnes, London: Heinemann Educational, 1977.

The Marquis of Keith in *From the Modern Repertoire, Series Two*, ed. Eric Bentley, Bloomington: Indiana University Press, 1952.

The Lulu Plays and the Marquis of Keith, translated and adapted by Steve Gooch, London: Absolute Classics, 1990.

The Lulu Plays, translated by Carl Richard Mueller, A Fawcett Premier Book, Tulane Drama Review Series, USA, 1967.

Spring Awakening, trans. Tom Osborne, USA: Riverrun Press, Inc. 1979.

Spring Awakening, trans. Edward Bond, Methuen, 1980.

Translation of Wedekind's diaries:

Hay, Gerhard, (ed.), Yuill, W.E. (translator), *Frank Wedekind: The Diary of an Erotic Life*, Basil Blackwell, 1990.

Books about Wedekind and his era:

Best, Alan, *Frank Wedekind*, London: Oswald Wolff, 1975.

Boa, Elizabeth, *The Sexual Circus: Wedekind's Theatre of Subversion*, London: Basil Blackwell, 1987.

Garten, H.F., *Modern German Drama*, London: Methuen, 2nd ed., 1964, pp. 87–96.

Gittleman, Sol, *Frank Wedekind*, No. 55 in Twayne's World Authors series, New York: Twayne, 1969.

———, *Frank Wedekind und Bertolt Brecht: Notes on a Relationship*. Modern Drama, 1967, 10, pp. 401–9.

Harris, Edward P., *The Liberation of the Flesh from the Stone: Pygmalion in Frank Wedekind's Erdgeist*. Germanic Review, 1977, 52, pp. 44–56.

Midgley, David, 'Wedekind's "Lulu": from "Schauertragödie" to Social Comedy', *German Life and Letters*, 38, 1985, pp. 205–32.

Natan, Alex, 'Frank Wedekind', London: *German Men of Letters*, vol. 2, 1963, pp. 103–29.

Pascal, Roy, *From Naturalism to Expressionism, German Literature and Society 1880–1918*, London: Weidenfeld & Nicolson, 1974.

Peacock, Ronald, 'The Ambiguity of Wedekind's "Lulu"', *Oxford German Studies*, 9, 1978, pp. 105–18.

Skrine, Peter, *Hauptmann, Wedekind and Schnitzler*, MacMillan Modern Dramatists, 1989.

Spalter, Max, *Brecht's Tradition*, Baltimore: Johns Hopkins, 1967.

Willett, John, *Expressionism*, London: Weidenfeld & Nicolson, 1970.

A Note on the Translators

EDWARD BOND was born and educated in London. His plays include *The Pope's Wedding* (Royal Court Theatre, 1962), *Saved* (Royal Court, 1965), *Early Morning* (Royal Court, 1968), *Narrow Road to the Deep North* (Belgrade Theatre, Coventry, 1968; Royal Court, 1969), *Black Mass* (Sharpeville Commemoration Evening, Lyceum Theatre, 1970), *Passion* (CND Rally, Alexandra Palace, 1971), *Lear* (Royal Court, 1971), *The Sea* (Royal Court, 1973), *Bingo* (Northcott, Exeter, 1973; Royal Court, 1974), *The Fool* (Royal Court, 1975), *The Bundle* (RSC Warehouse, 1978), *The Woman* (National Theatre, 1978), *The Worlds* (New Half Moon Theatre, London, 1981), *Restoration* (Royal Court, 1981), *Summer* (National Theatre, 1982), *Derek* (RSC Youth Festival, The Other Place, Stratford-upon-Avon, 1982), *The Cat* (produced in Germany as *The English Cat* by the Stuttgart Opera, 1983), *Human Cannon* (Quantum Theatre, Manchester, 1986), *The War Plays* (*Red Black and Ignorant*, *The Tin Can People* and *Great Peace*) which were staged as a trilogy by the RSC at the Barbican Pit in 1985, *Jackets* (Leicester Haymarket, 1989), *September* (Canterbury Cathedral, 1989); *In the Company of Men* (Théâtre de la Ville, Paris, 1992); *Olly's Prison* (BBC 2 Television, 1993); *Tuesday* (BBC2 Television, 1993). His *Theatre Poems and Songs* were published in 1978 and *Poems 1978–1985* in 1987.

ELISABETH BOND-PABLÉ, born in Klagenfurt, Austria, studied theatre and music at Vienna University (Dr Phil.). Theatre and book critic and feature writer for German language periodicals, papers, radio. Writes and edits books and anthologies mainly on theatre, music, cabaret etc. She moved to England in 1970 and married Edward Bond. Translations include Kroetz's *Homework* for the Half Moon Theatre, London and, with Tinch Minter, two plays by Marieluise Fleisser: *Purgatory in Ingolstadt* and *Pioneers in Ingolstadt*. Both plays were premièred at the Gate Theatre, London in 1991 and Elisabeth Bond-Pablé and Tinch Minter won the first Empty Space Award, presented by the London Theatre Review, for their translations.